This book was edited as a project
of the Ethnic History Program of the
New Jersey Historical Commission

WHOLESALE
SUGAR
MALT & HOPS
CITY CHECK

AMERICA
The Dream of My Life

Selections From the Federal Writers' Project's New Jersey Ethnic Survey

EDITED BY

David Steven Cohen

RUTGERS UNIVERSITY PRESS
New Brunswick and London

Photo credits:

p. i—Young Russian Jewess at Ellis Island, 1905. (*Lewis W. Hine Collection, United States History, Local History & Genealogy Division, The New York Public Library, Astor, Lenox and Tilden Foundations.*)

p. ii—Prince Street, Newark, in 1938. (*Newark Public Library.*)

Copyright © 1990 by Rutgers, The State University
All Rights Reserved
Manufactured in the United States of America

Library of Congress Cataloging-in-Publication Data

America, the dream of my life : selections from the Federal Writers'
   Project's New Jersey Ethnic Survey / edited by David Steven Cohen.
      p.   cm.
   Includes bibliographical references.
   ISBN 0-8135-1514-9 (cloth)   ISBN 0-8135-1515-7 (pbk.)
      1. Minorities—New Jersey—History.   2. Immigrants—New Jersey—
   History.   3. Immigrants—New Jersey—Biography.   4. New Jersey—
   Social life and customs.   5. New Jersey—Emigration and
   immigration—History.   6. Oral history.   I. Cohen, David Steven,
   1943-   .   II. New Jersey Ethnic Survey.
   F145.A1A47   1990
   305.8'009749—dc20   89-37770
                                                                  CIP

British Cataloging-in-Publication information available

For my daughter, Elena Louise Cohen

As in an orchestra every type
of instrument has its specific timbre
and tonality, founded in its substance and
form; as every type has its appropriate
theme and melody in the whole
symphony, so in society, each
ethnic group may be the natural
instrument, its temper and culture
may be its theme and melody and the
harmony and dissonances and discords of them
all may make the symphony
of civilization.

Horace M. Kallen
"Democracy Versus the Melting-Pot," 1915

Italian *bocci* game, Newark, ca. 1936. (*Harry Dorer Collection, Newark Public Library.*)

Contents

Public bathhouse on West Park Street, Newark, ca. 1910. (*New Jersey Historical Society.*)

Illustrations

Acknowledgments

First and foremost, I wish to thank the anonymous men and women who agreed to be interviewed by the New Jersey Ethnic Survey between 1939 and 1941. It is a brave thing to open one's life to examination by strangers. They took this risk so that we might better understand the immigrant experience.

I was fortunate to be able to locate Charles W. Churchill and Vivian Mintz Barnert. Churchill was the state director of the New Jersey Ethnic Survey, and Barnert was the supervisor of the subproject on African-Americans in Newark, Atlantic City, and Montclair. Both agreed to be interviewed, first by letter, then by telephone, and finally in person. Their willingness to relive these earlier years added to our understanding of how the New Jersey Ethnic Survey was conducted and the intellectual premises behind the project.

The true authors of this volume are the fieldworkers and writers who compiled these case histories and neighborhood descriptions. Fortunately, we have most of their names because the narratives were signed. They include Herman Bader, Mazie Berse, T. Giergielewicz, John Karpinic, Murray J. Koch, Rudolph E. Kornmann, A. Losi, Fred Madrygin, E. Norwich, Sinch O'Har, Ernest W. Pentz, Arthur Vermeire, A. Basil Wheeler, and Irving H. Zuckerman.

Other fieldworkers who worked on the survey include Salvatore Attansio, A. Carricchia, C. Hanlen, Sigfrid Hauck, William Hautau, Andrew Irshay, Harry F. Langton, W. L. McMillan, Stephen Palinkas, Joseph Mitruska, Harold Smith, and H. G. West. Emanuel Del Guidice was the office manager, and Harold A. Lett was the director of research. The typists on the project were Lena Sazer, Margaret Fitzgerald, Malvina Sachs, and H. Hames.

I also want to thank the librarians and archivists who conscientiously preserved these case histories over the years and who pointed me in the right direction to find related materials. They include Karl Niederer, Bette Barker, and Dan Jones of the New Jersey State Archives; Joseph P. Sullivan of the Manuscripts Division of the Library of Congress; the staff of Record Group 69 at the National Archives; Susan Pumilia and James Ward of the Passaic County Historical Society; Giacomo De Stefano and Thomas Peters of the Paterson Museum; Wilson O'Donnell of the New Jersey Historical Society; Robert Blackwell, Charles Cummings, and Paul Stellhorn at the Newark Public

Library; and Jerome Nathans of the Jewish Historical Society of North Jersey.

Joan Babbage of the Newark *Star-Ledger* assisted me in finding Vivian Mintz Barnert with her well-timed article, and Saul Schwartz of Livingston, New Jersey, saw the article and sent it to Ms. Barnert. The staff of American University in Beirut, especially Dr. Landry Slade, the assistant to the president, and L. N. Diab, the dean of the faculty of arts and sciences, helped me find Professor Churchill.

I also want to acknowledge the benefit I derived from conversations with Nan Martin-Perdue on the problems of interpreting the case histories from the Federal Writers' Project. Jerrold Hirsch gave the manuscript a thorough and thoughtful reading, and I am deeply indebted to him for his constructive criticisms. Rabbi Jack Paskoff of Anshe Emeth Memorial Temple and Professors Morris A. Moskowitz and Taras Hunczak, both of Rutgers University, graciously answered questions concerning their respective areas of expertise. Barbara Cate of Seton Hall University helped to refine the title.

Marlie Wasserman, Associate Director at Rutgers University Press, saw the potential book in this collection of life histories. Kate Harrie edited the manuscript, making good use of her knowledge of the Russian language and culture. Liz Schweber Doles contributed yet another bold and original book design, and Raymond McGill prepared the index.

Patricia Thomas retyped all the case histories into a word processor and made the innumerable revisions. Evelyn Taylor helped proofread. Finally, Howard L. Green, research director at the New Jersey Historical Commission, not only supervised the work on this project, but, even more importantly, believed in it.

Introduction

"America became the dream of my life," a Dutch shoemaker, living in Paterson, New Jersey, told a fieldworker from the Federal Writers' Project in 1940. His statement appears in a case history, compiled as part of the Ethnological Survey of New Jersey, or, as it was known to those who worked on it, the New Jersey Ethnic Survey. Between 1939 and 1941, fieldworkers hired from the unemployment rolls assembled approximately one hundred "case histories" (that is, life histories) of immigrants who came to America during the late nineteenth and early twentieth centuries and settled in New Jersey cities. The interviewees were Irish, Polish, Lithuanian, Russian, Dutch, Ukrainian, Jewish, and Italian, although not in equal or representative numbers. Most of them lived in Newark and Paterson.

The interviews were conducted before the days of modern tape recorders, so the narratives were written from notes taken by the fieldworkers. Thus, while these case histories are not the exact words of the interviewees, they are nevertheless based on the lives of real people, most of whom were elderly at the time the interviews were conducted. Their life histories take us well back into the nineteenth century, several generations earlier than the oral histories being compiled today. They add flesh and blood to the skeleton of facts and figures about immigrant life during this period. This body of material has been barely mined by historians. Although there are comparable unpublished collections, this is, as far as we know, the first publication of a statewide collection of Federal Writers' Project case histories from what was called the Social-Ethnic Studies program.[1] It represents for immigration history what the more famous Federal Writers' Project collection of slave narratives has meant for African-American history.

This material vividly conveys in human terms what it was like to leave one's country of birth and come to the United States. It may not tell us about the great transformation from rural peasant to urban industrial culture occurring in the nineteenth century in many European countries that was the context for the major internal migrations and external emigrations.[2] But it does tell us about the personal motivations and expectations of individual immigrants and the extent to which their hopes and dreams were fulfilled.

Many interviewees express economic reasons for emigrating. A Polish interviewee puts it succinctly, when he says that his father came to

1

America *za chlebem* (for bread). Another Polish interviewee says that "in 1893, wanting to better myself, I decided to come to the United States." He cites the belief in Poland and Europe generally that a common laborer who went to the United States was able to provide his family in Poland with many luxuries in a short space of time. An Italian interviewee cites a letter sent by an uncle in the United States saying "how much better everything was in America, how much more chance one had to make something of himself there." A Jewish resident of Paterson says, "Wages in Paterson were higher than those in Łódź, Białystok, Ozorkow, and other towns in Europe, and living conditions were on a much higher level here."

Others say they came to the United States to avoid persecution or being drafted into the military. A Jewish interviewee, whose family owned one of the largest clothing stores in Odessa, Russia, remembers the visit of the tsar in 1880, which was followed by a *pogrom* (anti-Jewish riot). His father decided to sell the business and move the entire family to Vienna. He had to bribe the "agents of credentials" on the Rumanian border because his two sons were of military age. A Jewish woman describes how she had a cousin who was killed in the tsar's army during World War I. She says that one young man in her village cut off his trigger finger to avoid military service; but was given a fifteen-minute trial by Russian officers, and then was taken outside of town and shot. Another Jewish interviewee says that the Russo-Japanese War (1904–1905) was imminent, and he did not want to be drafted, so he begged his American relatives to send him tickets to enable him to leave Russia.

Not everyone had such a sanguine vision of conditions in the United States. A Dutch interviewee mentions the divergent opinions of his uncle, who viewed the United States as a land of opportunity, and his father, who cautioned about how hard it is to start all over again in a strange land. Another Dutch immigrant has the opportunity to return to his native village of Filippine in the Netherlands on a furlough during World War I, but concludes that "it was a mistake for anyone to go to another country and leave parents and loved ones behind." One of the saddest life stories is that of a successful Jewish merchant from Odessa, who is convinced by his son to come to the United States and by Michael Heilprin, a Jewish-American intellectual, to go into farming in Vineland, New Jersey. He ends up losing a large amount of money in his unsuccessful attempt to engage in agriculture, and his family nearly perishes when his sons decide to rebuild the farmhouse wall just prior to the Blizzard of 1888. At one point, he visits the South Jersey town of Alliance, where he sees people who used to work for him doing better than he. The man curses the day he ever came to the United States.

The case histories also show the importance of letters home as a way of communicating about conditions in the United States and in Europe.[3] A Dutch interviewee says that he wrote a letter home every other week. The owner of a Polish employment agency says that once a Polish immigrant girl got a job as a housekeeper, she would send the passage money to other family members, until the entire family was brought over. These letters resulted in a "chain migration," that is, people from one region or city in Europe following neighbors or relatives to the same town or city in the United States. It is noted that whenever a letter would arrive from Łódź, Poland, all the Jews from Łódź in Paterson would gather around the person who received the letter to get the most recent news from home. Considering the importance of these letters, it is significant that the Yiddish film reviewed at the Little Theater in Newark was entitled *A Brivele der Mamen* (A Letter to Mother).

There is considerable information about the health and sanitary conditions in Newark and Paterson during the nineteenth century. A description of a Polish boardinghouse in Newark in 1890 informs us that there were either families or several men living in each of its eighteen rooms. There were five toilets in the backyard and no indoor plumbing. Pitchers of water were brought into the room by the boarders to wash themselves, and sometimes several people used the same water. Most of the rooms had oil lamps, although a few had gas lights. The result of these unsanitary conditions was that diseases such as tuberculosis and pneumonia were rampant.

Given these unsanitary living conditions, we readily see the importance of the neighborhood bathhouses. A Jewish woman says that when she arrived at her uncle's house in the United States, the first thing her aunt did was to take her to the Turkish baths to clean herself up from her long trip. There is also a description of the Clifton Avenue bathhouse in an Italian neighborhood in Newark. Six thousand people a week used the facility, including entire families.

Health conditions at home and at work were appalling. A shocking number of the interviewees had never seen a doctor or a dentist during their entire lives. Midwives were commonly substituted for doctors. One interviewee says, "In my case, the doctor would not have improved on my grandma, to say the least." There are accounts of immigrant with "nervous" conditions, probably due to the emotional pressures of adjusting to the new culture. There are also accounts of dangerous conditions on the job, such as those of the Irish steeplejack

who survived several falls from smokestacks and of the dangers encountered by Lithuanian workers exposed to acids and fumes in the
smelting works. It is not surprising, therefore, that the 1890 census
described Newark as "the unhealthiest city in the United States."[4]

There is considerable information on the adjustments immigrants
had to make to a new way of life and work in the United States. A
Dutch shoemaker laments the loss of old-world craftsmanship in the
United States, resulting from the decline in demand for custom-made
shoes. A Polish Jew from Warsaw, who worked in the sheet metal business, notes that in the United States "people want work done cheaply,"
resulting in "speeding up labor and using machinery." One of the biggest changes for Orthodox Jews in the United States was having to
work a half-day on Saturday, which is the Jewish Sabbath. The silk mill
owners in America did not allow Jewish weavers to have beards because they could get caught in the machinery. A Jewish woman who
worked in a paper-box factory says that for safety reasons she dropped
the custom of wearing a shawl over her head. It should be noted, however, that similar changes were taking place with industrialization in
Europe.

We also get information about economic arrangements made by immigrants. The case history of an Italian-American *padrone* (labor
agent) describes his multifarious business interests, including operat-
ing a boardinghouse, helping immigrants find jobs, banking (depositing
funds, but keeping the interest for himself), running a saloon, and even
arranging marriages. Boarding was a common living arrangement for
many ethnic groups, either in boardinghouses or with individual families. Each boarder in the Polish boardinghouse described in the case
histories would fill out an order slip for each meal, and he would pay
the storekeeper directly on payday. One study found that in 1860, almost 20 percent of the inhabitants of Newark's Fourth Ward, which
encompassed the central business district, lived in boardinghouses.
Both native-born and foreign-born workers lived in boardinghouses,
but the foreign-born tended to live in houses run by members of their
own ethnic group. In 1860 they were replaced by Italian owners. The
boardinghouses were not confined to one district, but were scattered
throughout the city.[5]

Crime was sometimes a means of economic betterment for some
immigrants. The case histories contain references to Jewish boys in
Newark who stole bicycles and tires, rented pushcarts and then sold
them, stole corn and potatoes from nearby farms, and made whiskey
from rubbing alcohol. One account describes the Third Ward of Newark as "a tough neighborhood" in which Jewish boys "pilfered junk to

make a few pennies." These passages are reminiscent of Saul Bellow's 1949 novel *The Adventures of Augie March*, which is about a Jewish street tough from Chicago.[6]

The case histories also reveal differences and clashes between the first and second generation of immigrants. A seventeen-year-old Polish-American girl named Jean Oleska tells us that her Polish-born father does not understand or appreciate American ways. While her mother does not speak English, at least she has conformed to American ways. A first-generation Jewish woman says that American children do not help much at home and do not respect their parents, as was the case in Łódź, Poland. A first-generation Jewish man tells us that Jewish boys in Poland were already married and supporting families at the age of eighteen, but in the United States all they think about are sports and play. He complains that his daughter spends more than she earns. Perhaps the most poignant example of this generation gap is the Jewish mother whose heart is broken when she learns that her daughter has been posing naked for photographers.

The conclusion of sociologists that rates of intermarriage varied by ethnic group is confirmed by the case histories.[7] The desire to marry their own kind was especially strong among the Jews and the Dutch. A Dutch interviewee says, "One thing about our people; they will not intermarry as long as there is a Hollander left." Being very religious, most Dutch young people met each other at church. In a number of the case histories, a Dutch man married the daughter of the family with which he boarded. One Jewish interviewee mentions a cousin in New York "who left the faith of Israel for that of his wife" and was considered "dead in the eyes of my parents." When intermarriage did occur between ethnic groups, it tended to be with someone of the same religion.[8] An example is Jean Oleska, the Polish girl mentioned above, who says that she is dating an Italian boy. When asked whether she would prefer to marry a Polish boy, she answers that she will follow the dictates of her heart.

There is evidence in the case histories of a continuity of tradition in the folklore and folklife of immigrants. One interviewee mentions itinerant rabbis who came to Paterson to put on programs of Yiddish and Hebrew songs and stories. A Jewish woman who spoke fluent Russian, but no Yiddish, learned Yiddish in the United States because she liked the old songs and wanted to join a Jewish chorus. Another Jewish woman says that her father used to tell her stories about the forest of Lithuania. "They were the most beautiful stories, and I never got tired of them," she says. These traditions were reinforced by Yiddish theater and Yiddish films. The account of the Yiddish film at the Little

Theater in Newark mentions how, when the cantor in the film sang, many of the men and some of the women in the audience sang and hummed along with him.

There are also examples of ethnic jokes and humor. A Jewish rabbi tells about a practical joke he played on his "greenhorn" wife: he tricked her into eating her first banana with a knife and fork, seasoned with salt and pepper. An Irish informant tells an ethnic joke about the newly arrived Irish immigrant who thinks that the telephone operator ought to know his "delegate" (that is, political boss), Bill Brennan; and there is another ethnic joke about the Irish immigrant who brings the closet door with his immigration papers pasted on it to the polling booth. This kind of humor helped immigrants cope with a new way of life in the United States.

Often it is the most ordinary remembrances that contain the most emotive aspects of the immigrant experience. There is the description by a young Jewish man of the personal meaning to him of a vacant lot in the neighborhood in which he grew up. "This lot held for me some of the keenest and most thrilling experiences of my early life," he says.

> It was here that we used to dig trenches and hurl at one another our heavy artillery of snowballs, concealing within them sharp pebbles and sometimes formidable stones. It was here, too, that the circus, for some three years consecutively during my youth pitched its camp to the enraptured interest of myself and my young friends. It was also into this lot that my young friend Herbert fell from the second story of his home and miraculously escaped with only a broken leg. Yes, it was this lot that held the lore and meaning of my early life, and it was to this lot that most of my early life was dedicated.

These case histories not only tell us about the times they describe, they also tell us about the times during which they were collected. Most of the immigrants were elderly at the time they were interviewed, so the interviews were really reflections back on their lives from the perspective of old age. Given the vagaries of memory, one cannot assume that the life stories are objective statements of fact; rather, they are reconstructions, or reinventions, of immigrant lives. The times in which they were interviewed certainly influenced the way the interviewees remembered their lives. The Great Depression, which hit immigrants in the United States especially hard, colored many of these case histories. There is the Irish man who says, "I'm a lone wolf since the Depression. This country is alright. Right now there isn't an opportunity to make a living." A Ukrainian man says: "I live in a house not fit for rats to live in. I am obliged to eat the cheapest food. . . . As you see, I am wearing rags. And my future? Only an undertaker can tell. I can't think of amusement or movies, because I never have any money. When I have it, there are bills to pay—more bills than I can pay. And so it goes, all year round." And a young Jewish woman tells the touching story of how her family, through hard work and saving their money, managed to gain their lifelong dream of a house in the suburbs. But her father lost his factory job because of mechanization, the mortgage company foreclosed on their house, and the family moved to an old house on a dead-end street. Before they moved, her mother wanted to dig up the plants given her on Mother's Day, but the real estate agent told her that it was not allowed.

Thus, there is a certain irony to the title of this book, "America, the Dream of My Life." There were many other causes than simply the Great Depression for the dreams that went sour, such as mechanization of factories and the lack of education of many of the immigrants. Historians have found that social mobility for immigrants was a very slow process. Often the most they could expect from an entire lifetime of work was perhaps to buy a house or to improve their job.[9] Rarely was it the rags-to-riches success that was popularized by the novels of Horatio Alger.[10] Nevertheless, the Great Depression was a low point in the lives of many people. Had these interviews been collected a decade earlier or a decade later, perhaps the tone of many of them would have been different.

Furthermore, with World War I still vivid in the memories of many of the immigrants and with World War II looming on the horizon, the case histories are replete with the prejudices of their day. A Polish newspaper editor says that the impression people have that Poles are street fighters comes from people confusing Poles with the other Slavic groups, such as Russians, Ukrainians, and "Liths" (his term for Lithuanians), who were, in fact, the enemies of the Poles. The fieldworker, who happened to be Jewish, notes that this newspaper editor had a violent dislike of Jews. A Jewish woman living in Paterson says that in Łódź, Poland, there were often fights between Christians and Jews. "They were always starting fights with Jews and resenting the Jewish presence very much," she says. Yet this same woman goes on to say that "there were too many colored people moving to the River Street section" of Paterson, which was one of the Jewish neighborhoods.

Some of these prejudices came from experiences of persecution in Europe, especially during wartime. A Jewish woman describes her family's experience during World War I in the following words: "During the war, we lived like dogs, running from one cellar to another—first to get away from the Cossacks and then the Polacks." Her mother and father were killed by anti-Semitic soldiers. Another Jewish family is separated during World War I, when first the Russians and then the Austrians came through her hometown of Lvov on the border between Poland and Russia. Yet another Jewish woman says that during the war the Germany soldiers paid for the food they took, but the Polish soldiers stole from the Jews and "the women suffered." The Russian soldiers, she said, were not so bad at first, until they began to lose the war. Such memories were not easily erased in the United States.

Other conflicts came, not from the Old World, but from groups that came into contact for the first time on the streets of the United States. A Jewish rabbi in Elizabeth, New Jersey, complains that boys who hung out on street corners made fun of his beard and his chanting of Jewish hymns in the evening. A Jewish woman in Paterson describes how "bands of loafer kids" came through the Jewish section of town, shouting "sheeny" and "Jew." The description of Prince Street in Newark notes how "race prejudice between Negro and Jew on Prince Street rarely breaks out into the open. It expresses itself with mild baiting between the two; the Jew jeers at the Negroes in Yiddish; and often the colored man's retort is couched in the same language." An Irish man from the Down Neck section of Newark says, "The Slovaks, the Poles, and the Lithuanians—yes, all except the Spaniards and Portuguese are all right." But he criticizes the Poles for changing the name of Sanford Street to Pilsudski Street in honor of the Polish patriot. Another Irish man says that when some Irish veterans gave blood to a Jewish war veteran, they told him afterwards "that he was a better man than he was before."

The prejudices were not just on the side of the interviewees. The fieldworkers, who were not fully trained in interviewing techniques, had prejudices of their own. A fieldworker named Zuckerman, who was evidently Jewish, attempted to interview a Ukrainian priest in Newark. The fieldworker's negative attitude toward the Ukrainians can be seen in his choice of words in describing the priest and his surroundings. He refers to religious symbols and paintings "littering" the walls and a frieze of Christ covered with scarlet red print "smeared with indiscriminate taste." He describes the priest as peering at him "as though he condescended to see us," and he comments on the priest's alleged "resentment at our apparent ease and utter lack of awe and mystification in his most august presence." He speculates that the priest was "unused to people who didn't scrape and bow." Zuckerman concludes by writing, "I've never before witnessed such smugness and superiority in clerical garb." He makes the mistake of telling the priest that he is Polish, rather than Jewish, not realizing the long history of conflict between Poles and Ukrainians in Europe. The priest responds by saying that Polish employers discriminate against hiring Ukrainian workers. When the fieldworker tells the priest that he works for the WPA (Works Progress Administration), the priest responds that "the WPA is run by Jews," and refuses to be interviewed. While this unsuccessful interview may reflect poor fieldwork technique, it tells us much about interethnic conflict during the 1930s.

The description of Prince Street, Newark, written by Rudolph E. Kornmann, is another example of biased reporting. Kornmann's description today might well be considered both anti-Semitic and racist. He writes about the Jewish pushcart peddlers: "Prince Street sells cheap, out of pushcarts, out of open barrels, along the sidewalk, and across seamy counters. . . . Prince Street sells cheap; it will sell even more cheaply, if you haggle." He writes that the former German residents of the neighborhood sold out "to others," ostensibly Jews, "who operated on principles of clever merchandising, rather than through personal appeal and neighborliness." He repeats the anti-Semitic accusation that Jews, through "a species of race solidarity" (a term that exposes his prejudice), had price and trade agreements to exclude non-Jews from trade. Kornmann calls the great migration of African-Americans from the South after World War I "the second invasion of Prince Street" (another loaded term), and he insinuates that the upstairs rooms are the haunts of African-American prostitutes. "Over the stores are rooms. Trade goes on there, too, though the faces upstairs are Negroid. Prince Street sells cheap—its merchandise fills the needs of every appetite, at bargain prices. And often it gives more than the buyer bargains for."[11]

Some of the ethnic bias in the fieldwork reflects divisions within ethnic groups. For example, there is a report on interviews conducted with German Jews. Evidently, the fieldworker was a Polish or Russian Jew. He explains the affluence of the German Jews by the opinion that there were greater opportunities for immigrants who arrived early in the nineteenth century. Those German Jews who came more recently benefited, in his opinion, from having relatives already in the business. The fieldworker is outspokenly critical of those German Jews who believed that Jews should not offend other Americans by being prolabor, and he condemns German Jews who wanted to restrict further Jewish immigration to the United States. He feels that these German Jews were influenced by Nazi propaganda into thinking that eastern European Jews are inferior. He is especially critical of a German Jewish rabbi who was anti-Zionist and "ignorant of Yiddish, as are most German Jews." The fieldworker characterizes the rabbi's feeling that no action should be taken against Hitler as an "escape from reality." This report suggests a deep division within the Jewish community between German Jews and Eastern European Jews. However, it should not be read as an objective statement of that division, given the obvious bias of the fieldworker.

The New Jersey Ethnic Survey was an auxiliary project within the Federal Writers' Project, which was created in 1935 in the federal agency named the Works Progress Administration (known as the WPA). The Federal Writers' Project's main priority was the researching, writing, and publishing of a series of state guidebooks. According to folklorist and historian Jerrold Hirsch, the goal of the Federal Writers' Project was not only to make work for unemployed writers, but also to "redefine" America in terms of three concepts: romantic nationalism, cultural pluralism, and cosmopolitanism.[12] Romantic nationalism was a movement, dating back to Ralph Waldo Emerson and Walt Whitman in the nineteenth century, that celebrated indigenous American culture, rather than imitating European culture, especially in the arts. Within the Federal Writers' Project, romantic nationalism was evident in Folklore Studies, under the national leadership first of John A. Lomax and then Benjamin A. Botkin. Cultural pluralism was a term coined in the 1920s by the Jewish-American intellectual Horace M. Kallen in reaction to the assimilationists who wanted immigrants to abandon their traditional cultures and become Americanized. Kallen argued for a democratic society in which each immigrant culture would retain its own identity. This celebration of ethnic diversity, Hirsch argues, was the notion behind Social-Ethnic Studies at the Federal Writers' Project, under the direction at the national level of Morton W. Royse. And cosmopolitanism refers to the conviction on the part of the organizers of the Federal Writers' Project that Americans would benefit from learning about other Americans different from themselves, thus "introducing America to Americans." These three assumptions, Hirsch argues, fit in perfectly with the liberal political ideology of the New Deal.[13]

While the concept of cultural pluralism was indeed a reaction to nativist distrust of immigrant groups, as manifested in the immigration quota restrictions of the 1920s, there was a certain idealism behind the concept. Kallen's original metaphor was that of a symphony orchestra in which ethnic groups maintain their own identities, yet play together in a kind of "symphony of civilization." Kallen mentioned both harmonies and dissonances, but the underlying premise was that the ethnic groups would at least get along well enough to make a peaceful, democratic society possible.[14] But, as historian John Higham notes, Kallen's cultural pluralism does not take into account the experience of African-Americans, and it is more a prescriptive ideal than a descriptive account of the history of interethnic relations in the United States.[15]

There is evidence that cultural pluralism informed the Social-Ethnic Studies project on the national level. In the "Manual for Social-Ethnic Studies," which Morton Royse prepared and sent to all the state directors of the Federal Writers' Project, he stated that studies of ethnic groups "should be functional, stressing cultural backgrounds and activities, not peculiarities and 'contributions.' "[16] Royse expanded upon this emphasis at a session of the American Historical Association in December 1938. A summary of his comments is included in Caroline F. Ware's *The Cultural Approach to History*.

> The concept of immigrant "contributions" implies that the culture of old-American groups constitutes "American civilization" and that bits of immigrant culture are added to it. The experience of the directors of the Federal Writers' Project casts doubts on this approach. In setting up a series of social-ethnic studies, they first attempted to use the "contributions" approach. After trying it out for several months in different places, they abandoned it. . . . Immigrants and children of immigrants *are* the American people. Their culture *is* American culture, not merely a contributor to American culture.[17]

Despite the apparent agreement among the national leaders of the Federal Writers' Project on the concept of cultural pluralism, Hirsch sees less unity in the individual state projects. In his survey of the various state guidebooks, Hirsch notes different points of view, depending on the state tradition and the contributors in each state.[18] The New Jersey guidebook, however, comes down squarely on the side of cultural pluralism. It tends to minimize interethnic conflict, stating that "relations between the various races and nationalities, on the whole, have been amicable in New Jersey." It mentions some "occasional cases of racial clash," such as riots between African-Americans and Italians during the Italian invasion of Ethiopia, violence in Newark's Chinatown during the Civil War in China, and a Jewish boycott of Germany and Italian stores over the issue of Fascism. But the guidebook returns to the inherent idealism behind the concept of cultural pluralism with the statement that "those who try 'real' Italian spaghetti, or 'genuine' Hungarian goulash, or who attend a Polish wedding or a Greek service as a spectacle, usually come away with a more enlightened view of minority groups."[19]

However, cultural pluralism was not the guiding principle behind the New Jersey Ethnic Survey. Under the state leadership of Charles W. Churchill, who later wrote his doctoral dissertation on the Italians of Newark (based on the Federal Writers' Project materials), and Vivian P. Mintz, who headed a special subproject on African-Americans in Newark, the main focus of the New Jersey project was to conduct a questionnaire survey on what was known in sociological circles of that day as "social distance."[20] This term was coined by sociologist Emory S. Bogardus to mean "a lack of understanding and fellow feeling" between "racial groups."[21] It should be remembered that despite what historian Thomas F. Gossett termed "the scientific revolt against racism," starting with the work of anthropologist Franz Boas in the early 1900s, sociologists commonly used the word "race" to refer to ethnic groups until World War II.[22] It took Adolph Hitler and the Nazi propaganda about the so-called master race to clarify social science thinking about the relationship between race and ethnicity.[23]

Whether the New Jersey Ethnic Survey should concentrate on case histories or on the social distance questionnaire became a point of dispute between Church and Royse. In a telephone interview November 19, 1987, Churchill told me that the case histories in the New Jersey Ethnic Survey were "anecdotal material we wanted to use to supplement our statistical findings—to put color into the material." Churchill went on to say that Royse wanted a different emphasis. "Royse and I had quite a bit of dispute about that. I was more for conducting a sampling study, and he wanted me to include more in the way of (case) history." When I interviewed Churchill in person on April 12, 1988, he expanded on his reasons for wanting to emphasize the social distance survey instead of the case histories: "Royse came in hellbent for case histories, and I wanted to do a survey. My argument was that you got your basic facts about the community by survey methods, and then you go into case studies to flesh them out."

Actually, Royse was himself under pressure from Henry G. Alsberg, the national director of the Federal Writers' Project, not to make Social-Ethnic Studies too academic. Jerre Mangione, who was an assistant to Alsberg, notes in his book *The Dream and the Deal* that Alsberg wrote to Royse criticizing the study of the Greeks in America for being of "a professional nature." "What does that mean?" Alsberg wrote. "Does it mean something the University of Chicago will like? In that case, it will probably be a dull affair. I hope you are impressing on the workers everywhere that these studies must really be human documents, otherwise they will become dry, academic pamphlets which nobody will read."[24]

At issue here was not solely whether the New Jersey Ethnic Survey should do case histories for a popular audience versus an academic survey of social distance. What was at stake was also whether the survey should adhere to the official line of the Federal Writers' Project, which was to emphasize cultural pluralism, or whether it would follow the University of Chicago approach to urban studies. Actually, the University of Chicago had pioneered in the use of case histories with Thomas and Znaniecki's classic study of Polish peasants.[25] Bogardus himself, on whose social distance concept the New Jersey Ethnic Survey so heavily relied, recommended the use of life histories. "Life histories treated in a social case-analysis fashion," he wrote, "will be revealing. A picture of the immigrants' longings, thwarted wishes, and unfulfilled hopes is essential."[26]

The University of Chicago approach to urban sociology, under the influence of its founder, sociologist Robert E. Park, tended to view the city, in the words of historian Maurice Stein, with "a slightly jaundiced eye."[27] Park saw the city as a place of rapid change and social disorganization. For the immigrant, the city was the place where uprootedness occurred, where the newcomers experienced a loss of their old culture and the disruptive challenge of adapting to a new culture. The result was poverty, crime, and discord.[28] Bogardus saw the immigrant as "troubled by dissatisfactions and unmet longings." Upon arriving in the new country, the immigrant was shaken loose from established moorings and exposed to prejudice and disillusionment.[29] The process was not unlike that described by historian Oscar Handlin in his descriptively titled book *The Uprooted*.[30] The University of Chicago view of the city very much influenced the case histories in the New Jersey Ethnic Survey because the social distance questionnaire was the context within which the case histories were originally gathered. Thus, there is a greater emphasis on prejudice than if cultural pluralism had been the guiding concept of the project.

The New Jersey Ethnic Survey existed for only a brief time, and it was constantly plagued by problems. Vivian Mintz was hired in June 1938, and Churchill joined the project the following fall. Churchill said that political problems complicated his being hired. He grew up in Jersey City, and the local Democratic party boss, who lived only four doors away, knew him to be a Republican. "Frank Hague was mayor of Jersey City at the time, and no one was appointed (to the Federal Writers' Project) from an address in Hudson County without being accepted by his organization," Churchill told me.[31] Churchill circumvented this problem, finally, by moving to Scotch Plains in Union County and then reapplying for the position.

The survey coincided with hearings conducted by the House Committee to Investigate Un-American Activities, known unofficially as the Dies Committee after its chairman, Democratic Congressman Martin Dies of Texas. The galleys from the New Jersey guidebook were introduced as evidence. At issue was the chapter on labor, which some members of the committee, including Republican J. Parnell Thomas of New Jersey, thought appealed to "class hatred."[32] As a result of the hearings, some sections of the New Jersey guidebook were deleted, and the state director of the Federal Writers' Project in New Jersey, Irene Fuhlbruegge, resigned.[33] Vivian Mintz Barnert remembers that in June 1940, in the wake of the Dies Committee investigations, everyone working on the Federal Writers' Project in New Jersey had to sign an affidavit stating that he or she had never been a Communist, Nazi, or alien. Much of the pressure came from Barnert's supervisors, who informed her that she had a number of Communists working on her project. Ms. Barnert feels that her project was singled out because she had many African-American fieldworkers.[34]

Throughout its existence, the New Jersey Ethnic Survey was constantly in danger of being abolished because of staff cutbacks at the Federal Writers' Project and also because it was not a main priority. By June 1939, Churchill had left, having made arrangements to use the Italian materials for his doctoral dissertation in sociology at New York University.[35] Vivian Mintz continued to work on the project, sometimes without being paid, until September 1940, when she married and left New Jersey to study social work at the University of Chicago.

In 1942, in the midst of World War II, the Federal Writers' Project was disbanded, and the New Jersey Ethnic Survey was deposited in the New Jersey State Archives along with other WPA materials. The archivists there brought the survey to my attention in 1985, when the New Jersey Historical Commission and the American Folklife Center were conducting a survey of folklife resources in New Jersey institutions.[36] In February 1987, the Historical Commission approved a proposal that, as a project of our Ethnic History Program, I would prepare a finding guide and determine whether there were materials in the survey suitable for publication.

The boxes contained a hodgepodge of materials, including the results of the social distance survey; draft chapters for a book on African-Americans in Newark; newspaper clippings; lists of ethnic organizations, newspapers, crime statistics, property owners, civil servants, and businesses; background material on ethnic customs, especially in the old country; typescripts of articles and chapters of books about ethnicity; a survey of radio-listening and newspaper-reading habits; population statistics; field notes and neighborhood descriptions; and outlines of books on a number of ethnic groups in New Jersey. In the middle of all this were the case histories. Although they may have been of secondary importance at the time they were collected, today they seem the most relevant material in the survey.

I tried to locate and interview the people involved in the survey. Because most of those who were interviewed were elderly at the time but most of the fieldworkers were young, I thought it more likely that we would locate the fieldworkers rather than the interviewees. Most of the interviews were anonymous, yet the case histories were signed by the fieldworkers. Also, the administrative files in the survey mentioned the names of the fieldworkers. Nevertheless, the only two people whom I was successful in locating were Charles W. Churchill and Vivian Mintz Barnert (her married name). I was able to trace Churchill because in 1970 he coedited a book on Arab communities in the Middle East.[37] He was listed as a professor at the American University in Beirut, Lebanon. The university provided me with his retirement address in Oceanside, California. Vivian Mintz Barnert was located through an article about this project in the Newark *Star-Ledger*, which was sent to her by a friend living in New Jersey. It turned out she also lives in southern California, but did not know that Churchill lived nearby. Both agreed to be interviewed first by letter, then by telephone, and finally in person.

These interviews solved at least one mystery about the New Jersey Ethnic Survey. I noted that although Churchill had written his dissertation about the Italians in Newark based on materials from the survey, there were no Italian materials in the files of the survey. Churchill explained that he had taken the Italian materials with him to Lebanon, where he taught for some twenty-five years. However, when he and his family were evacuated from Beirut in 1976 by the United States Navy, under a truce arranged with the Druse militia, they were only allowed one suitcase each. He had to leave all his research notes in Lebanon, including the Italian materials. My subsequent attempts to retrieve this material met with no response, and Churchill believes that it was probably destroyed. However, my research trips to Washington, D.C., to look at the administrative files of the Federal Writers' Project at the National Archives and the Federal Writers' Project materials from New Jersey in the Manuscripts Division of the Library of Congress led to the discovery of some Italian materials at the Library of Congress. These included the neighborhood description of Silver Lake, which was actually part of an earlier project called "Pockets of America"; field reports on immigrant banks and a bathhouse in the Italian section of Newark; and a fascinating case history of an Italian-American *padrone* (labor agent).

One unsolved mystery remains about the New Jersey Ethnic Survey. Most of the case histories are dated between 1939 and 1941. Vivian Mintz Barnert remained at the Writers' Project until 1940, but the New Jersey Ethnic Survey formally existed only from 1938 to 1939. When I presented Barnert and Churchill with the names of the fieldworkers who wrote and possibly gathered the case histories, they were not familiar with many of them. This means that they were not the same fieldworkers who worked on the New Jersey Ethnic Survey. Yet the case histories were considered part of the survey by whoever transferred the files to the state archives. Barnert and Churchill think that the bulk of the case histories may have been gathered by the regular writers for the Writers' Project, rather than their fieldworkers. Our attempts to find these writers have been unsuccessful, and there are no administrative documents in Washington because in 1939 the Federal Writers' Project was taken over by the individual states and renamed the Writers' Project. Were the case histories compiled after the official demise of the New Jersey Ethnic Survey because Churchill was so reluctant to do case histories at the time of the survey? Unfortunately, we may never know for sure.

I have only suggested some of the significance of these case histories. The careful reader, students, and scholars will note much more. They are a gold mine of information about the immigrant experience. In the last analysis, the case histories speak for themselves. For many of these immigrants, the dreams for which they came to America were fulfilled; for others, they were crushed by the hard times of the Great Depression. But for all of them, America was the dream of their lives.

Editorial Method

In editing the New Jersey Ethnic Survey for publication, it was necessary to decide whether to include all the case histories and neighborhood descriptions in their entirety or to omit some of the weak and repetitious material in the interest of producing a more popular publication. I decided to take the latter course, based on my conviction that this is in keeping with the original intent of the national directors of the Federal Writers' Project, which was to produce "human documents." Also, I had to decide whether this should be a book about ethnicity or about the immigrant experience. I decided that the strength of the material lay more in what it tells us about the immigrant experience. As a result, I decided not to include materials in the survey pertaining to African-Americans, even though this was a major subproject of the New Jersey Ethnic Survey. While the Federal Writers' Project made a point of including African-Americans in their "redefinition" of America, they were predominantly migrants from the South rather than immigrants from another country, and their experiences were sufficiently different to warrant separate treatment.

I also eliminated case histories that were either fragmentary, in outline form, or a combination of outline and narrative. While these often contain useful information, they are difficult to read. I also removed material within case histories that was repetitious. In some cases the fieldworker simply went through a questionnaire, writing down nearly identical descriptions of such topics as funeral customs and birth practices.

I did include the notes and comments of the fieldworkers, because these provide useful information about the context in which the case histories were compiled, including some of the prejudices of the fieldworkers. Also, I included two case histories that were substantively different from the rest in that they were not based on personal interviews. One was a profile of Charles P. Gillen, an Irish mayor of Newark; and the other was of Nathan Barnert, the first Jewish mayor of Paterson. I included them because they provide important insights into ethnic politics.

Some of the case histories were written in the first person, others in the third person. I have retained those differences. In some cases, the narrative switched from first person to third person in the middle. In those cases, I used the person that was dominant. I standardized the way the material was presented because there was no consistency in the originals. Usually, the interviewee's words were enclosed in quotation marks. I used the more modern style used in oral history collections today, in which the notes and comments are italicized. I also standardized the descriptions of the interviewees, placing them all in the beginning rather than at the end, as was the case in the originals. The originals also had the name of the interviewer, the date of the interview, and the name of the typist in the beginning. I moved the name of the interviewer and the date of the interview to the end and eliminated the name of the typist.

With a few exceptions the interviewees were anonymous. When the names were given, I retained them. In two cases, however, I made the narratives anonymous because some of the material in them was potentially libelous. Where dialect was attempted, I retained its syntax, but I used no dialect spellings, in keeping with approved practice of oral history and folklore transcriptions. To avoid confusion and to make the case histories more readable, I made both the verb tense and the person of the interviews consistent. The one editorial device I added was the titles of the narratives. With a few exceptions, these were not part of the original narratives. I tried, however, to draw the titles from some phrase or thought expressed in the case history.

Place names and foreign-language words presented a special problem. There was no uniform spelling in the original texts. The place names were complicated in that the same place was referred to by a different name in different languages. For example, the capital of Galicia is Lwów in Polish, Lvov in Russian, Lviv in Ukrainian, and Lemberg in German; the city in what is now western Poland is Poznań in Polish, but when it was part of Prussia it was Posen in German. What is today Gdańsk in Polish, was then Danzig in German. In Lithuanian, the city is Vilnius, but it is Vilna in Russian and Wilno in Polish. I used a standardized transliterated spelling depending on the speaker. That is, if the speaker was a Pole, I used the Polish name, and so on. With foreign-language words, such as those in Yiddish, which is written in Hebrew characters, I used a standard transliterated spelling.

On Ferry Street, Newark, ca. 1890. (*New Jersey Historical Society.*)

Morris Canal, Newark, ca. 1910. (*New Jersey Historical Society.*)

Employees of John Nieder, tannery, ca. 1890. (*Newark Public Library.*)

St. Gerard's Festival, Newark, ca. 1924. (*Newark Public Library.*)

View of Paterson from Monument Heights, ca. 1895. (*Passaic County Historical Society.*)

Interior of a dye house, Paterson, ca. 1900. (*Passaic County Historical Society.*)

Young girl tending a skein winding machine, ca. 1900. (*American Labor Museum, Botto House National Landmark.*)

Horizontal warping shop, Paterson, ca. 1920. (*American Labor Museum, Botto House National Landmark.*)

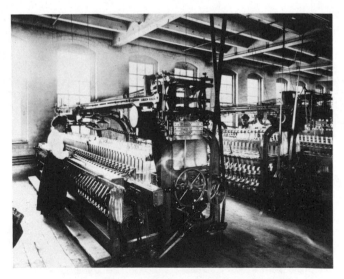

Ribbon-weaving shop, ca. 1910. (*Passaic County Historical Society.*)

Brochure for the Yiddish Film *A Brivele der Mamen*. (*New Jersey Ethnic Survey, New Jersey State Archives.*)

THE WORK

ORG

'CIRCLE CHORUS
FEB. 1923

The Workmen's Circle Chorus, Paterson, 1923. (*Heinrichs Collection, Paterson Museum.*)

Prince Street before World War I. (*Newark Public Library.*)

Jewish neighborhood on River Street, Paterson, 1933. (*Heinrichs Collection, Paterson Museum.*)

Tenth anniversary banquet of the Lodzer Young Men's Benevolent Association, Paterson, 1928. (*Passaic County Historical Society.*)

Jewish veterans at a Passover Seder, Paterson, ca. 1925. (*Heinrichs Collection, Paterson Museum.*)

WPA workers, Newark, ca. 1940. (*New Jersey Ethnic Survey, New Jersey State Archives.*)

Newark in 1800 was still predominantly an agricultural town of farmers and skilled craftsmen. Founded in 1666 by Puritans from Connecticut, the layout of its streets, with greens at either end of Broad Street, showed vestiges of a New England town. By 1850 Newark had become a city of immigrants and industries. It was the country's leading leather-producing center, and its other industries included jewelry manufacturing, carriage and harness making, and beer brewing.[1] The foreign-born popula-

---

Irish

---

tion of the city rose from only 18 percent in 1836 to 37 percent in 1860. Although first-generation immigrants were never a majority of Newark's population, the foreign-born and their children made up almost half the city's population in the period from 1850 to 1910.[2]

The transformation of Newark from rural town to industrial city coincided with the major immigration of the Irish to America. Between 1801 and 1900 more than a million people emigrated from Ireland, which was more than the entire population remaining in Ireland in 1900.[3] A disportionate number emigrated in the decade following the potato blight in 1845. There were equal numbers of male and female emigrants, and the overwhelming majority of the Irish who came to the United States were young, that is, under thirty-five years of age.[4] By 1860 there were more than sixty-two thousand Irish in New Jersey, which constituted more than 50 percent of the foreign-born population in the state.[5] In 1860, 24 percent of the household heads in Newark were foreign-born Irish, making them the city's largest immigrant group.[6]

The Irish in Newark tended to concentrate in a neighborhood between the Passaic River and the Newark salt marshes. It was originally known as Down Neck because the shape of the land resembled the neck of a bottle. Later, after the construction of the railroad, it became known as the Ironbound, because it was set apart from the rest of the city by railroad trestles. The neighborhood was a mixture of factories, working-class housing, and retail stores along its own main street,

Ferry Street. It was the neighborhood in which each new wave of immigrants settled. In the 1840s, Down Neck was predominantly Irish, with some Germans. By the 1880s it was becoming Italian, Polish, Lithuanian, and Russian. In the 1920s the neighborhood again changed as Spanish and Portuguese immigrants moved in. In 1939, the Federal Writers' Project's New Jersey guidebook described it as "a triangular section of lowland solidly built with workers' frame houses and blackened by the city's most important industrial plants. . . . Scores of small independent retail shops serve a population which seldom visits other portions of Newark."[7]

The Irish who came to Newark in the early nineteenth century found work as unskilled laborers and domestic servants. In the 1820s they worked on the construction of the Morris Canal, connecting Jersey City with Phillipsburg on the New Jersey side of the Delaware River, across from the Lehigh Valley. The route of the Morris Canal came through downtown Newark and Down Neck. One of the interviewees remembers swimming as a boy in the canal. In the 1840s the Irish worked on the construction of the railroads that eventually put the canal out of business. Unskilled Irish laborers also worked in Newark factories, expecially in the dirty jobs connected with hatting, leathermaking, and currying.[8]

The newly arrived Irish were not warmly welcomed by the native-born Protestants in the city. Newark's first St. Patrick's Day parade in 1834 was accompanied by catcalls from derisive spectators.[9] In 1853, Irish Catholics celebrated the installation of Newark's first bishop with a procession through the streets. The Protestants held their own counterdemonstration, which resulted in incidents of violence. In 1854, vigilantes attacked Irish laborers laying track on the Morris and Essex Railroad in Newark. When a fire broke out in a tannery that had a large Irish work force, only one fire company responded because the city's volunteer fire companies were predominantly native-born Protestants. Some of the violence was between the Protestant Irish (Orangemen) and the Irish Catholics. In September 1854, a group of Newark Orangemen, who were members of the anti-Catholic American Protestant Association, held a march past a leather factory where a large number of Irish Catholics worked. The Catholic workers attacked the Protestant marchers, who in turn sacked St. Mary's Catholic Church. Two tannery workers were killed in this incident, which became known as the APA Riot.[10]

The neighborhood saloon was an important immigrant institution in the nineteenth-century city. According to historian Rudolph Vecoli, "The saloon served the Irish neighborhood as a social club in which the

Hiberian wit and blarney reigned. It was also the precinct headquarters where political alliances were sealed with a toast to the Emerald Isle. The saloonkeeper, therefore, was an important personage in the social and political life of the Irish community."[11] During the 1850s there was a strong temperance movement in New Jersey that pitted the native-born against the immigrants. The Germans in Newark owned many of the breweries, and the Irish owned many of the saloons. In 1855 a prohibition bill failed to pass the New Jersey legislature by only one vote.[12] Nationwide Prohibition in the 1920s finally destroyed the institution of the immigrant neighborhood saloon.

In the late nineteenth century, the Irish became politically powerful in New Jersey. By 1870, they had become a dominant force in the city politics of Jersey City.[13] In 1890 there was an Irish congressman from New Jersey, two Irish state senators, and five Irish assemblymen. Also, in the 1890s two Irish-Americans from New Jersey were elected to the United States Senate.[14] By 1915, sixteen of the thirty-one members of the Newark Common Council were Irish. During the first decades of the twentieth century the political boss of Essex County (in which Newark is located) was James R. Nugent. Charles P. Gillen, who was profiled by the New Jersey Ethnic Survey, was a wealthy Irish businessman with extensive real estate interests and a vice-president of the Guaranty Trust Company. He rose to political power by challenging the supremacy of Democratic party boss Nugent.[15]

The Irish in New Jersey were especially active in the labor movement, both in the rank and file and in the leadership. As early as 1856, the Irish Laborers' Union in Newark went on strike for higher wages. Irish workers were also active in the railroad riots in 1877. Despite the Catholic church's hostility toward the Knights of Labor, Irish Catholics made up much of its membership in New Jersey. The Grand Master Workman of the Knights of Labor, Terence V. Powderly, was himself the son of Irish immigrants. Peter J. McGuire of Camden was an organizer of the Brotherhood of Carpenters and Joiners, one of the founders of the American Federation of Labor, and a lobbyist for the establishment of the national holiday of Labor Day. In Paterson, Irish-born Marxist Joseph P. McDonnell led a series of textile worker strikes in the 1880s and edited the radical newspaper the *Labor Standard*.[16] Thus, it is appropriate that several of the case histories reflect Irish union activity.

The Irish were also active in the Irish republican movement, which was the fight to gain independence for Ireland from Great Britain. Though the Catholic church condemned the Fenian Brotherhood, which was founded in 1859 as a secret society dedicated to overthrowing British rule in Ireland, the Irish joined the American branch of the society. The Fenians saw the Civil War as an opportunity to gain military experience, and they were active in the Union army. They also financed the construction in 1881 of the submarine designed by Irish-born John Philip Holland of Paterson, which was intended for military use against the British.[17] The case histories reflect the experiences of recent immigrants from Ireland who fought against the Royal Irish Constabulary (British military units stationed in barracks throughout Ireland in the period 1916–1920) and the Black and Tans (the British auxiliary police sent to Ireland in 1920, whose name came from the khaki coats and dark green trousers and caps they wore). Irish-American heroes were the leaders of the Irish republican movement: Daniel O'Connell (1775–1847), who was responsible for rekindling Irish nationalist feelings; Charles Stewart Parnell (1846–1891), who was chairman of the Home Rule party; and Eamon de Valera (1882–1975), leader of the Sinn Fein (which united various Irish republican organizations), president of the provisional government of Ireland and, later, prime minister of the Republic of Ireland.

The memories in the section are some of the earliest in the New Jersey Ethnic Survey. They take us back to a time when the streets of Newark were lighted by gaslight and when immigrants came to the United States in sailing vessels. Memories were dated by important events in the lives of people, such as the Big Wind off the Irish coast in 1839 and the Blizzard of Eighty-eight. By the time these interviews were conducted, Down Neck had changed from a predominantly Irish neighborhood, and there was already a nostalgia for the days when it meant something to be a Down Neck Irishman.

After the Big Wind **35**

After the Big Wind

This interview was conducted in the Twelfth Ward, Newark.
Father and Mother came over in a sailing vessel. I don't know how long it took them. Gollies, I can't tell you when they came over here. As a matter of fact, Mother and Father didn't know their own ages. They came over here before the Civil War—after the Big Wind.
At this point I asked him when was the time of the Big Wind. He did not know. A companion of his, who was sitting in on the conversation, said the Big Wind occurred off the Irish coast in the year 1839.
I asked a truckman once if he remembered the time of the Big Wind. "Indeed, I do. Sure, I played baseball at the bottom of the wind."
I know an Irishman who came into the saloon to telephone. It was the first time he used a phone. He wanted Bill Brennan. Another Irishman in the saloon told him just to ask for Bill Brennan. The Irishman called up Brennan. The telephone operator asked him for the number. "Number be damned," he said. "I want to talk to me delegate Bill Brennan. He lives at 240 Springfield Avenue. Ye ought to know him." No joke. It's the absolute truth.
The same man came to vote. The challenger challenged his vote. He said he wasn't a citizen. He brought the door of his closet with the citizen papers pasted on it. He couldn't take off the papers.
I put fourteen years on the election board. The biggest businessmen were the dumbest voters. The man who worked hard every day was the most intelligent voter. I could tell you plenty of stories of the election business. The workingman after a hard day's work reads the paper and learns what's going on and votes according to his conscience.
I asked him if his father served in the Civil War.
Father was too young to go to war. He went into business, married, brought up a family, served a term in the legislature. He refused to serve a second time. He told them, "You almost made a crook out of me the first time, and I don't want to serve a second time."
I asked him how long a term in the state legislature was then. He didn't know.
It was fifty-eight years ago. I was only five or six years of age. I remember Grover Cleveland in 1884, riding down Market Street in Balbach's carriage.[18] He was elected in 1884, beaten by Benjamin Harrison in 1888, and reelected in 1892.
Father was not very wealthy, but he did a fine job of raising the family of six. I could tell you plenty about people who trimmed him. He

always lived in the Ironbound neighborhood. He lived in this section from the time he came over here until the time he died.

"What was the district like when he came here?" I inquired.

Irish and German. I remember when there wasn't an Italian in it, this side of the railroad. There was only four families of Jews. We didn't have modern conveniences in the houses. Ferry and Market streets were the only streets paved. No, there was a side street paved. The only lights they had were lampposts—gas. The lamplighter used to go around with matches. He had to climb each lamppost, before he got smart enough to use a long light. We use to go swimming in the Passaic River with our birthday suits. I wish I had those days over again. That's when they caught shad in the Passaic. We only had to open a few buttons and dive in. Those were the good old days. We didn't realize it. Lots of time we'd be diving from lumber piles at Clark's lumber house, when a policeman would come along. We'd swim across the Passaic and sit on the other side till he went away. The old Down Neck, when the Irish and Germans were here, was the best place in New Jersey— no, I mean in the world. Where the steelworks are we'd have ice skating thirty-one nights straight with the moon shining every night, when I was a kid. In the Blizzard of Eighty-eight we walked on the snow and looked into the second-story windows in all the houses of Market Street. There were two horsecars stuck between Monroe and Adams streets on Market. After we got wet from the snow, we built a fire in the horsecars and dried ourselves, so we wouldn't get a tanning when we got home.

Since Father came here, we have every nationality on the face of the earth—everyone. I don't care who they are. After Father and Mother died, my wife died.

"Could you tell me something about your sisters and brothers," I asked.

We all live together like Mother Brown's cow, and Mother Brown only had one cow. I thank the good Lord that we are pretty well off.

At the mention of the word "Lord," the respondent made the following commentary on religion:

Whether a man is Protestant, Catholic, or Jew, he should follow his religious belief. The man who attacks religion meets a bad end. I'd hate to be in any man's shoes who dies when he has no religion. He'll have to answer for every idle word and deed before the final judge. It isn't anybody's business what his religion is.

I inquired about the different nationalities that have moved into the Ironbound.

The Slovaks, the Poles, and the Lithuanians—yes, all except the

Spaniards and the Portuguese are all right. When the Spaniards and the Portuguese moved into the neighborhood, the kids would rush home with their lanterns, and when they got to the door, they wouldn't stop ringing the bell until someone came to the door. They sure used to be scared.

My inquiry into nationalities caused him to begin a conversation on the changing of street names.

It was childish to change German names to American names during the war. Pilsudski, originally Sanford Street, was changed to Tyler in honor of an American general, and then changed to Pilsudski Street in honor of the Polish general.[19] You can't imagine how good it makes them feel. They have a swell church. The church, St. Casimir's Church, has the largest seating capacity of any church in New Jersey. They fill it in five separate masses. They have a parochial school.

At the beginning of the interview, the respondent was not very eager to talk about himself. At this point I asked him if he could tell me about himself. He gave the following account:

I graduated from St. James' and St. Patrick's schools. At that time there was only one high school, on the corner of Linden and Washington streets. Now they have dozens. I went to school at seven years old and quit at sixteen. When I went to school, I could read, write, and do a little figuring.

I put in over eighteen years for a concern in Down Neck. I was laid off at holiday time. The reason given was to reduce expenses. I put in twenty years and two months for a concern in the same neighborhood—gave them more than was required of me and was handed a check for two weeks' salary and let out without any rhyme or reason. That's the absolute truth. I know people who had worse experiences than I did. I know people who worked for fifty years, who helped them make their money, and were fired.

I went to work for a man named McGregor. I learned the plating business. I gave it up because of my health. I acted as bartender for three years, and then worked for another concern, in the printing business. In other words, you can say I worked eighteen years for one concern and twenty years for another. Once I worked as a shipping clerk.

I raised a family of four. We lost one. We have three youngsters living, two boys and one girl. My children are happy and successful.

Don't put my political affiliations. I wouldn't want to give my experiences as an election officer. They were terrible.

At this point in the interview, a radio was turned on in the room we were in. It was a news broadcast by Richard Brooks. He was reporting on the war situation.

I hate to hear about that war. I don't even read newspapers anymore. I am sick, sore, and disgusted about the war. I can't see how people can be so selfish. That's all it is—selfishness. Now they want to give them ninety days' credit to buy munitions. That means they'll finally get more credit, and then we'll be in it. Cash-and-carry is all right, but no credit.[20] The women have the right idea: not raising their sons to be shot. But I think, though, birth control is not right. There's an old and very good saying: Do unto others as you would have them do to you.

Ernest Pentz
October 6, 1939

Born in the Ironbound

This interview was made in the Twelfth Ward in Newark on October 6. The individual interviewed was a second-generation Irishman.

My people have lived here sixty years. Father came here when he was about twelve years old. His parents were here ahead of him.

"Did your father have any hardships?" I asked him.

No, Father did not have hardships. Father's father was an officer in the British army. He was in the army in the Civil War at the age of sixteen. He had two brothers in the old New Jersey regiment—volunteer stuff. He died at about forty-five years of age, and he left seven children. He was a hatter by trade. A hard-working man who supported his family in good shape.

Did they have unions in those days?

Yes, he was a union man.

Born in the Ironbound district?

Yep. Childhood was pretty good. People in those days did not bellyache the way they do today. This neighborhood was mostly German and Irish those days. I could have gone to high school, but I didn't want to. We used to swim in the Morris Canal. It is now Raymond Boulevard. The old canal bed was at Kresge's store.[21] Its source was at Lake Hopatcong. We used to get all full of tar. When the cop came, we used to run like the devil. The terminus was at the Passaic River. The canal was used for hauling coal. The barges were towed by a couple of mules.

In this whole territory the land was vacant, and people grazed their cows. When the section was laid, the streets were raised and the land had depressions. For recreation and fun, we made it ourselves. We made wagons. We had no movies, so we devised our own means.

My first job was at one dollar a week. The dollar was dirty. It always struck me funny. They thought they could make a wood carver out of me, but I found it wasn't in me. I wound up by serving my apprenticeship in the building line. Became a building mechanic—a bricklayer.

Ernest Pentz
October 9, 1939

Trying to Make a Living

The man I interviewed was standing outside the Carpenters' Union, 60 William Street. He did not want to give me his name.

My grandfather was born in Cork. My grandmother was born in Kilkenny. On my father's side it was McCarthy, and on my mother's side it was Fitzpatrick. My father was born in Newark, and my mother was born in New York. In those times they came over in sailboats; there was no steam. There isn't much that I know about them. They came over here to get anything they could, like we do now. My grandfather had a hide and fat business. The fat house was on the corner of Norfolk Street and Thirteenth Avenue. He was there for years. That's the Fitzpatrick I'm talking about now.

"Did your father have hard times?" I asked him.

No, he worked for years for the United Cigar stores. He was manager of a store. I am a carpenter, trying to make a living. I have three kids—they're all girls. I haven't lived any place else. I lived in Newark all my life. Thirty-five years.

Did you have a happy childhood?

Oh, sure, that's the trouble. I had it too easy. If I had had to work a little harder, maybe I would have got somewhere. Look at how these foreigners come over and make good.

My grandfather was worth over one hundred thousand dollars. I was born in our big house on Norfolk and Thirteenth Avenue. We had everything. We never wanted for shoes or clothing or eats. I never had an education. I didn't figure I needed education because I was well off. In those days, the people didn't think much about education. The property where the playground is on is where we used to have our house. The property is right near the Robert Treat school.

Ernest Pentz
October 10, 1939

Started as a Lamplighter

I started off to work for a quarter a week lighting lampposts—remember that?—in the old Sixth Ward. The next job I got was at $1.25 a week in the old American Hat Leather on Sixth Street. The next job was down in the Franklin button works in the Old Domestic at $2.25 a week. They raised me to $3.00 a week. Then from there to the Electric Cutlery works at $6.00 a week. From there I went to the Valley Forge Cutlery at $12.00 a week. I put in eight years in there. And then from there I started to play baseball. There I was an umpire. I put twenty-eight years in at baseball and six years as an umpire. I have wound up as a bartender, and I am still working as a bartender. I was born fifty-seven years ago in Newark.

Ernest Pentz

Born in the Old Country

A woman, sixty-three years old

I was born in the old country. I was almost thirteen years old when I came to this country. I haven't much to say, except that this country is alright.

In those days, children went to work young. Today, they can't go to work until they are eighteen. In Amsterdam, New York, fifty years ago, I recall a young Irishwoman of nine years of age worked in the Sanford Mills from six in the morning to six at night. I heard of her death just a little while ago. Women built up that mill.

My father was a union man. He belonged to the Knights of Labor. Before the union came in, my father worked for nine dollars a week and had to do stable work on Sundays. When the Knights of Labor came in, there was no Sunday work and the wages were raised to fifteen dollars a week and hours reduced. He was a brewery worker. I haven't heard of any strikes in the breweries until Hoffman's went on a strike.[22]

My husband is not at home, but he was born here. His parents were born here. He had a couple of uncles who fought in the Civil War.

All my life I have been hearing about war—the Boer War, the Spanish-American War, the World War, and the war today.[23] War is a terrible thing. Anyway, it has never reached us here in this country.

Ernest Pentz
1939

A Down Neck Irishman

The respondent is in his forties.
I'm an original Down Neck Irishman. I went to St. Aloysius School, and I'm interested in Irish literature and Irish games and pastimes. I attribute that to the interest my Irish parents had in Irish games and pastimes. I helped to organize Irish games and football—hurling.[24] I also helped to organize them in the state of New Jersey, and I was president of that organization for two years—1926 and 1927.

Ernest Pentz

Came from Ireland

I would judge the respondent to be in his thirties.
I came from Ireland in 1925. The place I came from in Ireland is a great historic town. There is a great improvement now, and they come from all over Ireland to this town. They are trying to canonize a saint. The town has been noted for its industry—for its linen. Since I left there, there have been big changes. Since I came here, I found this a wonderful country which cannot be excelled anywhere. I mean it can't be beaten anywhere. It's pretty hard to go into details.

Ernest Pentz

A Boilermaker

I was born May 17, 1888, the year of the Big Blizzard. In my home town—Nashville, Tennessee—the snow was up to people's necks. My father died when I was three months old, and I was raised in an orphan asylum until I was ten. Then I went to work in a bucket factory to support my mother. I was twelve years old then. Then, I quit the bucket factory and went to work as a messenger for the Western Union and the postal service. I worked part time in each one. I worked approximately a year for them. I quit and went to work in an apprentice shop for two years. At sixteen years of age, I left home and started working in boiler shops wherever I could find work. I rode freight trains all over the country. I went through Oklahoma and Texas and worked on bridges and railroads as a structural ironworker. Then, in Port Arthur,

Texas, I went to work for the Texas refinery. I served out my time as a boilermaker and got my card. Then, I went into the oil fields during the oil boom of 1912 and 1913, building oil storage tanks.

When the war broke out, I went to Virginia and worked for the Chicago Bridge and Iron works. I quit. I was in Hopewell, Virginia, for the DuPont people. That was the biggest gun powder plant in the country. They employed thirty thousand people during the construction of the plant. It was called the "Small New York." In Hopewell, I worked in the boilermaking division. I quit DuPont and went back to work for the Chicago Bridge and Iron works and helped build a steel water tower, one of the largest in the world. It was built to prevent fire. There were all wooden barracks.

Being shipped from Camp Lee to Philadelphia, we put a water tower in at the Philadelphia Arsenal in South Philadelphia. After completion of the job, I obtained a job as boilermaker in the Hog Island shipyards, the largest shipyards in the world. Fifty ships could be built there at one time. I worked there until the armistice. When the armistice was signed, it closed overnight.

From there I came to Newark and obtained work in the federal shipyards as a boilermaker. After working for two years, I went into the steeplejack business for myself, and I have been working in that business since—eighteen to twenty years.[25] I had two falls. One fall was a hundred feet. I fell off a smokestack at Napthea hat works, William and Main streets. After being laid up for three months, I had a job at Haledon, New Jersey, for the Manley Piece dye works and fell fifty feet off of a stack. Yet, I have no defect from either fall.

Now I find it hard to get a job, and I have to take work as a watchman on WPA.

Ernest Pentz

Only Way to Get Decent Wages

Interview with Mr. Clark, president of the Bartenders' Union of the American Federation of Labor

I was born of Irish parents who had come from England. Their parents came from Ireland. I went to parochial schools in Boston. I graduated from St. John's Academy, a preparatory school, and then spent two years in training as a textile engineer. This was the extent of my college education.

I worked for a textile mill as a draftsman. It was part-time work while going to school. I learned the rudiments of the textile industry. While I was working in the textile industry, the towns of Lowell, Haverill, and Manchester became towns of empty textile factories. They moved to the South, where they could get cheap labor. I found no jobs open and decided I wanted to see the world.

I got out of school in 1919. In that year I shipped out of Boston on a fruit steamer to Buenos Aires, South America. Since then I have been in England, Ireland, France—all the European countries. I've been in Singapore, Hong Kong, the Malayan straits.

I worked as a salesman, a cook, a hotel man—everything. I worked as a tree surgeon for the Davey Tree Surgery Company. I learned a great deal about trees from one of the greatest men in the business.

I got married in 1931. I settled down and took up organization as a life work. I was just a bartender when I started. I found that a union is the only way a man can get decent wages. With an organization behind him, a man has a backing. It is not a question of pressing an employer with a whole lot of grievances. We settle grievances by arbitration and by cooperation between employee and employer. First, it is our duty to keep our men employed—to see to it they get proper remuneration. We never force any man to join our union. We sit down with a man and explain to him how the union benefits him. If he doesn't understand, we don't want such a man. Such a man is liable to work overtime and for less wages. The employment situation is caused by such men doubling up and putting other men out of work. We don't use the old-time methods of force on an employee or an employer. In these days we use negotiation.

We not only help our own men, but we help the employer. We point out to the employer that only unskilled men, as a rule, will take low wages and work long hours and that these men make up the differences in wages by robbing the till. They do indifferent work and make the employer lose trade.

A union bartender always knows his business and gains the respect of customers. He knows that he has to be honest to keep his job and stay in the union. Not long ago, a tavern keeper came to us and told us that, since he hired one of our men, the receipts dropped thirty-five dollars a week. On the days the tavern keeper was away and the man was in charge, we sent some of our men to buy drinks. When we and the boss checked up, we found the bartender was putting the money into his own pocket. We fined the guy seventy-five dollars and had him expelled from the union. Sometimes we take such fellows back but never send him out on a job. They're kept on the books, but we never recommend them for a job. With a union bartender, a tavern keeper or a saloon owner knows he is keeping people working at good wages, and the difference he pays between good and low wages is more than paid up.

Our toughest nuts to crack are the employers who are always crying the blues. One tavern keeper was doing a $750 net business with the two bartenders and not paying them decent wages. We know that one week he paid cash for a car, clamped $2,000 cash down on two lots. He built an addition to his place and cried he was going broke. These fellows keep two sets of books. When we go and see them to get them to hire union bartenders, they show us the book with a lot of losses. We know that they have this other book with the profits. But with the consumption of beer, wine, and other liquors we know that their profit is higher than they say it is. We can figure out how much they make. They always talk about all the donations to charities they make. We know that they have been able to make all this money at the expense of the labor they hire. These are the kind of men we try to get to hire union bartenders and other union help.

We advocate a union man in every bar. We never ask a family who operates their own tavern or saloon. Some of them voluntarily join. I always have been an organization man. I started from the bottom. I came from middle-class parents. I didn't have the early hardships of many labor men. The CIO has lent a great stimulation to our union. We belong to the International Hotel and Restaurant Employees Association. A couple of years ago we had only 60,000 members. We now have 450,000 members.

Ernest Pentz
October 4, 1939

Chased Out of Ireland

The respondent is in his fifties.

I've been here over twenty-three years. I was chased out of Ireland by England. We licked them in the end. The commander I fought under lives in this country. That was 1915. I wouldn't mention his name. If I got down to tell you my own history, it would take a volume. I have been in this business almost since I came here.

"Anything else?" I asked him.

This was a good country until the politicians got ahold of it and put it on the bum.

Do you want to make any comments on Ireland?

The country is still beautiful. They will never be able to drain the Lakes of Killarney nor the river Shannon. I've been in Paris, Bordeaux, Marseilles, New York, Chicago, and I still think Dublin is the most beautiful city of them all. I still love the country of my adoption and would join the army to fight for it, but I think I am too old. You can add this: that the Dies Committee should continue its investigation, and all those with Communistic, Nazi, or Fascists convictions should be ferreted out.

I found it very difficult to get an interview from this respondent. He was very suspicious of the purpose of the interview. This is true of a great number of Irish from whom I have tried to get interviews.

Ernest Pentz

Fought against the Black and Tans

This interview was made in a tavern, and the respondent at the time was under the influence of liquor. Only through a friend of his was I able to get this interview. The respondent was a stocky man of medium height. I should say that his age was somewhere from thirty-five to forty.

My father was Irish, my mother was Irish, and so am I Irish. I am a union man and proud of it. I was in the Building Trades Council. I was in a union ten years before I came to this country and twelve years in this country. I worked as a laborer when I was first here. I belonged to a laborers' union. I was in a bartenders' local in Dublin—the best there was. I never scabbed in my life. I was a bartender at Number One Mill Street, Dublin. I'd rather go on relief instead of taking low wages. I'd always stick by the union and the Irish.

I got a bullet wound from the Black and Tans. I have a brother in the British army. He was caught in the draft. I fought against the Black and Tans, July 11, 1921. That's when the peace truce was signed with England and Ireland. I changed guards with the British groups taking over command. I went to Lanyford. When the Colones Barracks R.I.C. came in on a train, Commander Fitzpatrick was in charge. Fitzpatrick went to challenge the R.I. Constabulary. He got his brains blown out. We were behind him. We riddled the train with bullets of Thompson machine guns and Lee Enfield rifles. I left Ireland and came over here. I have been here twelve years.

Ernest Pentz

Active in the Republican Movement

This respondent did not appear to be more than thirty-eight or forty.
Well, during 1916 to 1922, I was active in the republican movement. From 1922 to 1927, I remained at home on a farm. In 1927 I came to Canada. I remained six months in Canada, and then I came to the United States. I worked as a conductor on the Hudson and Manhattan Railroad from 1927 to 1931. In this country I was in ten different states. In 1933, I started in the tavern business at this address.

I was active in all Irish movements. I had a unit in the St. Patrick's parade for three years. I am a native of County of Leitrim. I made a trip back to Ireland in 1929. I was then single. I got married in June 1932. I've got four kids, three boys and a girl. In 1937, I had another kid. I took my wife and three kids over to Ireland in 1937. I took my automobile with me and traveled in every county in Ireland. During the trouble in Ireland, I spent a year in jail from 1920 to 1921. I was eligible for a pension from the Irish government, but I haven't received it yet.

Ernest Pentz

The Blood of Irish Ancestry

You can blame the Irish for bringing Italians to Newark.

I have only been in Newark seventeen years. My grandparents came from Ireland. One came from Cork; the other came from Donegal. Father's side from Cork, and the mother's from Donegal. I don't have much about either of them. They settled in New York on the "Farms" at Forty-second Street. That's where they both met. New York at Forty-second Street was just a cow pasture.

Progress in those days moved fast. As the city moved uptown, they moved uptown. My grandparents on my father's side both died at what is Fifty-second Street. My mother's parents moved to what is now Long Island City. At that time, both my parents had grown and were married. My parents established their home in New York City. I think it was Fifty-eighth Street. My parents were married in New York City.

"Did your parents have any hardships?" I asked him.

In those days my father studied for law. A man to be a lawyer then had to spend a long apprenticeship. My father had children at the time. My grandfather died. He was a policeman. He saved the life of a great

Italian painter twice—once from drowning, once from fire. In gratitude the painter painted my grandfather's picture. Funny thing about families. We have things handed down from the past, and they're in the attic. Because of the misfortune of both his parents dying, my father had to seek a vocation which paid real money. He had brothers and sisters. Misfortune seemed to trail; and as misfortune of all kinds kept coming, the children kept coming. My father had fourteen children. The kids came along and grew and thrived. Although there was misfortune, we all got along. I'm the only one of all of them who didn't get an education. My brothers and sisters all went to college or universities.

As misfortune grew, my parents moved to Long Island City, which was then the country, and we kept on moving out as the city grew. We ended up in Jamaica [Queens], where my parents died, and where the main part of my family still lives. Of course, we had teaching in our home. The code we were taught was: first, be thankful for the religion you were lucky to be born in; second, be thankful you have been born an American; third, in your veins flows the blood of Irish ancestry.

Being one of a gang of fourteen kids—that's a lot of mouths to feed—I was near the tail end, when we were having misfortune. At that time Horace Greeley said, "Go West, young man." At eleven I left to rediscover America. I always kept in contact with the family when I was away.

In 1908, I joined the Sixty-ninth Regiment in New York City. That was known as the "Fighting Irish." The ban on Irish-Americans had been lifted, and I got in. It was originally known as the "Irish Volunteers." They were the Irish Volunteers in the Civil War. I won't go into that. It was absorbed by the National Guard. My kid brother, who was only nineteen years old and six feet one in his stocking feet, joined and laid down his life in France. Of course, I served in the war; and when I came back, I stayed at home a couple of years. I fell back in the old wanderlust. I didn't go very far. I came to Newark. Of course, after being here a short while, I married a girl from Newark. I then settled down and took on the difficult job of establishing a home.

I was not active fraternally until 1934. When a few of my Irish friends, who were veterans of the world war, saw that veterans seemed to be breaking into racial groups, I and five of my friends decided that the time was ripe to form a veterans' organization, which would be composed of men of Irish birth or heritage. And upon investigation, using the best statistics available, we found that in all wars participated in by this country, that men of Irish birth or heritage played the most dominant role. We found that in all the wars that never less than

65 percent of the enlisted men were Irish by birth or heritage. Even today, in the forces, not less than 50 percent of the men are Irish by birth or extraction. In realizing this fact, we formed the Irish War Veterans of the United States. To be eligible for membership in it, one must have fought for this country, provided that he is Irish by birth or extraction. We gave a Jewish veteran some of our blood. Afterwards, we told him that he was a better man than he was before.

We formed this organization, not so much primarily as a selfish thing, but more to bring to the realization what the Irish have done for this country. We took much time to delve into the history of the Irish in America and were surprised to find the history books in our own public schools, in a great many instances, did not have facts insomuch as the Irish were concerned. The best illustration that one could ask for is the case of Commodore John Barry.[26] They called John Paul Jones the "Father of the American Navy." This is an absolute falsehood. If one would go to Washington and go through the archives, they would find that George Washington appointed John Barry the head of the Navy. They left John Barry's name off the Navy monument in Annapolis. At the same time, if they will go to Constitutional Square in Philadelphia, they will find a statue of John Barry in the main entrance of Independence Hall. It was John Barry, a personal friend of Washington, who helped form our Constitution. Many a thing he did brought others in line.

So we finally formed the Irish War Veterans. We adopted as our insignia the shield of the United States superimposed upon a shamrock and these two superimposed on a golden circle. The three petals of the shamrock symbolized the army, navy, and marines; and by superimposing the shield on the shamrock, it shows that the Irish are constantly on guard and are always ready to defend it. It has grown into a national organization to let people remember what the Irish have done for the country.

After we were only formed a year, in 1935, we got the idea of bringing to life again the St. Patrick's Day Parade. In 1936, we had our first parade in forty-two years. We had fifty thousand on the streets. So as not to assume any selfish ideas in the matter, we called in all Irish groups to participate in this great enterprise, out of which was formed what is now known as the St. Patrick's Day Parade Committee, which has produced a parade every year, and which has increased in numbers each year tremendously.

I am now in the process of laying the groundwork for the preparation of a federation of Irish societies, the purpose of which will be to more closely tie the Irish activities together. I have had many trials and tribulations, which is only natural. Anything worthwhile always had its trials and tribulations.

Would you want to tell me something about your travels?

No, there isn't much that I have to say, only that I always wanted to work. I have always been independent. I'd rather refuse a piece of cake if I had to get it as a favor. I'd rather take crumbs instead. I'd rather get them by working. I realized later the value of an education. When I came to Newark, I saw the handwriting on the wall. I took a civil service examination and got in the civil service. My father always taught me that, when I did a job, always act as if you were working for yourself. I always hear the stuff about pull. It may be in some cases. If you work and show people you have ability, you usually come out on top. Business today is based on energetic, hard work. A good, energetic, conscientious worker never stays in the background. You know, most people are willing to work. Here and there are some grumblers.

At this point in the interview, the respondent took out his watch and quickly rose from the chair and excitedly said:

Gee, it's late. I've got to meet my boy for lessons. You are going to hear a lot about him some day.

I inquired if the boy was a musician.

No, he is a singer.

He handed me an album from a table nearby and opened the pages. While he was getting his coat on, I looked through it. It was filled with newspaper clippings and musical programs. The heading of one clipping read: "Ten-Year-Old Prodigy Will Sing at Memorial Park." There were scores of programs. One listed songs in French and Italian. In the meantime, the father had gotten on his coat and pointed to one of the songs on a program.

There's a song even opera singers find hard to sing.

My respondent then asked:

Are you going in the direction of Washington Street?

Yes.

We can walk down together.

As we walked together outside, I told him that I had been in the service.

Yes.

Yes. I was in the navy.

You fellows had a hard time. When I was in, I served two roles. I was in the Sixty-ninth, and they transferred me to the Lafayette Escadrille.[27] Before the war I was an automobile mechanic, and they needed mechanics.

We soon reached Plane Street. His ten-year-old son was there. He decided not to go as far as Washington Street. We shook hands, and, as I said goodbye to him, he said that he would be glad to give me the names of as many Irishmen that he could who would be interesting to interview.

Ernest Pentz

Belongs to a Lot of Organizations

My mother was born in Ireland in Dublin City. Her name was Annette Carroll. She was the daughter of Patrick Carroll and Marianne Bryan. My father was born in England while his parents were on a trip from Ireland. His father's name was John Crilly. He came to this country in 1892. My mother came the same year. They were married in New York City.

I was born in New York City, and when I was quite young, my uncle and aunt reared me. They had reared me really since my birth. I went to St. Aloysius School in Down Neck. My mother and father had five children. One died, my aunt and uncle took two, and my mother and father kept the other two. After graduating from St. Aloysius, I went to St. Mary's High in New York City, but I had to quit school on account of ill health. I lost a lot of jobs because of ill health. After trying every conceivable way of getting well, I went to a chiropractor. The improvement was so rapid that I was inspired to take it up myself. I worked during the day in New York, while I studied at night for four years. In addition to the degree of D.C., which is the Doctor of Chiropractic, I received a Ph.C., a Philosopher of Chiropractic, because I received over 95 percent in all my examinations.

My one ambition was to be a mechanical draftsman. I began to study at Newark Tech.[28] I couldn't finish it because of ill health. I wanted to study law, but I couldn't make the grade because of ill health.

I am past grand regent of Court Seton No. 72 of the Catholic Daughters of America, past district deputy of the Catholic Daughters, and president of Division Two of the Ladies' Auxiliary of the Ancient Order of Hibernians. I was county officer for four years in the Ladies' Auxiliary. I have just been elected to the office of Irish historian of the Ladies' Auxiliary of the Ancient Order of Hibernians of Essex County. I was on the original parade committee for the reorganization of the St. Patrick's

Parade, and I have been active on the parade committee ever since. I do not want to say any more, except that I belong to a lot of organizations.

Some people say chiropractors have no education, but I have had special courses at Upsala, New York University, and Columbia in psychology, public speaking, parliamentary law, social sciences, and business English.

Ernest Pentz

Active in Politics

Charles P. Gillen was born in Ireland in 1876. He came with his family to Newark when he was eight years old. He has lived in Newark ever since. He was educated at Seton Hall College. He entered the real estate business at age eighteen in 1894 under the name of Charles P. Gillen and Company. It continued under the same name to the present time. He became active in politics at age twenty-one and has been active ever since. In 1912, he was elected city commissioner on the Democratic ticket. He was turned down for renomination by the Democratic machine in 1915. He was the first office holder to be elected as an independent in the city of Newark, beating the combined conspiracy of the Republican and Democratic machines. He was reelected in 1917 as city commissioner under the commission form of government. He served from 1917 to 1921 as mayor of Newark and was reelected city commissioner in 1921, again in 1925, and again in 1929, serving until May 1933. He was appointed a member of the Newark Housing Authority in March 1939, which office he still occupies. He served in elected city office for much longer than any other public official in the city of Newark.

Most men who become very active in politics, particularly those who run for office time and again and who have much to do with campaigns and politics in general, gradually lose their business or give it up. Mr. Gillen was one of the few public men who never neglected his business for politics. For the forty-four years that he devoted to real estate business, from the time that he was eighteen years old to the present, he was always extremely active. For the past twenty-five years, he has devoted most of his real estate efforts to the development of tracts of lands of which he was part owner. He was part owner and developer of the last three residential tracts developed in Newark— the Monticello Park on South Orange Avenue, Stuyvesant Acres on Stuyvesant Avenue, and Mount Vernon Park on Chancellor and Lyons avenues. Beside these, he developed many smaller tracts. Many hundreds of buildings were erected on those tracts.

He was always very active in all social activities of the city, belonging to many organizations and mixing with all classes of people at all kinds of social gatherings. He was one of the organizers and first vice-president of the Guaranty Trust Company and was a director of other banks, building and loan associations, and mortgage companies.

His political career was one of the most turbulent and strenuous in the history of New Jersey politics. Always a Democrat, he refused to be bossed or "machine-controlled." During his first term as city commissioner of public works, he gained the enmity and open antagonism of the powerful Public Service Corporation and all its affiliates by opposing certain of their demands.[29] At that time, the influence of the Public Service Corporation was so great in New Jersey that it overshadowed almost everything; both party machines of the city and state government were absolutely subservient to the will of this company. Nearly everyone who fought against all of their demands was retired from public office or taken into the employ of the Public Service Corporation. Mr. Gillen fought them openly and also fought the Pennsylvania Railroad on fare rates. Challenging them to combat, he ran for office time and again; he was elected and reelected by the people on that issue. In these fights, he was also opposed by the powerful Democratic and Republican machines, who were very friendly to the Public Service Company. At the end of his first term, the Democratic machine refused to renominate him. It was tied up with the Public Service and other big interests that were under the control of the Public Service, with the Republican machine and a paving ring, which controlled all of the paving contracts. He denounced all these interests, made a smashing campaign, was reelected by a great vote. He won in spite of the full force and antagonism of the Democratic organization. His victory terminated the rule of the powerful Democratic boss, Joseph R. Nugent. In later years, he helped to lead the Democrats in many of its campaigns. Serving as mayor during the war, he assumed the leading part in all activities of the city to help the nation in the world war. His administration, during the war and the three years following, was filled with a multitude of activities of all kinds, made necessary by extraordinary conditions existing during that period. As commissioner he fought incessantly against all extravagances. He did everything in his power to prevent the large number of public improvements undertaken by his fellow commissioners, which were not necessary, on the grounds that the city would be forced to borrow so much money for these unnecessary improvements that it would reach the stage of bankruptcy. The improvements he fought against were passed over his opposition and were made at a cost to the city of approximately $40 million. These expenditures impaired the city's credit and eventually got the city into all sorts of financial difficulties, from which it is now trying to free itself. Mr. Gillen's stand on these matters has been fully vindicated.

Like many other Irish-Americans, he took a leading part in all movements to bring about Irish freedom. He heard Charles Stewart Parnell at his own home in Ireland, when he was a small boy. His father was an ardent Irishman, who remembered seeing Daniel O'Connell when he [the father] was a child. He welcomed many of the famous Irishmen who came to Newark on various missions for the aid of the Emerald Isle, including Eamon de Valera, the prime minister of Ireland. In his business and social relationships, he became acquainted with many of the prominent Irish-Americans of Newark of the last half-century, including well-known politicians, newspapermen, manufacturers, the leading contractors of New Jersey, lawyers, and clergymen. With these men and many others of the Irish race, most of whom are gone to their rewards, Mr. Gillen had many dealings and was associated in many movements for the building, progress, and growth of the community.

A Lone Wolf

This respondent is in his sixties.

When the immigration boom was on, thousands went to Canada, a couple went to Australia, and some went to all parts of the world. You get the fever too. You leave. Sometimes you give up a good home. You find you've made a mistake. If my friend was here, he'd give you a good interview.

I'm only here by myself. Nobody belongs to me. I'm a lone wolf since the depression. This country is alright. Right now there isn't an opportunity to make a living. Lots of us fellows have it awful tough. It's a feast and a famine. You have a chance to get your head above water, then you sink again. The guy that has steady employment doesn't even know what is going on. It'll take me too long to tell you about myself. We have to take the good with the bad.

Ernest Pentz

I talians are one of the largest, if not the largest, ethnic group in New Jersey today. They began to emigrate from Italy in large numbers in the late nineteenth century due to a series of changes Italy was undergoing. One of these was rapid industrialization, which resulted in factory-made goods replacing handicrafts. Also, agriculture was becoming more commercial, which undermined the position of the landless peasants. Furthermore, the political unification of Italy in 1870 increased the tax burden, especially on the southern provinces.[1]

Italians

Between 1899 and 1910, more than two million Italians came to the United States. Eighty-four percent of them came from southern Italy. This early migration was overwhelmingly male, relatively young, and mostly unskilled. Forty-three percent were laborers, and 32 percent were farm laborers. Many of them did not intend to stay. It is estimated that of all the Italians who arrived in the United States between 1887 and 1907, 44 percent returned to Italy. New Jersey was a major destination for many Italians who came to the United States. By 1900 there were more Italians in New Jersey than in any other state except New York and Pennsylvania.[2]

Of all the cities of New Jersey, Newark had the largest number of Italians. They came from the provinces of Benevento, Caserta, Salerno, and Avellino. Most were Avellinese, especially from the towns of Caposele, Teora, and Vallata. Later arrivals came from the provinces of Messina and Palermo in Sicily and Matera and Potenza in Basilicata. Initially, they settled in colonies consisting of people from their own town, and they established mutual aid societies that provided sick and death benefits to their members and sponsored festivals to the patron saint of their town. After World War II these mutual aid societies were replaced by organizations that spanned the entire Italian ethnic group, such as the Italian Catholic Union, the Knights of Columbus, and the Holy Name Society.[3]

The early group of Italian immigrants in Newark dug ditches for the new gas and water mains being installed. They also worked as street sweepers, sewer cleaners, and track walkers. The height of the Italian immigration to Newark coincided with the building boom. Many Italians found work in the construction industry, both as skilled stonemasons and as unskilled laborers. They worked for the railroads, removing the grade crossings (the intersections where the tracks and streets were at the same level). They also worked for Public Service Electric and Gas Company, removing overhead wires, burying electric power lines, and laying track for the trolleys. About 1910 they began to replace German and Irish workers in the leather factories. There were some skilled tailors, hatters, and dyers, as well as skilled craftsmen in the construction trades such as stonemasons. Also, there were some Italian ethnic bankers, tavern owners, boardinghouse owners, and storekeepers. The Italians had a virtual monopoly on barbering in the city.[4]

The Italians in Newark were excluded from political power by the Irish and Germans until 1933, when a coalition of Jews and Italians united to elect the first Jewish city commissioner, Meyer L. Ellenstein, and the first Italian commissioner, Anthony Minisi. In 1948 two Italian-Americans, Peter W. Rodino and Hugh J. Addonizio, were elected to Congress from Essex County. The first Italian mayor of Newark was Ralph A. Villani, who was elected in 1949. Addonizio later became mayor in 1962.[5]

One of the great finds in the New Jersey Ethnic Survey is the case history of an Italian *padrone* (labor agent) in Newark. This document tends to confirm some of the statements about the institution offered by historian Humbert Nelli. He argues that the padrone system was rather informal. The padrone, according to Nelli, was little more than a labor agent, mainly involved in railroad and construction work. The padrone knew the employers and the American system of work, and he could speak both Italian and English. There was not always a clear line of demarcation between the padrone and the banker, which is clearly seen in this case history. By 1910 the padrone system was in decline, primarily because the immigrants became more settled, more familiar with English, and more affluent and because reformers wrote articles exposing the abuses of the system.[6]

Equally rare is the brief description of the Clifton Avenue bathhouse located in the Italian neighborhood of Newark. The immigrant bathhouse was an important urban institution, which has not yet been studied by scholars. The public baths are a very old institution that can be traced back to the ancient Greeks and Romans. Yet the immigrant baths in American cities were established to fill a very specific need during a time when few tenement houses had indoor plumbing. They represent, not only a part of the immigrant experience, but also an important phase in the development of urban public health.

There is also a description of the Italian neighborhood of Silver Lake on the boundary between Newark and Belleville. This was a region that the urban sociologists at the University of Chicago called "the zone of emergence," that is, a suburb into which immigrants or their children moved as they emerged from the ethnic neighborhoods of the inner city. Silver Lake was described in 1939 by the New Jersey guidebook as a neighborhood "with comparatively modern bungalows and six- and eight-family houses built within the last quarter of a century to house the section of the Italian population which first became economically able to move from the downtown slum area."[7] The description provides evidence of the maintainance of ethnic traditions in suburban ethnic communities, including reading ethnic newspapers; eating ethnic foods; planting gardens with grape arbors; holding saints festivals; listening to the operatic music of Guiseppe Verdi, Gioacchino Rossini, Gaetano Donizetti, and Vincenzo Bellini; and joining ethnic societies, such as the Figli di Italia (the Sons of Italy, an Italian-American mutual aid association founded in 1902). There is also an indication of how the Italian-American community was divided on the confrontation between communism and fascism that was taking shape in Europe at the time.

Finally, there is a report on another rarely studied immigrant institution—the immigrant bank. Such banks were common among immigrants from southern and eastern Europe. According to the Dillingham Commission, the United States Senate commission chaired by Senator William P. Dillingham to investigate immigrant living and working conditions, in 1910 there were approximately twenty-six hundred such banks in the United States, of which about eighty were in New Jersey. Many of these so-called banks were informal arrangements that were not incorporated and had no capital besides the deposits of the immigrants. Often they were adjuncts to steamship ticket agencies, employment agencies, saloons, boardinghouses, real estate offices, or barber shops. Besides holding the savings of immigrant workers, these ethnic banks also wrote letters, received mail, and sent money home for their depositors.[8]

Conflicts between ethnic groups were an integral part of the urban ethnic scene. A rare description of a fight between the Irish and the Italians in Newark is contained in the unpublished recollections of Peter B. Mattia. Born in the mountain town of Calabritto in the province of Avellino, his father came to the United States in 1872. After living in New York City for a year, his father came to Newark, where he found work as a woodchopper and sent for his family to join him. Peter Mattia grew up in Newark, working first as a barber and then as a portrait photographer. He kept a notebook of his remembrances dating back to the 1880s. In it he describes the so-called River Street fight. He said that "Irish bums" would hang out at a beer saloon named the Tub of Blood on Commerce Street near River Street. Italians began moving into the neighborhood about 1876 or 1877, and the Irish would harass them, threatening to throw them into the Morris Canal if they refused to pay the price of a pint of beer. In response, the Italians sent word to the Italian neighborhood of Five Points in New York City, and a gang of Italians arrived by train, armed with pokers and knives and led by an Italian nicknamed Il Brigante (the bandit). The next day several Italians were sent past the Tub of Blood, and they were chased by the Irish "hoodlums." The Italians led their pursuers through the Italian neighborhood, where the Irish were ambushed. "No one was killed and no Italian was hurt," Mattia writes. "The Italians who were arrested were released in the custody of police chief William Corbitt, who was Irish and a resident of the neighborhood. He was much pleased to see that gang disappear."9

Silver Lake

On the Orange branch of the Erie Railroad, a short distance west, where Newark is divided from Belleville, is a small station called Silver Lake, marking one of the most colorful localities in the whole of Essex County. Not so long ago, before the turn of the century, it was a common practice for many of the local fishermen to try their skill at a nearby lake. The southern part of this body of water stretched irregularly along a line north of Bloomfield Avenue—from North Sixth Street west to North Thirteenth Street, and from Heller Parkway west for a distance of one hundred yards. This lake was called Silver Lake.

At the northern part of the lake, where today Heller Parkway meets Franklin Street, an old dam impounded the waters, and above it stood an abandoned mill. One stormy summer evening in 1889, the dam was torn down, and the waters rushed out into a break northward into the Second River. What was once a picturesque lake became a muddy swamp with a dirty creek meandering through it.

During the 1880s and 1890s, when the immigrants to the United States overflowed from New York City to the surrounding territory, some enterprising businessmen considered it extremely profitable to reclaim the swampy bed of the former Silver Lake and its adjoining land. What formerly had been a garbage dump became, as soon as the reclamation project started, the scene of a veritable real estate boom. The unattractiveness and low land values kept the well-to-do, native-born elements away and attracted those of foreign birth. Hundreds of poor, Italian, immigrant families—former inhabitants of congested slum areas—bought land and built their homes.

At the beginning of the mass settlement, the overwhelming majority of inhabitants were of Italian origin, although in later years many Negroes moved in, until today they form about 10 percent of the population of the territory. Today, there are approximately five thousand inhabitants in the Belleville part of Silver Lake and an equal number in the Newark section. The comparative isolation from the larger community has accentuated the tendency of the Italian immigrants of this locality to live in a manner not unlike that of the old country. This condition is even truer in the Belleville area. The Newark area takes in the southwestern part of the Eighth Ward. The population is predominantly South Italian. Ignorant peasants for the most part, the men usually work at heavy manual labor.

The sore spot of this area is on and near North Sixth Street, east of the site of the former lake. Here there are several blocks of old stone tenements, poorly ventilated, where frequently large families live in flats of three and four rooms. There are no playgrounds in this neighborhood for the children. The main source of social, cultural, and religious activities is the Roman Catholic church. Supplementing this function of the church are the various national organizations.

The Belleville section of Silver Lake is not as densely populated as the Newark part; and, in contrast to the latter, it is a clean, though poverty-stricken, community. The entire area is treeless due to its former swampy character.

Because most of the structures were put up by the people who were to inhabit them, most of the houses in this locality are one-family frame or brick dwellings built along irregular and unconventional lines. The ingenuity of the Italian immigrant in building his home is not only characteristic of the Silver Lake inhabitant, but of the vast majority of Italian laborers who work in the building and contracting industry. Thus, if one man made more money than another, he demonstrated his ability to keep up with the Italian equivalent of the Joneses, by building a more comfortable house and putting a few more frills on the exterior. The majority of the residents own their own homes, and those least fortunate economically live in little better than wooden shanties. Most of these houses consist of only two or three rooms, possessing few of the more modern conveniences. Many years ago, the Belleville Silver Lake section was a rural community, but the only remnants of its former rural state are a few intensively cultivated fields of corn, tomatoes, string beans, etc.; a dairy of twenty or thirty cows; and a half-dozen goats. Behind most of the houses are carefully cultivated vegetable gardens, where such common staples as tomatoes, squash, mint, parsley, string beans, and lettuce are raised. Another feature of the gardens are the grape vines. In many of the gardens the vines are arranged in an arborlike form, and, during the summer months, the men love to sit and play cards and drink wine in the shade of the vines.

The majority of the Italian inhabitants are laborers from the southern provinces of Italy. They are poorly educated and equipped to do only the heaviest of unskilled work. The depression was a great blow to this population, when building came to a standstill, from which it has yet to recover. Deprived of employment, the people were compelled to seek relief and relief work. Many of them were deprived of their homes after paying on them for many years. Although many of the people in Silver Lake have lived there for two and three decades, they were discharged from their WPA jobs for not being American citizens. The most widely read newspapers are the Italian *Il Progresso* and *Corrierre Americana*.

Although the bulk of the inhabitants are poor, there have been several individuals who have "made good" in this Little Italy. One of them is a contractor, another a saloon keeper, and the third a huckster. The contractor owns a great vacant field, which borders the northern side of this pocket community. At the southeastern part of this vast, hilly field, one encounters a scene reminiscent of the "Tobacco-Road" South—an old, jagged wooden fence encases a dilapidated structure, which houses several Negro families. The Italian atmosphere of the neighborhood is emphasized by the romantic names of two streets—Florence and Naples streets—and by "Pizzeria" (pie shop) signs painted in several store windows.

One of the most colorful characteristics of this neighborhood is the gay religious festivals which various societies give in celebration of their patron saints. Before the depression, these festivals were more frequent than they are today. At these festivals—which are of a carnival nature—thousands of people gather in the evening after the procession is over to hear the band play the melodious music of Verdi, Rossini, Donizetti, Bellini, and other favorite Italian composers. The band is seated on a large stage brightly decorated with gold and silver tinsel and varicolored papers. The street where the platform is situated, as well as the adjoining streets, is brightly illuminated by hundreds of electric bulbs arranged in rows of large arches.

Usually when a festival is held, the society sponsoring the affair foots all the expenses and makes all the arrangements; and, from the profits, a voluntary contribution is made to the parish church. During the morning and afternoon of these festivals, a statue of the saint is carried in a long procession winding through all the neighborhood streets. A uniformed band leads the procession, with another band about halfway back. The members of the society take a leading part in the parade, but other members of religious organizations also participate. As the procession goes through the streets, contributions are made, and for every five dollar bill that is pinned to the saint's clothes, the band plays "Marcha Rigali," the Italian national anthem. Following the saint are those who have made vows to him, either walking barefeet, carrying huge candles, or shouting religious invocations.

St. Anthony's parish church—a small frame structure built thirty-seven years ago—is the principal social agency of the community. Today, a new and much larger church is being erected to improve the facilities of the older building. When Italian immigrants from the native town or region first arrived here, they formed societies and clubs among themselves. These societies were usually named after the members' native town or after the town's patron saint. On the individual, separated from the larger American community, these societies exert a powerful influence, by providing him with religious, social, and cultural outlets. Some of the more outstanding societies are Holy Name Society, St. Bartholomew, St. Gerard, La Madonna Adoloratta, and Figli di Italia.

Lately, it has been alleged that leaders of the Figli di Italia, as well as leaders of several other organizations, have displayed pro-Fascist sympathies. The Madonna Adoloratta, a society solely of adult women, is distinguished by the black dresses which its members are compelled to wear on any of the society's formal occasions.

Of late, there has been a sharp break in this rigid, old-country, church-dominated community. A group of more progressive adults have formed a branch of the International Workers' Order, and it is said that there is a unit of the Communist party active as well. These represent the beginnings of a general questioning of the authority hitherto exerted by the church and the national-language organizations.

Clifton Avenue Bathhouse

Opening and closing hours are weekdays, 1:00 P.M.–8:30 P.M.; Saturday, 11:00 A.M.; Sunday, men only 5 A.M.–11:30 A.M.

Members of both sexes have access to the bathhouse. There are available forty-eight showers for men and twenty-seven showers for women; there are also sixteen small tubs for the exclusive use of children under ten years of age, these being located entirely apart from adults.

A common sight at the bathhouse is to see an entire family, ranging from grandfather to grandchildren, arriving for their baths; for the bathhouse is made use of equally by all generations of Italians. Many Italian mothers come daily with their children to bathe, their desire exceeding their actual need, according to the attendant.

However, the bathhouse is used by all nationalities and races in complete unity and respect for each other. Each person will wait his or her turn to enter a shower, and there are times when persons have had to wait as long as an hour or even more, but this has not caused any trouble to any of the attendants as yet. The many different nationalities always seem to be in a good mood and get along very well with each other. While disorders of any kind are immediately curtailed and offenders are liable to arrest, most people who use the bathhouse have a sense of appreciation for its existence.

According to the attendant interviewed, there are about six thousand persons who use the bathhouse weekly. Of this number, the Italians outnumber all others by about two to one. This is because of its location on Clifton Avenue, in the center of the First Ward, which is predominately Italian.

An Italian Padrone

I was born August 14, 1872, in the small village of Oratina, in the province of Campobasso, Italy. I was the third child in a large family of nine children. My father was a farmer, but he did not own his farm. He rented it on a profit-sharing basis. The farm was small, and, as I remember, sometimes we had hardly enough to eat; especially if, for some reason or other, the crops would not come up to the real padrone's expectations. You may be sure that his share would never suffer and that my father's share would be reduced, if necessary, to meet the owner's quotient. My father, two elder brothers, and I worked and cultivated the entire farm, except at harvest time, when my father would hire several men and women to help us, especially with the corn and wheat crops; for they were the main sustenance of the farm. He paid the workers with grain or corn. And, as for my elder brothers and myself, we got paid in the form of a new suit or a pair of shoes, providing crops had been good and Father could manage to sell part of our share of the crops, which didn't happen every year, you may be sure.

There were so many of us that he would take turns in clothing us, by which I mean to say that he would buy a pair of pants now, a pair of shoes later, a shirt at some other time, and so forth. But Papa did the best he could for us from what he had. As I look back, it was a dreary existence for us all; but somehow, we seemed to be contented with our lot, especially my mother. She worked hard caring for us all. But, when Sunday came, our family with several other families would congregate at a given point about a mile from our home, and we would walk about two more miles to church for Sunday mass, and there meet most all of the villagers, whom we all knew well. The women would get together to exchange greetings and gossip, and older men would also congregate for about the same reason.

Well, anyhow, work on the farm was hard and I didn't care for it much. So, one day my uncle, who was in America, wrote to us. In this letter, he wrote about how much better everything was in America, how much more chance one had to make something of himself there.

He also asked my father if he cared to come to America. He said that he would send money and that later both he and my father would send for the rest of the family. Father didn't care to come to America, but he was willing to let my older brother go. By the following month, my uncle had received and answered our letters. He lost no time in sending passage money for my brother to come to America, but, as the time approached for sailing, my brother decided that he didn't want to leave his home and parents. Then came the chance, for it was for some time that I had hoped for something to happen to change my circumstances and condition. When I asked my parents about going to America in place of my brother, Papa consented; and arrangements were made for me to leave.

I was at that time fifteen years of age. Well, I kissed my father and mother and the rest good-bye and sailed here to America. That was in February 1887. I didn't know it at that time, but it was the last I ever saw of my mother and father; for, in spite of all the attempts made later to bring them here, my family never cared to make the trip. And I, in turn, never seemed to have the time to go back. Something always seemed to come up. Now I am old and do not wish to go anymore; for my parents are dead, and, although I still have brothers and sisters, we hardly ever correspond.

Well, when I arrived here in America, I was kept in quarantine at Ellis Island until my uncle came for me, which was about twenty-four hours after I had arrived. When I arrived in Newark with my uncle, I was very happy because it wasn't congested like New York. It was more like my home in Italy, for in the old Woodside section of North Newark in those days, it was semi-country with plenty of trees and open fields. However, four days after my arrival, my uncle secured a job for me on the Erie Railroad as a laborer in track repair at $6.25 per week. I went to work, and I soon found out that the work here was just as hard as that on the farm; but I didn't mind it much because I would receive what seemed to me like a lot. I had never gotten any wages of any kind before, so that you can understand how pleased I was when I received my first weekly pay. On arriving at my uncle's home, I also found out that my uncle was charging me $1.50 for board and lodging, which meant $4.75 out of my weekly pay was left for me to do as I pleased.

As time went on, I became accustomed to my surroundings and soon made friends with other Italian boys about my age, who were also working for the railroad, and life seemed a bit rosier for me. From time to time, I would have someone write to my parents for me, for, having no schooling, I was unable to write. In most of my letters, I would send some money to them. For about a year or two, things went along like this, and, in the meantime, I was learning a little English, more than most of my *paisani*, or countrymen. I had received several increases in salary, so that in three years' time my salary had gone up to nine dollars per week, and sometimes I worked Sundays, for which I was paid extra. At this time, I was saving my money as much as I could, for I neither gambled nor drank, and I was content with my lot; and, on my eighteenth birthday, I received a pleasant surprise by the "big boss," or foreman, of our crew. We were very busy cutting through a branch road, and more men had been hired, and my boss had to have an assistant to handle a forward crew of about fifteen men to prepare the road bed; and, as I was quite adept at it, he selected me as his assistant; and, too, I was able to understand him, something most of my countrymen could not do. When my uncle heard of this he was glad; but that same week, he notified me that I would have to pay $2.50 for board and lodging in the future, to which I agreed. So I looked forward to a better board in the way of more and better food; but, in this respect, I was soon disappointed, for the quality of the food did not change nor the quantity, but I didn't complain to my uncle or my aunt. I reasoned I was making more money, and I didn't mind paying it to my uncle. Still, in those days, board and lodging in any of a dozen houses of similar standing was $1.50. That was a standard price. However, since I had become assistant boss on the railroad, I suddenly found myself very popular and in demand by my fellow workers and countrymen, which, at first, I could not quite understand. But not long after, I fully understood, so much so that it started me thinking.

During the course of our working day, there were many occasions for various men to call on me in reference to work, and they would almost always address me as padrone. It got so that in about a year, I really was "padrone this" and "padrone that." Without realizing it fully, I had acquired a moniker which carried more meaning than I realized at the time. Before I fully appreciated it, I became quite a leader among our entire Italian group, for so many had come to me for employment. Fortunately, I had been able to secure work for them, so that it further increased my countrymen's esteem for me.

So one day I realized I could be happily married on my present salary, which was about fifteen dollars per week; so I expressed my thoughts one evening at a local gathering saloon to my numerous friends, more or less in a joking way, but I didn't do anything about it. But my friends did, for in about a month's time I had received several photographs of girls of my hometown and other towns adjoining; so that I was not long in selecting one which appealed to me, and arrangements were made immediately by her brother, a friend and an employee in my crew. Soon after, his sister arrived at Ellis Island. We both went over to receive her, and I lost no time in getting married, for I had prepared a home for us all—a six-room, cold flat—with an understanding that her brother was to board with us. That day and several days after were spent in celebrating our marriage, and almost everyone came to see us and bring their various gifts of money and good wishes.

Well, not long after that, everyone wanted to board with us. So I bought beds, and I furnished, at one time, bed and board for about twenty-four men. I also furnished, at extra cost, their wine for their meals. Well, conditions being what they were, most of my countrymen soon were entrusting to my care all of their savings and not expecting any interest in return. I, in turn, invested in real estate and deposited in various banks all of their savings and mine, too. Besides this, from time to time, I would furnish in part, or all, necessary expenses for many countrymen to come to America; and then, on arrival, I would put them up at my place, which by this time had become a center of activities, and also provided jobs for them, so that eventually they would repay me for all the money I had advanced them, at figures which I quoted, with no questions asked by anyone. I enjoyed their faith so, that I was respected as a father in general, and I also arranged and promoted a number of matrimonies. I selected and bought all necessary furnishings for such an occasion. Then, too, as time went on, some of my boarders having saved quite a lot of money, I would induce them to buy a small home, which I would sell them, for I had acquired seven or eight of them. They were small homes, with about six or seven rooms to most of them, and they were all located alongside of the railroad yards, all in a row. I had bought them gradually and bought them quite cheap; so that, when any one of my friends and boarders accumulated enough money with me as the savings bank, I would induce him to buy one of my houses, which most of them were happy to do so. If they were not married, I soon would arrange for them to be married, and promote the entire affair to their and my satisfaction.

This condition prevailed for quite a long time, till I decided that I should own a saloon for the betterment of everyone concerned and for a greater financial income for me. In due time, I secured a license and opened a saloon in one of my properties. Later, I also established a grocery store, in which I sold Italian and American merchandise, rounding out a means of supply of foodstuffs and other wants for my employees, friends, and boarders. During all these years, no one ever regarded me as anything but a benefactor; and, to this day, I enjoy all of my friends' respect. My counsel and advice are sought by them, wherever they feel they need it.

The world war was the beginning of the end of my enterprise, for everyone was making a lot of money, and with that they all seemed to scatter. Some went to war, and some went to work in the shipyards and ammunition factories, and they didn't need me anymore. However, I take pride in one fact—that most all that could come back to me have come many times, and I feel that I have served and helped them well; and I do admit that, because of them and my circumstances, I benefited greatly, financially and morally. I have absolutely no regrets. I would do it over again if I had the same chance.

A. Losi
Ernest Pentz

Italian Banking

Italian immigrants came to this country in ever-increasing numbers from 1871, when thirty reached New York, until 1910, when ten thousand arrived in Newark and brought the city's Italian population up to sixty thousand. But the Italian immigrant was not a financier. He knew very little about money; he had never seen it in large quantities. He had never seen anyone, except the very infrequent signore and signora in his province, who had money in large quantities. When he dreamed, the extent of his dreams were one hundred lira, which he would secrete in a sock or a tin box and bury in the earth.

But when he arrived over here, he began to earn money in such quantities that he was very glad to write home to his father, his mother, his aunts, his uncles, and his cousins: "See. The streets of this strange land are paved with gold. Truly, a man is paid as much here for one day's labor (sixty-nine cents) as he would make in two weeks of toil over where you are." This kind of letter, written by the hundreds and thousands, was more responsible than any other factor for the terrific tide of Italian immigration that swept over this country in the next forty years.

Men who had never in their lives seen as much as five dollars before found themselves at the end of a month's hard labor with as much as twenty dollars. And the sole fact of possession of so much blunted any ideas they might have had as to what to do with it. Most of them carried it on their persons in a money belt, especially when they were living in the laborers' shacks along the right of way they were building for a railroad. It is a splendid tribute to the innate honesty of the Italian that very few of their laborers were ever robbed by violence. There were few thieves among them. There were, however, confidence men—"city slickers." These were smart Italians who had found a way of earning a good living without working for it. They would go into a construction camp around payday with a large bundle of counterfeit Italian money. And they would approach a laborer, especially a laborer who was known to have quite a bit of money. "Today," they would say, "I want you do me a favor. I need some American money very badly. I have lots of Italian money, but no American, and I must have one hundred dollars by tonight. Now, look here. If you will give me ten dollars in American money, I will give you twenty or thirty or fifty dollars in Italian money. It won't make any difference if you hold it for a while. When you cash it you will have that much more." If Tony was greedy, he would advance the American money and never know the difference, until he went to cash it. Then it would be too late because the man for whom he had done the "favor" would be a hundred miles away.

In Newark, in the very early days, the Italians would bring their money to the leading man or men of the "Little Italy." This was usually a saloonkeeper or a groceryman or a contractor. If he had a safe in this store or office, he was the man. Angelo M. Mattia held much of the money for the inhabitants of Newark's first "Little Italy" around Boyden Street. So did Alphonse Ilaria, "King" of that "Little Italy." When the Italians by their labors got so much money that they were forced to become "bank conscious," they carried it over to New York, where they deposited it in a bank owned and operated by a man named Cantoni. This man was a very honest banker, and nobody ever lost a penny. Indeed, he took it upon himself to become financial adviser to many of his clients and helped them to understand the laws of money.

The first Italians who started banks in Newark were not so trustworthy. If you mention the first Italian-American banks in Newark to an Italian old-timer, you will note that his eyes will slowly turn bloodshot and his voice begin to rumble with strange noises. He will tell you about a man named Romano. "I do not know what his first name was, but I know where he is, if he's dead." Romano started a bank on Fourteenth Avenue, near Prospect Street in 1887. He had the perfect front of the confidence man. He was handsome, smooth, and suave. Every Italian who had any money brought it to him to keep for them. He kept it for a year and then ran away with it in the autumn of 1888. The Italians then went back to Cantoni in New York, though many of them were obsessed by a terrific distrust for all banks. These hid their money in their socks and buried it behind the plaster of their walls. There is an Italian, ninety-four years old, living in Newark today, according to Dr. Mattia, who keeps his money thus. He has lost two hundred dollars to rats that have gnawed and eaten that much in paper bills. And once, he had to tear away the walls of rooms on two floors because his cache slipped down. But he wouldn't put what he had in a bank if he was paid 100 percent interest.

The next Italian American bank to open up was owned and operated by "a man named Perolli." He opened a bank about 1883 somewhere on Market Street. He also departed with a large share of the wealth of his Italian depositors and has not been seen or heard from since. But Newark was compensated for these two thieves by the bankers Salvatore D'Auria and Vito Marzano. These two men opened banks in different sections of the city at about the same time. Both prospered, as did their depositors. D'Auria's bank, still on the site of the original building at Garside Street and Seventh Avenue, and Marzano's bank, on Market Street, were the first two Newark banks ordered to open after the "Bank Holiday" of 1933.[10] These two men and their sons own and control financial institutions that are as strong as Gilbraltar was, before Mussolini became annoyed with it.

The emigration from Poland between 1870 and World War I has been called the emigration *za chlebem* (for bread) because it was primarily motivated by economic considerations. It had three phases. The first phase began in the 1870s and was primarily from German-held territories; the second phase, beginning in the 1890s, was from the Russian territories; and the third phase, which was mainly from 1900, was from Galicia. Many of the Galician and Russian Poles were young men and women who left their

Poles

families in Poland and intended to return to Poland. The German Poles tended to be better educated and more quickly attained middle-class status in the United States, while the Russian and Austrian Poles remained disproportionately in unskilled occupations.[1]

Obtaining statistics on the immigration of Poles during this period is complicated in that Poland did not exist as a separate country in the nineteenth century. Having reached its greatest size and power with the Union of Lublin in 1569, which united the Kingdom of Poland with the Grand Duchy of Lithuania, Poland was divided up in the late eighteenth century by its three neighbors—Austria, Russia, and Germany. In the first partition (1772) Prussia annexed the western portion of Poland, Russia took part of its northeastern tier, and Austria took the southern province of Galicia. In the second partition (1793) Russia annexed most of Lithuania and the Ukraine, and Prussia took Danzig and most of the country west of Warsaw. In 1794 Thaddeus Kosciuszko led an insurrection against the partitioning powers, but it was suppressed. In the third partition (1795) Russia took the rest of Lithuania and the Ukraine, Prussia annexed central Poland, and Austria took the rest of southern Poland. Following the Napoleonic Wars, the Congress of Vienna combined much of central and eastern Poland into the so-called Congress Kingdom under Russian rule. During World War I the Germans drove the Russians out of Poland, and in 1918 Poland became an independent republic with Jozef Piłsudski as its head of state.

Poles began moving into Newark in the 1880s. They first settled near the German neighborhood on High Street and South Orange Avenue, but soon a second settlement was established in the Ironbound. In 1882 they formed the King John III Sobieski Society, named after the Polish king who fought off the Turks in 1683. The members of this society founded St. Stanislaus parish in 1889. In 1908 a second parish was founded in the Ironbound, named St. Casimir after the patron saint of Poland and Lithuania. It is estimated that by 1938 there were about 35,600 Poles in Newark. At that time Poles were already moving out of Newark into the nearby suburbs of Irvington, the Oranges, Nutley, Springfield, the Caldwells, Maplewood, and Belleville.[2]

Like other ethnic groups, the Poles established mutual benefit societies, which are reflected in the case histories. These societies usually provided sickness and funeral benefits to their members. Some offered banking services to their members. In some cases, as with the Polish-American Building and Loan Association, founded in 1899, these ethnic banks evolved into incorporated savings and loan companies. It has been noted that these ethnic associations often served a dual function—consolidating ethnic identity at the same time they furthered the acculturation to the American way of life. For example, the Polish Falcons of America was founded in Chicago in 1887. The Falcons was a fraternal athletic organization that emphasized Polish nationalism. According to historian John Bukowczyk, organizations like the Falcons represented self-conscious ethnic identity in the United States that was instrumental in establishing the Polish nation after World War I.[3] But the original military-type training, consisting of gymnastics, horseback riding, marksmanship, and fencing, was gradually replaced beginning in the 1930s by the American sports of baseball, basketball, and later even bowling and golf.[4]

There developed a distinct immigrant middle class, which is demonstrated here by the case history of the Duckiet family. The Polish middle class ran various types of businesses, such as bakeries, butcher shops, saloons, boardinghouses, and funeral parlors. According to Bukowczyk, to make a living by burying the dead violated rural Polish taboos, but in the United States this became a major Polish business activity. These Polish-American businessmen functioned as go-betweens for the Polish immigrants: they "wrote and translated letters, extended credit and advice, held money, brokered jobs, found housing, arranged steamship tickets, and served as general 'agent' for their inexperienced countrymen and countrywomen."[5]

Bukowczyk notes that, unlike the Italians, the Poles had no padrone system (ethnic labor contracting).[6] However, a comparison of the descriptions of the Polish boardinghouse and employment agencies in this section with the case history of the Italian padrone in the previous section shows that there was not much difference between the two. This is consistent with historian Humbert Nelli's observation that there was a greater similarity between ethnic organizations of different ethnic groups in the United States than between old country and American institutions within the same ethnic group.[7]

Polish Customs

Mr. Smaga of 335 Lafayette Street, Newark, volunteered to tell of the various customs of Poland. The most important section of this story has been taken down word for word. Mr. Smaga spoke Polish to describe some of the more difficult passages. He spoke continuously for two and one-half hours.

Say, for instance, when a child is born in a poor family. My family comes from the village, not the town, and are farmers. Take the story of my house. We had a farm and we all lived in one room. We only had two beds. The rest of the children lived on the floor on straw. Some slept behind the stove.

When a child is born, no doctor is used over there. They call a woman, you know, a midwife. She did not have a license, and she did not know anything about medical care. Maybe American people don't know that, but when a child is born in Poland, he is wrapped up in muslin from his neck to his feet to keep his body straight, so that he will not have bandy legs or a big belly, and to keep his shoulders straight, too.

The father and the mother got together with the godmother and godfather to decide the name of the child. On the Catholic calendar, there are certain names for each day. For example, January 26 is Saint John's Day, therefore a child born on that day is named after him. After the second day, they take the child to church and give him a name. When they come home from church, they have a big party. They invite ten or fifteen families, have music, coffee, tea, and *schnapps*—this is the first thing—and have a good time.[8] Sometimes they get drunk before they go to church and lose the child someplace. They come back and look for child and find him in a ditch some place. (*This has actually happened.*) The priest comes to the christening too. The richer classes of people have it better. The poorer class only has a party and some fun.

All the sons, they take care of family. If the child is small, the father's brother takes care of things. Or if a widow gets married again, the stepfather takes care of the child. Like where I come from, under the tsar. When Father died, I was twenty-two. I was discharged from the army to take care of Mother and the rest of the family. I was sixth in the family. All my other brothers were out and married. So I had to take care of the family. I had to take care of the family until my brother grew old enough.

For instance, we did not need any trades on the farm. Some of us learned to be a shoemaker, a carpenter, or a blacksmith, or mason, or bricklayer. It was very hard to learn a trade. If I wanted to learn a trade, I would have to go to a master craftsman and work three years for nothing. He wouldn't teach you the trade, but make you wash floors, peel potatoes, and take care of the house and clean it. We learned whatever we could at night. After three years, they put you to work with whatever trade you took, and you stayed another three years. Father had to pay so much. As soon as I know something, Father stops paying, and the boss pays little. When you get to be seventeen or eighteen, you get a diploma and you are a tradesman. Then you go to the city and look for work. You can't get a job without a diploma. Yes, you have to send money home till you are twenty-one. You are already a tradesman, and you got to go to industry and live separately from your family. If you make eight or nine rubles a week, you got to send five rubles to Father. After twenty-one years, you don't have to send money to Father. If you want to send it, all right, but nobody forces you. Most children do that. They send money to Father and Mother because they paid for his trade. They always must help family, but after they become twenty-one, they got to join the army. If the father is fifty years of age, the first son doesn't have to go.

See, we people have different stories when you get married here or there. Old-fashioned people, according to who like it, do this. For instance, if I have a couple of acres of ground, and I like a girl and want her, and she does not want me, and she does not own so much ground as I do, she has to want me because her parents force her to marry me. The boy and girl never saw each other before they get married. Father and Mother on each side make all the arrangements. When they get married, she cries and says, "I don't like him." When she keeps it up, the father and mother whip her and make her do it.

Mrs. Smaga's sister got married in this way. She loved a poor boy, but her parents forced her to marry a widower with three children. Her sister cried day and night because she did not want to marry him. Her father said she would have a good living. After they got married, the father was very sorry because his daughter's husband was a drunkard and wife beater. He was sorry for what he did, but it was too late.

When they get married, they don't live good. They live like tools, rubbing against each other. This is the bad side. The good side is just like here. Boy meets girl, and after five months they think of getting married. You can't get married till you get permission from your mother and father. There is no length of time before they get married. It's all according to how much money they got so they can live.

Weddings are different than here. Weddings start Tuesday evening. Young people just come and they play all night and drink. Five o'clock

Wednesday night, they go out and invite families to the wedding. Fifty families get together and around ten go to church to see them get married and come back. The orchestra plays, and people dance, and they give a dinner. Around nine, they give supper again and make collection, not like here. Everyone who attends takes the bride and dances around the table, and everybody sings and claps and puts their rubles in one big plate on the table. Anybody who wants to dance with the bride has to pay. Everybody dances and everybody pays. Midnight it ends. Thursday morning, they all come back again and have breakfast. They dance till the afternoon; and when the drinks is finished, they make a collection to go on. Friday morning the wedding is finished. Friday afternoon and Saturday they rest. Sunday they again bring music and more drinks and finally finish up the wedding for good.

When a person dies, the system was: don't call any doctor or anything. We don't know if they died; maybe they are sleeping. We have no undertakers there. Somebody comes and washes the body, and the carpenter makes the coffin. The body lays at home. Soon as they die, they put him on straw on the floor. The next day, they put him in the coffin. The day before the funeral, the family makes small crosses, six by four, and sends them to the farmers as invitations to the funeral. The farmers pass it on to each other; instead of only sending it to one, the cross goes to everybody.

The third day, the people get together. Nobody stays up all night. When somebody dies, nobody lives in the house, because they are afraid. The priest comes and makes a ceremony and speech, and they put the body in a wagon and go to church. From the church they go to the cemetery. The priest comes there and makes another talk: "When you go to heaven, and when you go to hell." There are more talks, and then you go in the ground, and everything is finished. You don't pay anything for the land or grave there. You have to pay the priest, even if you have to sell your last cow.

From the time you are eight years old, you got to go to learn some religious questions: how God built the world, when he built it, how many days he took, etc. This is the Old Testament. In the New Testament you got to learn Jesus' story. Even before you can talk, you got to pray twice a day in the house. Every summer for three months, every day you got to go to learn religion. You got to learn everything created. It goes like this for three summers. You got to prepare for your first confession when you are ten. The priest asks you questions about yourself; for instance, "Are you a good child for your mama and papa?" "Do you like your brother?" They ask you also "Who created the world?" and about Jesus. You got to go again to learn for your Communion.

About twelve, they asked you already about girls. "Do you put your hand some place or not?" This is no kidding. When the children make their Communion, the priest gives them a party, and he gives them a Bible and rosaries. You got to go at least once a year to confession. If you don't go it will be too bad for you. Sometimes the neighbors will be angry with you. If you don't have religion, somebody will burn your house, and you will not have any friends.

When you get to be eighteen, the priest asks you more about girls. When Easter comes everybody must go to church. There are big churches, and the rich are the only ones that have benches; the poor people must stand up. If you do something bad with the girls, you have to lay flat on your stomach for one-half hour in the church and pray. It was cold, and we never had any heat. So the priest gives you two or three weeks of prayer for punishment. Also, the priest every Sunday gives the women a lecture. He preaches mostly on the Ten Commandments. Don't kill anybody, and don't go to sleep with anybody else's husband, or you will get a lecture from the priest. Some women do this. The priest stands up and hollers about these things. Some women who did these bad things get hysterical and get down on their knees and start to chant. The priest sees this and says, "See that!" When a child is born, you have to get a certificate from the priest. When you die, the priest has a record. When you marry, the priest has a certificate. The government has it too, but the priest comes first.

Poor people like plenty of holidays. Poor people work for somebody. You don't work by the hour or week; you work by the year. In Poland, there are forty religious holidays besides Sunday. The poor people like this because they go to church and pray and they have plenty of time to rest.

Sinch O'Har
October 26, 1939

A Prominent Pole

Any request for a biographical sketch is both flattering and embarrassing. I am at a loss to determine what may be of interest to anyone else. Perhaps some of the items mentioned may be of some significance as an expression of adjustments or reactions to surrounding trends and forces.

Father came to America as a young immigrant from the former

Austrian section of Poland za chlebem, just before the Spanish-American War. His destination was the Rondout section of Kingston, New York, where a village pal—a tailor—had preceded him. Father's choice lay between the brickyards along the Hudson or cutting ice in the river. He chose the latter. During the summer, it was removed from the huge icehouses, loaded upon barges, and towed to New York City.

Father married soon. Mother came to America at the age of twelve with her mother and stepfather. Grandmother is still living; my mother died in 1922. Mother quickly learned English, spoke it fluently and without a trace of accent. As children we spoke English at home with Mother, but only Polish with Father.

I was born in Kingston, September 29, 1900, delivered by an unlicensed midwife and my arrival not duly recorded for posterity in the official records, much to my subsequent annoyance. Apparently, there were some doubts as to my survival because, contrary to custom, I was promptly christened the following day in the local Polish church.

When I was a year old, Father heard of better pay in Newark, and we moved to the Ironbound section. Father worked during my boyhood as a molder, even when he risked a business venture in acquiring a grocery store when I was about six or seven. Mother managed the store, with some assistance from Father, after working at the foundry. The store had some old stock. I still remember surreptitiously disposing of packages of shredded coconuts. The neighborhood was German at the time. The store was disposed of at a loss after a year.

I started school at the Hamburg Place Public School, subsequently changed to Wilson Avenue during the war. The first day was a disappointment. The teacher tackled reading. No mollycoddling. It was about "a kid, a kid I bought for two pieces of money." I quickly memorized it and was terribly disappointed when reading stopped with the boy just in front of me. I spent three years there and retained only two impressions fairly vividly: one of no subsequent consequence, the second a class in drawing wherein I achieved a crayon drawing of an apple as the main feature. Since I transferred to a parochial school for the remainder of my elementary work, this remained a frustration until about twenty-five years later, when I developed an adult desire to dabble in watercolors and smudge everything with pastel.

St. Casimir's parochial school was a new school. Classes were rather disorganized and mixed. Two grades were simultaneously conducted in my class. I passed three years in St. Casimir's. A change of pastors occurred in 1913, and my parents were urged to send me to a newly organized prep school—St. John Hanty College in Erie, Pennsylvania.

This was accomplished through the assistance of a scholarship. The course was five years—more on the Austrian model approximating that of the gymnasium curriculum, with five years of Latin; three of Greek; Polish, five; mathematics through trigonometry; German for three; history from ancient to U.S.; and English; also courses in zoology, botany, chemistry, and physics. Quite a dose in comparison with the usual pulp in high school. The courses in English and American literature were very thorough.

Subsequent college work at the University of Pennsylvania in this branch seemed like the proverbial "fresh air" courses. I graduated in 1918. I entered University of Pennsylvania college course of three years. I detoured to the University of Paris for one year, then returned to school and a job in Philadelphia, where I entered the Temple University School of Medicine. During my first year in Philadelphia, I became attached as a part-time worker at the Smithwark Neighborhood House for classes in English and Americanization work. I became a resident for the last six years in Philadelphia and did varied social work in the evening, subsequently managing a men's club. I had varied and interesting experiences on the South Philadelphia riverfront. I had frequent opportunities for speaking.

I married Irene—— of Philadelphia upon graduation, then interned at St. Michael's Hospital, Newark, with several months' residence in Essex Mountain Sanatorium for the Tubercular and Essex County Isolation Hospital. At the end of 1928, I entered into the private practice of medicine as a general practitioner in the Ironbound section in a Polish neighborhood. The start was encouraging, but the depression has acutely affected the neighborhood and all business and professions in it. I became active in political and social organizations. I was instrumental in organizing all Polish societies into a central committee of Polish societies. I acted as president for several years. I initiated cooperation with the Ironbound council of school, social, and governmental agencies. I am active throughout Essex County with other Polish groups. I organized the Pulaski memorial observation in 1929, subsequently copied and enlarged in scope, and an art exhibit in Newark Museum in 1929. I organized the Polish Arts Club of New Jersey with regular meetings at the Griffith Auditorium for Polish cultural activities with arts and music. I had an unsuccessful venture into politics in 1934, but subsequently I was elected into the 1939 New Jersey legislature on the Republican ticket. I was characterized in a Newark Ledger editorial as showing "independence and intelligent interest in labor and social questions."

Lost All Ambition

I was born and raised in Poland, in a little village near Września, a city in the state of Poznań, in 1890. There were ten children in our family. My father worked at farming. He had eighty acres of land; this he would till and toil from early morn till late at night. I still remember how tired and drawn he looked. We were too young to understand or be of any assistance. As each one of us grew older, we helped our parents plow the land, sow seeds, dig potatoes, and weed the fields. We were neither poor nor wealthy. My parents tried their utmost to give their children some sort of an education, but at that time it was quite difficult. They did the best they could; they were understanding parents. My three brothers and myself took up farming. The two younger brothers took up a trade—one a butcher, the other a shoemaker. The others were too young, even up to the time when I left Poland.

While I was still a boy in Poland, we were under the Prussian rule. The Polish children were eventually forbidden to learn the catechism and to say their prayers in Polish. We were forbidden to learn anything about Polish history or to speak the Polish language. Everything was in German. This naturally led to a revolt on the part of the children in the town of Wrzesnia, who, upon refusing to pray in German, were brutally beaten by the teacher. The parents who protested were thrown into prison, but the strike of the pupils spread until it included one hundred thousand children. I was one of them. I recollect the brutal beating I received at the hands of a German teacher. The Austrian regime in south Poland was corrupt, but in general not violent. The Russian rule in eastern Poland was coarse and brutal, but the German efforts to denationalize the Poles in the most ancient of Polish territories—that is, western Poland, the section seized by Prussia to dispossess the Poles of land and deprive them of their language and nationality—were cold and heartless.

My father and others who protested were thrown into prison, beaten cruelly, and held for three months. My parents' home was ransacked for some evidence pertaining to the freedom of Poland. The Germans found nothing. After my father was released, his health was slowly failing. He was a heartbroken man. With so many children to clothe and feed, I knew some would have to leave and shift for themselves and make room for the younger children. My mother was a good-natured, hard-working woman. She labored in the field alongside of my father from dawn till dusk and then came home and did other tasks.

I thought America would be the right place to come to. So many people had left for America, and they wrote very highly about it. After a long conversation with my parents, they finally agreed with me and granted me permission to come to America. They were happy in my choice and helped me financially as much as they were able. I was twenty years old when I arrived in America in the year 1910. The money my parents gave me just about covered my passage. I arrived at a critical time. My father asked me to look up my cousin and stay with them a while, until I was familiar with the surroundings and American ways. I lost the address and found myself stranded, not knowing a living soul.

While I was at Ellis Island, someone spoke in Polish, and from sheer joy tears welled up in my eyes to hear my native tongue again. I went up to them and explained my situation. They were a young bride and groom from Bristol, Connecticut, and were expecting her sister from Poland, but were bitterly disappointed because she had not arrived. They gladly offered their assistance and took me in as a brother, bedded and clothed me until I was able to find work. I can never repay their generosity to me. I was out of employment for five months.

I succeeded, however, in finding employment in a foundry. It was very hard labor. I worked there a month and a half and could not stand the strenuous work any longer. By that time I was well acquainted with the Polish people, and through a friend I found a much easier position in a shoe factory. The hours were quite long but so much easier than the foundry. I worked there for one and a half years. I started a savings account and had a small amount saved. The young couple who had befriended me would not accept any payment from me. They took a liking to me and counted me as a brother. Their sister never arrived to America; she had to take her mother's place after her death.

One day, they received a letter from friends in Buffalo, New York, saying that work was picking up. Naturally, I decided to go and try my luck. To my dismay, I found it no better there. I found a position in a restaurant as a dishwasher for a few dollars a week. Of course, this helped a little, because I didn't have to spend the little I saved. From Buffalo I went to Detroit, Michigan, and found a position again in a shoe factory. Having a little experience in that line, it was much easier.

While in Michigan I met a young Polish girl, who was an employee at the shoe factory also. After knowing each other for two years, we were engaged and began to plan for the wedding. About two weeks before the wedding, she received word from her brother in Poland, stating their parents were taken as prisoners to Siberia by the Russian government, who claimed that they belonged to the Polish revolutionists. My fiancée took it so to heart that she collapsed and suffered a heart attack. She died a few days before the wedding. I could not forget the tragedy for a long while. She was always on my mind. Even today I still speak highly of her. I am a brokenhearted man. I could not find another girl to take the place of my first sweetheart, and I will be faithful to her to my dying day.

I lived in Detroit up to 1915. Later, I came to Jersey City and made it my permanent home. I found work in a sugar factory, then the cigarette factory, and finally I was employed at the docks. Now, at forty-nine I work a few hours a day wherever I find any work. I speak English poorly, but I am an American citizen. I lost all ambition after my future wife's death.

Prior to the war, I received a letter from one of my brothers. I communicated frequently with my family. They knew about the tragedy before my wedding. They asked me to come back to Europe and live with them. In the twenty-nine years since I had left, Poland was now well built up and was fast becoming a modern country. My parents died a few years ago. One brother is a wealthy butcher, the other a well-known shoe craftsman. My youngest sister married a wealthy farmer; the others became farmers and worked the eighty acres together. My brother wrote that if they all could live and support themselves, there would be sufficient for me too. I knew I wouldn't be able to face them, knowing I was a failure. My appearance did not worry me anymore. After the death of my sweetheart, everything was closed to me. In answer to my brother's letter, I wrote I was quite happy and doing well for myself. I was sorry I was not fortunate to see my father and mother before their death. The last letter I received from Poland was in July 1939.

The people who befriended me have four children and are quite happy. Their son has entered college to become a doctor, their daughter a pharmacist, while the other two girls are attending the grammar school. They are both in the eighth grade. It makes me happy that they are blessed with such good children. My wish is that they will always be happy and never suffer the tragedy I suffered.

Heartbroken and Disillusioned

Mrs. J. entered America in 1913, at the age of twenty-two. Her sister, who had married in America, financed the passage. Upon arriving in Newark, Mrs. J. lived with her sister until she received employment as a domestic in a Jewish household. She worked at this position three years, in which time she was able repay her sister and managed to save some money "for a rainy day." Mrs. J., who had emigrated from a small suburb on the outskirts of Kracōw in the Galician region, was confused at the hustle and bustle of urban life in Newark. She admitted it was a pleasant type of confusion.

In 1916, through an intermediary, Mrs. J. met a widower with four children. After a brief courtship she married this man, who was about fifteen years older than she. There was very little harmony in the household. In the second year of her marriage she gave birth to a baby girl. After a bitter struggle lasting about eight years, the woman gave up trying to live with her husband. She packed up, took her child, and fled to a domestic job in the city of Rochester, New York.

During the second year of her new life as a domestic, Mrs. J. fell in love with a Polish leather worker. She left her job and cohabited with him. The woman began to lead a satisfactory life. Their union was tied more firmly by the birth of a baby girl. They lived a pleasant existence for nine years. Suddenly the man became ill, and after a short illness he died. As this was the woman's one real love affair, his death left her heartbroken and disillusioned with life.

Two years ago, her older daughter married and left her mother, leaving a dark void in her life. This daughter now has a baby and has returned with her husband to her mother's house. The mother is delighted with the reunion and has lost some of her bitterness. Her future life will be built on the foundation of helping her daughters to live happily.

John Karpinic
December 9, 1940

A Peaceful, Law-abiding Citizen

Well, what do you want to know? My life story, you say? I haven't much to tell. I was born in East Galicia, under the reign of mean Austrians. My living has been a mere struggle for bread. For years my parents wanted to till the soil, but never had a chance to buy any in the old country. When we came here, back in 1908, they tried to get a homestead, but all the good land was already taken up by that time. So when I was of age, I went to work on the railroads, washing cars. This is hard work, but I did not mind it until I had a little accident—my right arm was broken and I was laid up for seven months.

Sometimes I think life isn't worth a damn for a man like me. I am not educated. My work is unskilled. I get little money, just enough to pay rent and buy food. I can't say I am living a normal life. Look at my wife and my kids—undernourished, seldom have a square meal, and I don't always have three a day myself. Can you blame me for taking to liquor? Of course, I haven't much money for that neither. But a few of my friends treat me sometimes—and that's the only time I forget how miserable I am.

Sometimes I think Bolsheviks had the right idea. They say nobody is unemployed there in Russia. Maybe if I was there I wouldn't starve so much half of the time.

I was on WPA until about a month ago. They laid off a lot of men on my job and me too. I did not get any relief yet, but they promise and promise. My wife was there many times, and I got sick of going down there. Those people down there think a man can pay his bills with promises.

I never bothered anybody, but there are a lot of people who seem to be interested in everything I do—investigators, bill collectors, landlord, groceryman—they all want to poke their noses into my private life. Private? I wish I could enjoy a day of privacy.

The only period of time in my life I really enjoyed was when I was a boy—carefree, no financial troubles, no one dependent on me for a lot of things I cannot get.

Listen, fellow, they call me a "peaceful, law-abiding citizen." I would like to know what peace and law mean. I haven't had a day of peace in my life. As for law, that is made only for big fellows who elect their own judges and appoint their own juries. People like me cannot get justice in the courts or out of them.

Now, crazy Europe went to war. Maybe we will too. I just as soon be in war as live the way I do. I have really nothing to live for—not even a chance for a decent job.

No, I don't mix with Communists, Socialists, Fascists, and their kind. They have nothing for me, neither. They're always scrapping over one thing or another. They don't agree among themselves. Moreover, I don't know what they are all talking about. Some people go crazy on Marx. I wish I was as crazy about something. I wouldn't waste my energies on Marx. But, of course, I am not educated, and—

My children probably know more about the world than I do.

Yes, that's what I'm missing worst—education. But I never had a chance to go higher than the fifth grade. My folks were poor. I went to work when fourteen years of age.

Please do not ask me more questions. So many people nowadays ask questions. Nobody seems to give any answers. Excuse me.

With these words, the respondent got up and walked away from me. He did not seem to feel well physically and was somewhat psychologically unstrung.

A. Basil Wheeler

Worked as a Laborer

I first came to Pennsylvania. I moved to Newark in 1912. I worked as a laborer in the foundries and the steel mills. In Pennsylvania, most Poles were mine workers. Some were organized in the trade unions, but very few were skilled workers. Some learned a trade in the Russian army, but very few. In the army they were drilled in the cavalry and infantry and had no time to learn a trade. Seventy-five percent left Poland so that they wouldn't serve in the army. Friends in the shop spoke up for them for jobs.

The majority of the Poles belong to the unions, but many still do not understand the meaning of a union. A lot of second-generation Polish girls work in RCA. I know three from one home that work there. They work on the assembling of radio tubes and lamps. They belong to the UER and MWA.[9] Many Polish girls work in Western Electric, where there is a company union. Wages are pretty good there, and it will be hard for the CIO to organize it. There are quite a few machinists in the A.F. of L. Quite a few Polish hatters still work. Many work in the leather business. Almost all the tanneries have moved to Massachusetts, so a lot work in the slaughterhouses and fertilizer factories. Many Poles are found today in the shipyards and the steel mills. There are a lot of Poles in the Franklin, New Jersey, zinc works and in the Calco Chemical Company. Also, in the Martin-Dennis Chemical Company shop, located in Woodside, New Jersey. There are many second-generation Polish foremen in the airplane factories. Many Poles could not get foreman's jobs because of difficulties with the English language.

Is there discrimination against Poles? Yes and no. In a way, you can't say it. Couldn't prove it, but there is one discrimination. A lot depended on for who you worked and where. In the organized shops, everyone was treated alike. In the unorganized shops, the native American or German bosses were partial. I worked in Ford from 1921 to 1925. There were lots of orders then, and they didn't care who they hired. Today, things are different. Ford wasn't bad until they had the speedup there.[10]

A lot of the Poles I knew worked as freight handlers on the railroads, and a few worked in the railroad repair shops.

Ernest Pentz

Owner of a Polish Employment Agency

Miss Nalikowski's mother opened the agency in 1904 for farm, hotel, and restaurant workers. Her mother told her that many immigration officials got in touch with her when Polish immigrants arrived at Ellis Island. These immigrants were taken care of by Polish homes, and she got work for them. Most of the women did domestic work and still do. Today, they earn thirty-five dollars to sixty dollars a month. In 1910, there were plenty on hand to get work, but today they are scarce. She declared that she always remembered the Polish women, working in order to help the husband. During the depression, they have been very proud and would do everything possible to avoid getting on relief, even if they only got a dollar a day.

Miss Nalikowski related her experience with a large number of the crew of the Batory liner, the Polish steamer which was interned in New York City when the Germans invaded Poland.[11] It was the job of her agency to get work for a large number of them. She said a few of them were excellent chefs and could arrange meals of rare quality and in an original manner. She was at a meal where one of the Polish chefs prepared a lobster salad. Pieces of doughnuts were artistically arranged on the red lobster. Hidden underneath the lobster were as many portions of food as there were guests. She said she had never seen such an arrangement before nor enjoyed a salad so much. When jobs had been secured for these men, the first thing they did was to go to night school to learn English and to improve themselves. She was impressed by their general high level of intelligence.

At the close of the interview, Miss Nalikowski informed me that the New Brunswick Laundry hires thousands of Poles.

Ernest Pentz
February 24, 1941

The Johnson Agency

When I entered the employment agency, a man, not very much past thirty and of medium stature, was talking to a well-dressed Polish woman, who was about forty-seven years of age. Their conversation was in Polish. Later, he was on the phone, describing in glowing terms the splendid ability of this Polish woman as a housekeeper and as a superb cook. No one could have spoken better of an individual.

The employment man told me not to bother about his name except to call him Johnson. My purpose in calling on the agency was to secure information on Poles who secured work and to learn about some of their early struggles. I learned that Mr. Johnson was a third-generation Pole. My interview was interrupted several times.

He said that his grandmother, one of the early Polish immigrants, had been in the employment business in 1890. She established the agency in 1904. She secured help mostly for domestics. Most of the demand was for Polish women. This was one of the principal agencies for the newly arrived Polish immigrants. Many of the Polish men were hired for farm work if they could not secure work in industrial plants.

In 1909, many Poles lived in overcrowded quarters, but the boardinghouses were only for those Poles who had no parents or friends. Sometimes the agency would make connections with the boardinghouses when calls for workers came in.

In reference to Polish immigrant women, the respondent said that once a girl got a job here, she would send passage to another sister. Sometimes they would get the whole family over here. The mother and the father would be the last ones to come over here. The woman played a large part in building up family resources. Most of them worked in factories. It was not uncommon for both to work and to have a next-door neighbor to take care of the children. Many Polish women worked at night in office buildings, while the husbands stayed at home to take care of the children. The respondent emphasized this was the very poorest class of Poles.

"When Polish people got their own money, they bought a 'shack,'—I mean, a two-family house. They furnish the house. Sometimes even if they own their home and the family gets pinched for money, the Polish women go out to work to keep the family together. The Poles are very conservative."

I asked him about conflicts between the first and second generations.

He replied that only a few parents objected to children adopting American customs. "When there is crime among the Polish second generation, it is because the family is poor, and it can't give the children the luxuries other children have. It is a question of not having."

He said he never knew much about church conflicts, except that there was trouble when an assistant pastor at St. Stanislaus Church was discharged from his position.

Ernest Pentz
January 2, 1941

Owner of a Polish-American Newspaper

"Early settlers came to nobody. They had to go on their own. Soon they organized the Polish community and built the St. Stanislaus Church on Belmont Avenue. This was their first settlement." The next settlement was in the Ironbound district. From the Ironbound and from Belmont Avenue, many of the Poles moved out in the direction of Irvington. In Irvington they have their own colony.

Very few Polish children attended Polish schools. "Nine hundred families belong to Irvington. Only fifty of their children attended Polish school the last year."

"Poles don't have any more difficulty with the language than any other foreign group. I have an editor who has been in the United States only three years, and he speaks and writes English better than a lot of Americans."

On the role of the saloon, Mr. X vehemently denied that in 1912 the Poles had only the saloons to go to for recreation. He said that they had their church, their Polish Falcon halls, and their Polish educational hall. He added that the Poles had their Polish movie house in 1915—the Polonia Theater at Court and Belmont avenues.

He declared that Poles do not hold on to their money, but spend their money freely. They are well-known for their hospitality, and they leave all their money in this country. They like to enjoy themselves.

Some of the additional information he gave me was the following: There were no church adjustments nor church conflicts. All Poles are devout Roman Catholics. "The reason some people think Poles got into fights and broke bottles is because Russians, Ukrainians, and other Slavs who were responsible for these acts were called 'Polacks'

'Hunkies' for whom the Poles took the blame. These groups were bitter enemies of the Poles. The 'Liths' were also their enemies."

He said it was untrue that Poles had been more disposed toward Poland than America. He said Poles had always placed America first in their minds and hearts. He declared that a Polish-American club with fourteen hundred members existed in 1902. In 1898, there was a (Republican) Polish-American club headed by Johnny W. Jurkokowski.

"Because of Americanization, Polish schools did not meet with much success."

I had informed Mr. X that I had been at the Johnson Employment Agency. When he learned this, he said that they wouldn't give me an honest picture of the Polish people. He declared that the head of the agency was more for Hitler than he was for Poland. Mr. X had a violent dislike of Jews.

Ernest Pentz
January 2, 1941

The Choice of the Polish People

Mr. Stanley J. Doman, a second-generation Pole, was born in Wilkes-Barre, Pennsylvania, on July 20, 1911. When Mr. Doman was seven months of age, his parents moved to Jackson Street in Newark. After living in this city about seven years, his parents decided to move back to Pennsylvania. Mr. Doman attended the Wilkes-Barre public schools. When he was thirteen years of age, his parents moved back to Newark. This time they decided to live permanently in the Ironbound section of this city.

At the age of fourteen, Mr. Doman began working with the Sherwin Williams Company as a shipping clerk. He worked for this company about a year and then left for Chicago, where he took a two-year course in automotive engineering at Greers College. He studied during the day and worked nights in order to pay his tuition.

Returning to Newark after the completion of the two-year course, Mr. Doman received employment with the White Motor Company in Newark. He remained with this firm for four years. In 1932, he enlisted with the United States Army and was stationed in Hawaii. While in the army, Mr. Doman became quite adept at boxing in the middle-weight division. He cherishes proudly a trophy he received for his distinction in boxing.

In 1934, he settled down in Newark and became a student of civic affairs. One of his favorite methods is checking and saving newspaper clippings. He also likes to talk with all kinds of people, not discriminating because of race, nationality, or creed. Mr. Doman married a Polish girl on May the 17th, 1936, in St. Casimir's Church. At the present time, he is the proud father of a husky four-year-old son. In 1936, he became interested in the trucking and used-car business. This is his present occupation. The used-car business has always fascinated Mr. Doman. He admits that, if he is elected as a commissioner in Newark, he will always find time to dabble with automobiles after doing his regular work. Mr. Doman's favorite sports are boxing, bowling, and football. He is a member of the A.F. of L. and St. Casimir's parish.

Although he is still a young man—thirty years of age—he is keenly interested in politics. In comparing Newark with other cities, he feels that he can be of great value in the reduction of taxes and dealing with other civic problems. Mr. Doman began his campaign as a candidate for city commissioner last year. Upon learning that the Polish societies on January 9, 1941, were banding together under the name of the Newark Municipal League in an effort to elect a Polish candidate into the city commission, Mr. Doman believed that he should be the man. The Newark Municipal League originally had decided to pick one man out of four candidates and back that man with all their might. The four candidates were Assemblyman Wegrocki, Stephen Lorenz, William A. Rucki and Dr. John B. Przybylowicz. Mr. Doman appeared at the meeting and pleaded his case, hoping to receive the backing of the Polish societies. According to this man, the committee has not as yet chosen a candidate, and his chance of being the choice of the Polish people is good.

John Karpinic
February 18, 1941

Wanting to Better Myself

Mr. Sypniewski first joined Organ Dramatic Society in 1893. In 1899, he joined the Moniuszko Singing Society. In 1902, he joined the New Life Society, which met at Pasek's Hall on South Orange Avenue. In 1899, he helped found Polish-American Building and Loan. In 1909, Mr. Sypniewski joined Society of Polish Tradesmen, which met at the Polish Home on Beacon Street. He had two sons. One died young; he sent the other to public schools. This son graduated high school and

went to AIB. When Mr. Sypniewski left for the United States, it was
with the thought of earning a quick fortune and returning to Poland to
live like a gentleman.

I was born in Poznań in 1887. My father was a forester on a private
estate. I went to public school from age six to sixteen. This included
about two years in a business course. After I got out of school, I went to
work as an apprentice clerk in a dry goods store. I worked there for
three years and then went to Berlin to get further experience. I got a job
in a woolen goods store operated by Germans, and I stayed in Berlin on
this job about four years. From Berlin, I returned to Poznań and worked
in the same store for two years.

In 1893, wanting to better myself, I decided to come to the United
States. I crossed with four other young fellows from the same town.
The reason for migrating to the United States was the high opinion
held in Poland and Europe generally concerning the United States; to
wit, that a common laborer who went to the United States in a short
space of time was able to provide his family in Poland with many luxuries. Of course, this led an educated person to believe that he could do
much better in comparison.

On my arrival, I went to live in Bloomfield with friends from my
hometown. I stayed there a year. While staying in Bloomfield, I married
a German girl who had been born in the United States. She died a half-
year after the wedding.

All this time I couldn't get work because of the hard times during
Cleveland's time.[12] When I moved to Newark, I got a job in Branch
Brook Park with the city. At that time, most workers in the park were
Poles, and I got my job because I was able to speak German to the
foreman, who was a Czech. The job paid $1.25 for a ten-hour day. I
worked in the park about four months, then I got a job in a traveling-
bag factory and stayed there eleven years. In 1906, I went to Buffalo and
opened a bookstore and newspaper agency for *Ameryka-Echo*.[13] I
stayed there till 1908 and then returned to Newark. On my return, I
worked as a representative for a Buffalo brewery for two to three years.
I left this about 1911, entered the real estate and insurance business,
and have remained in same to date.

Work Couldn't Be Had in Poland

I was born in 1886 near Białystok. My parents were farmers who owned
a thirty-acre farm. I went for two years to school in Warsaw. Then I

returned to Białystok and went to work for my father on the farm, from when I was fourteen until I was eighteen.

At the age of eighteen, I decided to go to the United States to get work because it couldn't be had in Poland. I had heard good reports about the United States—that work was plentiful. On my arrival, I had about one hundred dollars. I settled at Glen Cove, Long Island. A week after my arrival, I got a job on a farm at eighteen dollars per month. I took the job to see how farms are managed in the United States, and I kept it one month. Next, I worked a summer in a brickyard at three dollars per ten-hour day. In the winter, brickyards are slow, and I went to work in coal mines in Pennsylvania for three months. In the summer, I returned again to the brickyard.

In 1916, I came to Newark and took a job in a spring-mattress factory and stayed there for ten years. While working in a celluloid factory, I took a Palatine Correspondence School business course at night for five years. I learned English by myself. About 1925, I opened a butcher and grocery store in Newark and kept it for eight years. After that, I went into the packing business—food and condiments. I joined St. Valentine's Society (PRCU) in 1920. This was my first membership. Later, I joined the Polish Falcons, and recently, in 1927, I joined the Polish-American Businessmen's Association.

Mass Meeting of the IWO

Four hundred and fifty Poles, Russians, and Ukrainians, representing sections of the International Workers Order, a fraternal organization for labor, packed the Ukrainian Hall at Fifty-nine Beacon Street, Friday, October 27, 1939, to protest the invasion of their country of birth—Poland—by the German army.

F. Haracz, the national head of the Polish section of the International Workers Order, was the main speaker for the evening. He spoke of the feudal setup of Poland and the sympathy the Polish government expressed for the Nazi regime during periods of world crisis. The Polish leaders, he said, did not grant democracy and independence to their people. The recent government was following the policy of Polishification and did not permit the various national minorities composing the Polish nation to speak their native tongue or to allow freedom in extending their native culture. He compared this method with the policy of Russification of the tsarist regime when Poland was a part of Russia, and explained that the same results have been produced—that the nation will not have national unity of its peoples. When Czechoslovakia was denied existence, the Polish government was one of the first that asked for a share in the plunder. Furthermore, he stated, England and France had no intention of defending the independence of the Polish nation. They did not contribute one bullet with which the Poles would defend themselves.

Dr. Adolph Wegrocki, a prominent leader of the Polish community and a candidate for reelection to the state assembly, was scheduled to speak. Due to a conflict in campaign meetings, he did not appear.

Seamen from the SS *Piłsudski*, a ship that left the port of Gdynia at the outbreak of the war, were presented to the audience for a brief address. The federal authorities are discussing their status as refugees, and at the present time the seamen are being housed by a Polish Seamen's Home in New York City.

Sinch O'Har
October 27, 1939

Follow the Dictates of Her Heart

Miss Jean Oleska, a senior in high school, is the youngest of four children in her family. The children include one girl who is married, two boys, and Jean. Jean was born in Newark in 1923, on Main Street in the Ironbound section, and has lived all her seventeen years in this city. When this girl was about six years of age, her family moved to uptown Newark into the Thirteenth Ward and has lived in that vicinity ever since.

Jean's parents were born in Poland on the outskirts of Warsaw. Her father immigrated to New Brunswick, New Jersey, in the year 1913, where he met Jean's mother, who also had come to America in the same year. Although her father worked as a farmer in Poland, in America he became a painter. Their first child—a girl—was sent to parochial school, which she attended to the fifth grade. From the fifth grade, she entered public school with her sister and brothers.

Jean feels that her father still does not understand or appreciate American ways. Her mother, however, although unable to speak English, has conformed to the American pattern, creating understanding between Jean and her mother. About ten years ago, the family became completely disorganized. The father was so abusive that mother and daughters were forced to leave the house and live separately for nine years. Now the family has united once again, and some sort of harmony prevails. The father has become quite industrious, although he still likes to drink "for his health" because of the effects of his painting profession.

Jean, who is her mother's favorite, frankly admits that her mother has spoiled her. Her mother gives her anything she desires and does not insist upon Jean doing any housework. I asked Jean if she would like to go to college after finishing high school, if it were possible. She replied that college was not for her; it would do her no good. Her highest ambition is to be a stewardess on an airplane or a nurse, although she admits this will never happen. She said that, when she completes high school, she will probably work in a factory a year or two and then get married about the age of nineteen or twenty, have two or three children, and remain a housewife the rest of her life. At present, she keeps company with an Italian lad of twenty-one, whom she firmly believes will be her future husband. I asked her if she would not prefer to marry a fellow of Polish descent like herself. She replied that she would follow the dictates of her heart, and the fact that a fellow is German, Italian, or any other nationality would not make any difference. Asking her if her parents would have anything to say in directing her choice, she said absolutely no—that the choice was up to her and no one else.

If events ever become amiable in Poland, Jean would like to visit the country, staying about six months in order to better visualize the country from which her parents emigrated.

J. Karpinic
November 4, 1940

Left to Seek His Fortune

Mr. Mieczyslaw Straszynski was born in the Galicia region of Poland, which was under the rule of the Austrian king. The section of Galicia from which he originates was poor. The best products were shipped to Austria; Galicia took what was left. There was no choice. However, the Austrians were by no means physically cruel to this region of Galicia. As long as the people recognized the Austrian flag, there was no trouble. His schooling was in Polish and German. Whenever possible, the schoolmaster tried to avoid singing the Austrian anthem.

His parents were farmers with a few acres of land, which yielded

food for his family, and no more. If the year was good, the extra products were sold in the market. This was not too often. He left Galicia
after he realized that he would not progress much higher than his father. His father sent him to a nearby town, where he was a painter's
apprentice. When he acquired the essentials of painting and saved what
money he earned, he left the country to seek his fortune in America.

He left Galicia in 1907. This was the period of time when America
was receiving thousands of foreigners to her shores. He took his ship at
Rotterdam, the Netherlands. The ship's first stop was Ellis Island. After
a routine examination, he was permitted to land at New York. He did
not stay in New York City because he had an uncle living in Newark.
He obtained work in Montclair as a painter, but continued to live in
Newark.

He married in 1915 and settled in the Ironbound section of Newark.
At this time, the Ironbound section was thinly populated. Most of the
people living here were of German descent. In 1917, a son was born.
Mr. Straszynski had no political interest at this time, being busy with
supporting his wife and child. His social recreation consisted of trips to
the seashore with friends, automobile rides, and home entertainments.
His religion is that of the Catholic faith.

He had little difficulty in adjusting himself to the English language.
He attended night school for a short period of time. As he worked in an
English-speaking section, he learned the language easily. At home, he
lived among the Germans, Slavs, Irish, and Italians. In Galicia, he
learned German and Russian. He also learned Ukrainian. The city life
of Newark was a great change from the farm life in Galicia, but this did
not cause him any emotional strain. He quickly adjusted himself to the
modern conveniences. Having none in Galicia, this was easy. The
world war gave him a great deal of work because he was employed as a
painter, painting ships at the Port of Newark.

About this time, he joined several Polish organizations—a sick benefit club, a glee club, and several social clubs. At the present time, he is
only active in the sick benefit club. He is an active member in the
painters' union. He is happy to state that he has been a member for
over thirty years. He is not employed twelve months of the year because his work is seasonal. During good times, he would work about
nine months of the year. This is far from the fact now. His sole aim in
life was to save enough money to send his son through grammar
school, high school, and college. He did all these. His son was graduated from college in 1938. He buys the Polish newspapers and listens to
Polish programs on the radio regularly.

Born in America, but Raised in Poland

Mr. G. was born in America in Jersey City. He was taken to Poland by his mother at the age of four with his two brothers. The eldest brother lost his eye when six years old while playing with other children near a building under construction in Jersey City. The contractor's carelessness in not having a watchman on duty while children were playing caused the child's misery. The youngsters thought it a splendid idea to make snowballs out of the unfinished lime and began throwing it at each other. Unfortunately, Mr. G's brother was the victim; it burned his left eye immediately. He has a glass eye today.

The parents were overcome with grief, and the mother suffered from nervous prostration. Her husband sent her and the three children to Poland, with the hope that she would someday forget and return in better health. She was ready to return to America, but, unfortunately, war broke out in 1914. She was stranded in Dobrzyń, a city in the state of Warsaw in Poland, then under Russian rule, with three children and without funds or aid from anyone.

Mr. G's ancestors were descended from nobility, dating back as far as the eighteenth century. In 1863, Mr. G's great-great-grandfather, then living in Lithuania, fought in the revolution for Poland's independence. The Lithuanian government confiscated his wealth and property, leaving him a pauper. They dynamited his palace of eighty rooms and took his title of count away from him. He left Lithuania and came to a small town near Warsaw, and there with his family he began a new life. He had a strong willpower, and he hungered for Poland's freedom with all his heart and soul. He fought in many battles, and he died in 1892, fighting for Poland.

After serving his six years' term in the Russian army, Mr. G's father was released and returned to his hometown, where his wife and son were waiting patiently for him. A month later, following his return from the Russian army, war broke out between Russia and Japan, and he was called to the colors. Not wishing to fight for Russia, he planned to escape. His father gave him money, and luckily he got through Germany to Bremen—Germany's seaport. There he had to bribe the German guards to get through, and he successfully escaped to America.

While in the Russian service, he was a cornet soloist in the tsar's private band. He soon found a part-time position in America as a cornetist in a small orchestra. The little he earned helped to keep the wolf from the door. His trade was cabinetmaking. Finally, he was fortunate to find a steady position at twelve dollars a week. This was considered a good salary in that day. At the end of summer in 1905, he had sufficient funds to cover his wife's and son's travel expenses to America. His wife and son first set foot on American soil in November 1905. They were a happy family because they were united once again, but the most important thing was they were free from Russian domination and brutality.

In 1906, Mr. G. was born, and in 1910, Mr. G's mother gave birth to her third and last child. Late in 1910, Mr. G's mother left for Poland with her three sons and was stranded in war-torn Europe. They suffered agonies and had to run away from one village to another. They were hungry, sleepless, and desperate. Starvation and disease were around them, death staring them in the face at any moment. They lived like hunted animals. Mr. G. was eight at that time, and the horrors of war will always stand out in his memory. He knew the meaning of war even though he was only eight years old. His mother knew she could not feed her children any longer. Those people who had more than others helped the needy. She knew death stalked everywhere, and, after three months of constant wandering, seeking, and hiding, she decided to return to her hometown and face death there. They knew no fear; it was either life or death.

She had expensive jewelry—gifts from her husband—which she treasured dearly. When hunger gnaws at one's stomach, jewelry can't feed it, and she gladly exchanged her jewelry for money from a wealthy man. With this small sum she bought a little store. This kept her and her three boys from starvation. The little profit she made was certainly welcomed.

During the four years of European war, the people grew accustomed to it; to them life or death had no meaning. Mr. G's mother was robbed a few times by the German, Austrian, and Russian armies when they invaded. What did they care about a poor mother's heartbroken plea. They would sneer. Pleadings and tears were no help. They treated the people cruelly—in fact, beastly and coarsely. Farmers suffered intolerably. Their horses, cattle, and all their worldly possessions were gone. Death was better than life. If they opposed, they were shot anyway.

No wonder, when Poland gained her freedom in 1918, the new Polish government found nothing but barren soil. There were no horses, cattle, or plows—no seeds of any kind to be sown. They had to buy seeds and seek loans from other nations to rebuild Poland over again. Roads were ruined completely. For 150 years, Poland was under Russian, German, and Austrian pressure; they plundered and burned and murdered the Polish people. Two years later, after Poland gained her freedom in 1918, another war broke out between the Bolsheviks and Poland. Whatever was rebuilt was in ruins again. Before this last war, in 1939, Poland was on her feet again. She had one of the largest seaports—Gdynia, on the Baltic—the fifth largest on the continent. Modern buildings. It was indeed a beautiful country, but crushed now.

Mr. G. attended school with his brothers. His mother worked harder than ever so her boys could receive an education. Mr. G. graduated from the primary grades and had two years of business college; but he could not attend any further because of his mother's illness. The eldest brother was the breadwinner then, and Mr. G. also had to find work to support the family. He found a position in a large store where eighteen clerks were employed. He worked himself to manager in a short time.

Since Mr. G. was an American citizen, he had a desire to come to America to see the country where he was born. According to his mother's stories, America was a wonderful place in which to live. He thought he could help his mother more if he had a good position here. He also wished to see his father, from whom they had not heard in years. He left a good position in Poland and came to America in 1929. Born in America, but raised and educated in Poland, he couldn't understand or speak the English language. He found it quite difficult to find a position. However, he was quite happy because he had found his father, who was a sick man.

He had to find a position as soon as possible. His first position was teaching in the Polish night school. This, however, did not bring in enough income, so he obtained a position as a reporter for a Polish paper. Dissatisfied, he tried other places, and after six years, he succeeded as a salesman in a large concern. He completed his salesman's course at the Sales Analysis Institute in the state of New Jersey.

Mr. G. married a Polish girl who was born and educated in America. They have one child. Their desire is to see their little daughter grow up and, with God's help, complete her high school and college education, which is a necessity today. Mr. G. sent money to his mother and brothers. He had sufficient funds to pay for his youngest brother's passage to America. He is also an American citizen. But his brother did not like America. He grew homesick, stayed only six months, and returned to Poland, where he married his childhood sweetheart. They had a little girl just before the war broke out in 1939.

Mr. G. has not heard from his mother or brothers to this day, and he doubts very much if they are alive. He has tried to communicate with them in every way possible, but without success. His father died of a heart attack in 1938, without seeing his granddaughter for whom he so anxiously waited. Mr. G. resides in Jersey City. He speaks English well, and he is an active member in a few large organizations.

T. Giergielewicz

The Duckiet Family

The Duckiet family lived in Frysztak, Poland, which was called Austrian or Little Poland. They were wealthy businesspeople of this town. Mr. Duckiet passed away in 1887, and his money was divided among his five children. The oldest son, Walter, came to Newark in 1888, locating and starting a boardinghouse and meeting hall on Thirty South Orange Avenue. This was the first Polish boardinghouse in Newark. Another son, Leon Duckiet, arrived in this country on April 2, 1890, and also located in Newark at the age of twenty-four. The Duckiet family had a large department or general store in Frysztak, Poland, where the children worked with their parents. Mr. Duckiet also owned several properties in the same city. Leon Duckiet spent three years attending gymnasium.[14] His brother and sisters also attended gymnasium, so the entire family had a fair education. From all appearances Mr. Leon Duckiet seems to be of a very high moral character.

The children of the Duckiet family were all born in their homes without the help of doctors. At the last moment, a midwife was called in, who had the help of the nearby neighbors. Conditions were not very sanitary, and there were a great many deaths at childbirth among the poorer people. Families as a rule were large; there were five children born in the Duckiet family. The children of the Duckiet family attended several years of gymnasium, but this was not so among the poorer people. It cost money to get a higher education in Poland.

The standard of living in Poland was according to the income and wealth of its people. Those who had money lived in sections where they had their own well; in other sections, there was a water pump or well for every few blocks. Oil lamps were used for lighting, and most of the heat came from wood brought in from the forest. The wealthy people had a slightly better standard of living than the poor people. They had various means for earning a living. There were a great many farmers and cattle ranchers. There were also many mines and oil wells near Frysztak. There were mostly Poles in this section, with some Germans and Austrians.

The Duckiet family left Poland after the death of the father, the estate being sold. The children all had money, and they decided to come to America. There were not very many Poles leaving this section of Poland in the 1880s. A few wealthy people who wanted a change came to America. There were a great many jobs open, and there was a great demand for foreign labor in Newark in the early part of the 1890s. Foreign labor worked for less money than the local labor. There were certain factories in Newark where there were bad odors, such as in the leather tanneries, and there was some difficulty holding men on the jobs.

Leon Duckiet started as an apprentice in a tailor shop for six dollars a week, and in a very short time his pay was increased to nine dollars a week. Two years later, he earned fifteen dollars, and, in 1894, he left this work and secured a job in a hat factory, earning thirty dollars a week, working twelve hours a day. He spent twenty-four years in this hat factory. In 1918, he left, going into the insurance business, and he remained in the insurance business for one year. Then he became a salesman for a grocery house catering to the Polish trade, in which he remained until he retired several years ago.

When Mr. Duckiet first came to Newark, he boarded with a private family on Morton Street near Broome Street. There were two other boarders who shared the same room with him. He lived here for one year, then moving to Howard Street and then to Jones Street. This is the section where all the Polish immigrants lived in Newark at that time. Mr. Duckiet did not want to spend more than he earned, and every time his earnings were increased, he moved to better and more private quarters. Several years later, after his marriage, he moved to Bloomfield, where he built his own home, which he still owns.

As a young man, Mr. Duckiet was very active in Polish-American political affairs. He spent many of his evenings in the private parks and beer gardens. He met a young woman there on many of his evenings, and, after keeping company with her for a year, they were married. Mrs. Duckiet came to this country when she was nine months old and received her education in the schools of Newark. They had a very large wedding in Duckiet's Hall, and the Polish people in that section of Newark were invited. Mr. Duckiet was twenty-nine when he married, and his bride was twenty-four. They were very happy at first. They separated twelve years ago, but they still have the greatest respect for each other. Their grown children married professional men.

The most modern method of the Poles meeting their prospective brides in Newark in the 1890s was by going to the beer gardens and private parks, where the younger Poles congregated in the evenings.

Dances were held there every night. Mr. Duckiet saw his prospective bride here most every night, danced with her, and then he would see her home.

Several years after their marriage a son was born, who died nine months later. Then twin girls were born. Both girls became high school graduates. The family is strongly against intermarriage. The girls married Polish men who were born and brought up in the German section of Poland. There were no difficulties with their children over American ideas because of the fact that Mrs. Duckiet and both daughters were brought up in this country and received their education in American schools. The children do not observe any Polish habits or customs because they consider themselves to be and act like Americans.

Several times a year, Mr. Duckiet attends Roman Catholic church, but he sees no great attraction there. In 1890, Mr. Duckiet started the first Polish political club in the city of Newark—the Polish National Republican Club—and he has been active in politics ever since. He always votes for the best man, and he is 100 percent for democracy. He is very bitter against dictatorship and loves our form of government.

Mr. Duckiet is a very old and healthy looking man, and he is very active for a man over seventy. He claims to have never been ill in his life. He is a man of about five feet seven inches tall, is stocky, and weighs about 165 pounds. He is cleanshaven and has very bright eyes, white hair neatly combed, and a rosy complexion. He is well-dressed and has the appearance of a retired businessman. He is very pleasant and witty and seems to get a lot of pleasure from life. Mr. Duckiet is a great baseball fan and attends quite a few games. He spends a great deal of his time in a saloon, where he plays cards and greets the customers as they come in. He likes to drink whiskey.

Murray Koch
February 3, 1941

Polish Boardinghouses, 1890

In the year of 1888, Mr. Walter Duckiet, who had come from Frysztak, Austrian Poland, a year previous, started a boardinghouse and meeting hall at Thirty South Orange Avenue. Mr. Duckiet's father died in Frysztak, leaving him quite some money, and he left for the New World. Coming to Newark, and not wanting to find a job, he decided to go into the boardinghouse business. The Poles who were coming here were unable to find places to live. There were eighteen rooms in this boardinghouse, of which about eleven were occupied by families and the other seven occupied by boarders, three or four men to a single room. There were about five toilets in the backyard, without plumbing. Once a month, Mr. Duckiet would give notice to his boarders to leave the house, in order to clean out and empty the toilets. This would leave a very bad odor in those days, as there was no running water or sewers. Mr. Duckiet had two sinks in the boardinghouse, and there would be long lines waiting for a pitcher of water to bring to their rooms for washing. Many times, several people would wash in the same water instead of going for fresh water. A few of the more expensive rooms had gas lights, but most of them had oil lamps. Rates were one dollar to two dollars a week. Conditions in general were very unsanitary and un-healthful. Most of these boarders ate in the dining room, which was situated on the rear of the first floor, and the boarders ate according to the salaries they earned. There was another large Polish boardinghouse on South Orange Avenue, between Broome Street and Prince Street, that had twenty-two rooms. Both of these boardinghouses were filled at all times.

Almost every Polish family in town had from two to five boarders. There would be about two or three boarders in one sleeping room. There was one tenement house on Morton Street, opposite the public school, that held eighteen tenants, who were all Polish families. It is believed that this building housed 150 people, mostly boarders. There were eighteen booths in the backyard as toilets without water or sewers. At night, they would enter these toilets with lamps or candles. There were also a great many Polish tenements on Beacon Street. Hall-ways were dark and dirty, and the rooms had no heat. Most of the Pol-ish families would get their boarders from the enquiries made at Mr. Duckiet's boardinghouse. Jobs were plentiful, and the Poles were never out of work at this time unless they did not want to work. There was a demand for foreign, Polish labor; they were hard workers, working long hours for less pay than American help. Then there were certain shops, such as the hat factories and tanneries, that had a bad odor, and the Poles agreed to work in them. Many of their wives worked by taking in washing or going out to do housework.

The Poles were great ones for going out for walks in the evening or on Sunday. There were a few public parks and several beer gardens with dance halls, that were called "parks," and they were great places for men to meet the ladies. Many a Polish romance started here.

Murray Koch
January 30, 1941

Everything Was Taken from Us

I was born in Warsaw, Poland, in the year 1885. Warsaw was then under Russian rule, and I can clearly remember the difficult time my family had under such rule. We were not permitted to speak the Polish language, to celebrate Polish holidays, or maintain Polish customs under the Russians. My father was a clothing merchant of good circumstances, but the exorbitant taxes and the many restrictions seemed to weigh upon him heavily by the time I reached my fifteenth year. It was not long thereafter that he passed away.

After my father died, my brother and I were the only ones home with Mother, my two older brothers being in the United States. I got a job in a small machine shop in Warsaw and became well acquainted with different kinds of tools and their uses. The little money we made, together with what my brothers in America sent home, kept us going. However, when I was nineteen, my mother died. My brother and I decided to go to America to join our brothers in New York.

I know very little about my birth except that a midwife attended. I had three brothers, two older and one younger than I. None of us know our exact age, nor is there any written record, although we do know that we are one or two years apart.

Most of our learning was received at home under the supervision of my mother. While working at the machine shop, I learned quite a bit of mechanics. In Warsaw there were many schools, but, for some reason, my parents would not let us go to school. The people in Warsaw were mainly of the middle class, who earned a livelihood by selling, working in machine shops, farming, building, and by various other trades. Most of them went to school at one time or other or were taught the Polish language and customs at home. They knew how to read and write in Polish as well as Russian.

When my brother and I reached New York, my oldest brother met us and took us to his home in Jersey City. It was not long thereafter that I received a job as a real estate agent with a New York firm. My duty was to work among the Polish people and get them interested in New Jersey real estate. Being well versed in the Polish language, I was welcomed everywhere and soon was making a good salary.

I was invited to attend a wedding of one of my friends at the Polish Home in Jersey City, and it was there that I met a girl who is at present my wife. We went together for about a year to various house parties, weddings, dances, and church gatherings. At the age of twenty-one, I became a married man. My brother, who ran a tavern in Jersey City, decided to help me financially. It was through his aid that my wife and I finally entered into the grocery business, having a little store on Jackson Street, Jersey City.

The business was very good, our marriage seemed to be successful, and soon thereafter a son was born. Although my wife was born in America, she knew how to speak the Polish language as good as I, and to write it better than I. Since we talked in Polish at home, our son picked up the language very quickly and knew it very well by the time he entered public school.

During the year 1916, I was offered a good business proposition by a big concern to take over a certain tavern in Paterson. All I had to do was to pay the monthly rent, and the brewery would furnish me with all the fixtures and other necessities. I sold the store in Jersey City at a good profit and moved with my wife and son to Paterson. The tavern and restaurant combined did a very good business. I profited a great deal by the transaction, but, in the year of 1921, I had to sell out because of the Prohibition law. My wife and I thereupon invested in property in the city of Paterson and also in Asbury Park. We received a good income therefrom and lived comfortable for a number of years. However, about 1930 the income stopped, the property was very difficult to rent out, and taxes began to mount. Finally, the bank in which we had our money closed, and, within a few years, everything we had worked for was taken from us. I managed to secure a job as a machinist in the Pollock Manufacturing Company of Kearny at twenty-six dollars a week; and I still maintain this position, setting up different mechanisms from blueprints.

I attend church pretty regularly, although sometimes I cannot because of my work. I do not belong to any political party, and I vote for whoever I think is best suited for the office. Due to financial losses and worries, my health has steadily decreased, and in the last few years I have had quite a lot of trouble with my stomach, which necessitates my keeping a strict diet. Now and then for recreation I play a little cards at the Polish Home or attend a theater, and once in a while I go bathing at the seashore, when I can afford it.

E. Norwich

All My Life in the Polish Falcons

I was born in Galicia on March 1, 1898. My father owned his own land. He was carpenter, cooper, and jack-of-all-trades. I was taught all these things by my father. He wanted me to learn a trade early in my life. The other side is different. When you are nine or ten years old, you can't play hookey like here. You got to work and study. I went to school at the age of eight, from eight in the morning till four in the afternoon. After school, we had to watch cows and work on the farm. When I was thirteen, I belonged to the volunteer fire department. At eighteen, I was a member of the Polish Falcons. The population of my town was 196. We had two schools, but no theaters or dance halls. Parties were run in houses. We had to travel three miles to the theater. The Falcons was like the Boy Scouts. We hiked, organized sports, and had the same fun as boys do here.

At the age of sixteen, I went to Germany to attend a gardeners' school. I was there three years. After those years, I came to the United States on March 31, 1907. I liked farming, but there was not enough for us all. My life on the farm was better than in Germany and than when I first came to the United States. At home, I got plenty to eat and had clothes, but this could not last for long. On the other side, we drank very little. When I first came here, it looked bad to me, and I could not get a job. Teddy Roosevelt was president. I came to Newark, and it was two and a half months before I got a job. I've been in Newark ever since. My big problem was my inability to speak English. I attended night school, and in one year I was able to get around.

My first job was in the rivet works on Lafayette Street. The salary was $4.50 a week. We worked ten hours a day and six days a week. When I was young, I seldom went out. I stayed home to learn things. I was also a member of the Polish Falcons. In 1908, I was gym teacher in Nest Number 104. At that time it was Nest Number 2. In 1910, I was in a Falcon school for four days. This was a drill school. In 1912, I went to Philadelphia to attend a drill school. One of the instructors came from the other side. I was there five weeks. This was done to build our bodies. In 1914, I attended another drill school in Passaic for two weeks. We marched, sang songs, and learned rifle shooting and military drill. I was very interested in military books, and I spent much of my time studying these books. From 1910 to 1926, I worked hard to build the Falcon organization.

At the time the world war broke out, many Poles from Newark went to fight for Poland. I collected cigarettes, money, etc., for the boys on the other side. I got married in 1911, so I was unable to go there. In 1924 and 1925, I went to a Falcon school in Whippany, New Jersey, to teach children how to read and write Polish. In 1926 and 1927, I taught children Polish on South Market Street.

Today, I can't get a job. The gardener trade was bad in this country, and I never worked at it. If I had the brains I have today, I'd have stayed on that job. I had plenty of bad luck, but I never left home. I became a citizen in 1927. I am still active in Polish organizations, but now I have cooled off. I am not so active as when I was younger. There are different people now. Before, all kinds of Polish groups stuck together, better than like now. Today, there are too many politicians, and they don't understand what they are doing.

I have four children. They all have something to eat. One is married and three stay with me. Only one boy works, and he only makes ten dollars a week. I look for a job in all my spare time. All my life I spent in the Polish Falcons. I have plenty of pictures and can show you about these early days of the Falcons. I save all material on Poles—books, letters, papers. For five years I saved every issue of *Sokol*.[15] They asked me for these copies because they did not have them. This has been too much hurry up, and I can't remember everything. You will have to come some evening to my house, and I could talk to you more.

Sinch O'Har
October 10, 1939

No Beer, No Work

I was born in 1891 on my father's farm in Ostrołęka, province of Białystok. My schooling was under the Russians. There was great hatred of the Russian rule. Schools in the cities and towns were taught in Russian, not Polish. The farmers got together to teach children Polish. They did it undercover. If they got caught, the punishment was severe. I went to "undercover school" for eight winters. We started work when we were eight years old. All summer we worked.

In 1909, when I was nineteen, only two more years before I had to join the army, I sneaked across to the German border and then came to the United States. I landed in New York and went to Massachusetts, where I had a brother. I got a job in a textile mill for a while. In 1912, through my friends, I got a job in a brewery.

In Poland there were few roads, and everything was muddy. We had no electric lights and gas. My father owned his own farm and hired people at harvest time. The rest of the year the family took care of the farm.

In 1914 I wanted to join the army, but I was rejected because I could not speak English. In 1916 I got my papers. In 1917, I was called into the army when the United States entered the war. I was two years in the army and spent one year in France. I say "war is hell," as Sherman said. It was terrible. I don't wish no one to go to war. It is a terrible sight. The air battles and gun battles are still in my mind. I was in the artillery. I was deaf for three months from noise. I remember men yelling, "Stop that noise!" These men lost their minds. There were many experiences I had. Everybody knows stories of the war. Many books have been written on it, yet this does not stop war. There is nothing pleasant about it, and I don't wish to say anything more about it.

In 1919, I came back to the United States from France. The army was demobilized. Prohibition came into being, and I lost my job. No beer, no work. In 1917 I got married, the same year I went into the army.

In 1919, I got a job at General Electric in Massachusetts. In 1924, I came to Newark, and I've been here ever since. I worked in General Motors in Harrison from 1925 to 1936—the longest I ever worked in one place. I got two boys—one born in 1920, and the other in 1924. In 1936, I opened up a business for myself—a tavern. I didn't make much headway, and I sold the business in 1938. I wanted to open up another business, but I couldn't find what I liked. I always wanted to be in business, but I never knew how to do it. You got to be experienced. I discovered it only now.

I was always a member of the Polish Falcons. I feel very bad about what happened to Poland. I have two brothers and one sister still on the other side. I haven't heard from them for a long time. It has always been the trouble for centuries. I blame the Polish diplomats; politicians always don't mean well. The people of Poland were always contented. Why can't they be left alone? They just got on their feet from the last war, and the same thing happens.

Sinch O'Har
October 10, 1939

Ninety Percent Are Democrats

Mr. X and his aides were discussing the intricacies of auto mechanics when I entered the business office of his establishment. A shifting of eyebrows greeted my hello. My entrance did not disturb the conversation, so I comfortably seated myself in a corner chair, waiting for some one to ask me the purpose of my visit. The conversation continued for some three minutes, in which time a person waiting to be recognized becomes impatient and annoyed to be so neglected. At last, Mr. X asked what he could do for me. I felt relieved. His approach was not the same he would use to a customer because I had some charac-teristics of a salesman—I carry a large notebook, and I was seemingly ready to discuss business.

I was hesitant in reporting my visit to Mr. X before such a group of attentive listeners, and I asked for the privilege of talking to him pri-vately. He ushered me into a room that was used as a display for cas-kets, where I whispered the intentions of our work, etc., and I asked him to give me a biographical story of his life.

Before half of my purpose could be described, he broke in with, "Are you sure I won't be stuck for any money?" Being convinced of my guarantee that no such motive existed, he invited me to see him the following day, as he was busy at the time preparing assignments for his workers. The next day, the greeting was more cordial. He arranged for us to talk in a small office next to the embalming room.

Mr. X is sixty-six years of age, about five feet in height, and he weighs close to 150 pounds. His walk has been slowed by his years of hard work. His smile, when noticed closely, expressed a beam of satis-faction because he was flattered to relate a story of his life that might someday be published in a book.

He impressed me as not being a person who exerts a dignified and important influence in the life of the Polish community. Though he is regarded as Pan X, by the rank-and-file Poles, he is not placed in the same high esteem by his fellow men in business and professional cir-cles.[16]

Mr. X came to this country when he was a mere child, yet he has great difficulty in speaking English. He entered the Renouard Em-balming School in New York. Mr. X became the first Polish undertaker and embalmer in Newark and its vicinity. His contacts and work have provided him with many opportunities for advancement. Any Polish worker can record more progress in mastering the language than he. When I asked him to spell a Polish town or a Polish organization that he is a member of, he could not do it verbally, but had to write it down on paper first, very doubtfully, following the same form as a child in school.

During the process of the interview, Mr. X very proudly showed me his scrapbook. He agreed that this scrapbook can remain in my pos-session until I get a more detailed story of his political life. He is a member of twenty organizations, and he is doing the impossible by acting as president, secretary, treasurer, etc., in a good many of them. His children must play an active part in keeping his records and orga-

nizational activity efficient. He showed me documents taken from the huge safe in his office, delegating him as a representative to conventions, banquets, etc. One invitation made him glow with pride—it was a printed invitation by President and Mrs. Roosevelt asking him to a White House luncheon.

Always active in political circles, Mr. X served in 1932 as a member of the New Jersey legislature. He is a member of the Democratic advisory board, was elected as a Democratic elector in 1936, and at present is the Polish Democratic leader in Essex County. Mr. X was a delegate to the National Convention of the Democratic party held in Philadelphia in 1936. To prove it, he spread out a copy of a Philadelphia newspaper with the following big-type headlines: "MR. X FROM N.J. ARRIVES." The story of his arrival was missing, only the headline was preserved. He claimed the pages of the paper were stolen from him by jealous individuals—his former friends who envied his growing progress in politics.

In the display room there are two large oil paintings hanging on the walls. One is a picture of Jesus Christ on the cross; the other portrays General Piłsudski with his army.

"Yes sir," he said, "these pictures are expensive stuff. How much do you think I paid for them?"

I looked admiringly at the "expensive stuff."

"You like it, eh? Well I paid three hundred bucks for 'em."

All my future visits were informal ones to gather additional material. His career is a very interesting one.

I was born in Fryzstak, Galicia. It was a little city. It had markets and everything. We lived alongside a school. My father was a tailor. His name was Albert; my mother, Amelia. I remembered a monument of St. Florence, which was near the school. We used to play around this monument.

I came here as a boy, five years, seven months old. I was born in 1873—December 18. I went to St. Peter's School on Belmont Avenue for three years. From there, I went to the Morton Street school two years At eleven, I worked at Johnson and Murphy shoe factory on Market Street.

I got a job at Fritz tailor shop on Richmond Street. It was the time of the Big Blizzard—March 12, 1888. I worked there for four years. At nighttime, at eight, it started to snow. We got up in the morning, and we could not leave the house to go to work. Nobody could get to work. We had sleds, pulled by horses, to get out. When we had to go uphill, another team of horses had to be used.

I worked at Seitz's hat factory on Blum Street for twenty years. At this time, I took an interest in undertaking business. While working, I ran the undertaking business.

When I was a boy about sixteen, I was the first altar boy when the Polish people organized their church. They had the first mass on William Street, called St. Mary's Church. It was held in a hall. From there, we moved to St. Peter's Church on Livingston Street. There we had masses every day. And then we bought a Baptist church on Belmont Avenue—St. Stanislaus parish today. Next to that was a tailor shop. The parish bought the tailor shop and made that the first school for Polish children. On top of that was where the priest lived. In 1889, we built the St. Stanislaus Church. It still stands today.

And then I got mixed up in politics. I belonged to the Republican party on Jones Street. There was no Democratic party. I was one of the representatives, and I was treasurer. I was one of the organizers of the Pulaski Fife and Drum Corps. We put up a slate. I put up for the clubhouse and upkeep, I paid for the instructor, I was one of the organizers of the Polish Calvineers, and I belonged to different organizations. My funeral parlor was on Livingston Street.

At that time, I was an office boy in a funeral home, carrying ice to bodies. We did not embalm them in those days. I had to help myself out. My father died when I was five. I'm married now forty-six years. I met my wife on Lincoln Street. I have six boys and a girl.

I started in politics at the time of Grover Cleveland. Those were hard times. We had to go out and get soup in pails and one loaf of bread a day. I am a Democrat since the time of Roosevelt. Conditions were caused by lack of production. There was not enough of food to go around. Today, we can do the same thing with five men that we did with a thousand men at that time. Inventions, that's what makes it. We used to go around with young fellows. We went Christmas calling and to parties. I used to take interest in Polish shows. We used to run them in Krueger's.[17] All the young fellows used to go out every day to different places for enjoyment.

When I joined the Democrats—I have always been active in politics—they selected me to serve on the election for the assembly. I was a legislator in 1932. When they ran us a second time, we all got beat. I was a delegate to the Eighteenth Amendment repeal, and I was a delegate to the national convention in Philadelphia. I was one of the electors in this state in 1936. I ran for sheriff in 1938, but I was defeated. There was a recount. I take part in all Democratic organizations and do hard work. You try to do the right thing for them, and they don't recognize it. I won't mention anything about money.

I belong to all the Polish organizations around here. I work in church services, in the Polish church and American church. I belong to the Polish Calvineers, the Pulaski Fife and Drum Corps, St. Casimir's Church, the Polish National Building and Loan Association, the St. Stanislaus Benefit Society, the White Eagles, the Polish Falcons, the John Sobieski Society, the Kosciusko Society, the St. Martins Society, the Wolnosz Benefit Association, the Holy Name Society, the Polish-American Democratic Club, the Elks, and the Young Men and Ladies Rucki Association. I am the owner of the property of the Young Men and Ladies Association. I bought a Russian church and turned it into a clubhouse.

I met my wife when I was twenty years old. Together we used to go to different parties. This is how we met. I am in the undertaking business forty-five years. In the old days, we put the bodies in the icebox the day before the funeral and then put the body in the casket the next morning. I went to embalming school in New York. After I got through schooling and could see my way, I retired from the factory where I was working and set up my own establishment.

What made you go into politics?

Oh, for my pastime. I took an interest in it.

What did you do when you were a legislator?

Well, I passed laws. What do you think? I worked for the bill appropriating money for the Pulaski Skyway. I helped to pass law for the Sons of Poland to organize outside of state. I ran for freeholder in 1934, but I had no chance.

Do the Polish people always vote for you?

Ninety percent of Polish people are Democrats. They have given me all their support. I have always been loyal to them.

Tell me more about politics.

In politics, we daren't say anything out of school. I can't think now. I'm too busy. The proper way would be to do this from childhood up. I know I'm the oldest Polish resident in Newark.

Sinch O'Har
October 11, 1939

Took Up Barbering

The informant has three children—two boys and a girl. One boy is in the aviation corps in Illinois. He completed high school and went two years to college. The girl is finishing high school and wants to be a teacher. The other boy is in his first year of high school. In 1910, the informant joined Polish National Alliance in Milwaukee and has remained a member to date. At present, he belongs to eight to ten Polish societies.

I was born 1892 in the town of Skulsk, in the province of Łódź (Kalicka Guberniya). Father was a flour miller and had his own mill. I attended school till 1909 and finished gymnasium—eight years in all. I took a business course. After getting out of school, I worked for Father for one year. In 1910, I left for the United States because I didn't want to serve in the army. I went to the United States because my brother lived there in Wisconsin. I joined my brother there. He had his own bakery business. I stayed with him one year and then went to a Catholic seminary for two years. I left the seminary because of the dissatisfaction of the heads of seminary over a piece of poetry by Maria Konopnicka that I had placed as the editor in the Polish-language paper.[18] The reason for their dislike of the poem was that it was on the papal index.[19]

After leaving the seminary, not having a trade, I took up barbering in Wisconsin for one year. In 1915, I joined the United States Army because work was scarce and I couldn't speak English too well. I thought I could improve myself in the army. I stayed in the army three years till the armistice. After leaving the army, I took up barbering in Milwaukee again for four years. Then I went to Detroit because my wife came from there. I got married in 1920. I also had a barbershop in Detroit. I stayed there five years.

Next, I went to Los Angeles and stayed two years. After losing all my money—$14,500—I went to Cleveland. In Cleveland, I also worked as a barber. I stayed there two years and then went to New York City in 1928. In New York City, I had my own shop on Third Avenue. In 1930, I came to Newark because my wife didn't like New York City. I didn't return from Los Angeles to Detroit because I felt ashamed to return broke. I have stayed in Newark ever since as a barber.

Fred Madrygin

The Standard of the *Pan*

Dr. X has shown much interest in the progress of our survey. He willingly sacrificed valuable time to discuss matters relating to the Polish community. He is a doctor by profession. Dr. X is solidly built—about five feet, eleven inches tall with broad shoulders—and weighs about 180 pounds. Many of our conversations dealt mainly with Poles in politics, leads for the survey in contacting prominent Polish organizations, and opinions on international events.

In the communities of the various national groups, any son who succeeds in either the medical or legal professions is looked upon as an authority on all subjects. In his opinion, there is one thing that has created a little disappointment among some of the Poles. He does not live up to the standard of the *pan* in employing a cook, a maid, and assistants in his office. His wife does the cooking, answers the phone, and replies to the doorbell. In Poland, a doctor would lose all his prestige and would show futile accomplishments if he did not have servants in his hire. Dr. X feels that he has hardened the Poles to his way of living and that this matter is not mentioned to him as often as it has been in the past years.

Fred Madrygin

Didn't Want to Leave

Mrs. X was born in 1876 near Warsaw. Her father was an organist, and her grandfather was a landowner near Warsaw. She went to school four to six years, but she studied mostly at home. She studied to be a dressmaker. She married when twenty-two and settled in Warsaw. Her husband was a cabinetmaker and later worked on the government railroad. In 1913, they came to the United States to join their daughter and see their grandchildren. Her husband didn't want to leave Poland. She was the only one of five sisters to come to the United States. When they came to the United States, her husband worked as a cabinetmaker and she as a self-employed dressmaker. They settled in Brooklyn because her daughter and cousin lived there. They moved with their daughter and son-in-law to New Jersey in 1920. They have lived here since.

Fred Madrygin

Learned about Hatting

I was born in Newark, July 24, 1911. The day I was born, my father was repairing shoes. When the news reached him that it was a boy, he dropped the shoes and bought my sisters new shoes. I was the only boy born in the family and the last. When very young, I was always sick, but I turned out to be quite healthy today. When six years old, my mother passed away during the flu epidemic. Therefore, I was brought up by my father and my four sisters, and I believe they have done a good job.

I attended the Morton Street Grammar School, from which I graduated. In my school days, I was very active in all events. I was assistant chief on the police force, and I belonged to the Just-For-Boys Dramatic Club, organized by the Newark Evening News. I always managed to get one of the leading parts.

After finishing grammar school, I went to Essex County Boys Vocational School. During that time, the school organized a student council body similar to the City Commissioners in Newark. Each department, such as police, etc., had a head. As assistant campaign manager for a school chum who was elected to that body, I became by appointment deputy commissioner of the police force. We held court every afternoon. It was my job to penalize the various offenders with such penalties as sweeping the school grounds, picking up papers, and paying cash fines. After my second year at Vocational, I was made shop foreman in the class and held that till the finish.

Finishing vocational school and seeing my buddies having cash in their pockets, I had an urge to go to work, which was my big mistake. I started to work as an errand boy for the A & P. I got a very small salary. Later, I was made a clerk. Having worked for them three years, my salary still was very small. I was given the opportunity to work for the Ferry hat company in Newark. Starting at the bottom, I learned practically all there is to know about hatting. After a few years, Mr. Charles Ferry, president of the company, called me in his office and asked me if I would care to learn one of the most important branches in the hatting line—dyeing. Being thrilled at the chance, I was sent to a school in New York run by the National Aniline and Dye Company with my expenses paid plus a salary. I studied there for six months.

On my return, I was put in charge of the dyeing department, with about thirty men under me. Having quite a difficult job, I had to work late hours, including Sundays, to straighten out my formulas. Things were running along fine. But then business dropped considerably, the plant went into receivership, and finally it was closed down. I was out of work for about three weeks. The plant was taken over under a new management, hiring their own crew of foremen; I had to go to work as a starter.

Having always made pretty good money, and growing into manhood, I married a very charming girl—Mary, from Irvington, who came from an excellent family. I opened up my own apartment and was very happy.

During these years, I was always interested in some Polish organization—one in particular, the Sons and Daughters of Poland. Having a newspaper of our own, I was made the business manager. This newspaper has received many compliments, not only from the Poles in the United States of America, but in Europe. It was put on display in Warsaw during the Polish Youth Congress there in 1931. Mr. A. Gorelski, who was the president, was sent to this congress by the Republic of Poland. This organization, having grown considerably, planned on expanding in Newark, where it was organized. Mr. Gorelski, with many associates, including myself, spent many a night organizing other groups in New Jersey, such as in Elizabeth, Hillside, Irvington, and Nutley. I was transferred to the Irvington group, where I lived at the time. I was elected president after its second year in existence, and I have held that office for two years.

During the two years, I have been instrumental in putting out a little pamphlet of our own, titled *The Crystal*, including all activities and reports of various members, good and bad. After some time, I joined the Irvington Falcons, which is a nationally known organization. I was made treasurer and hold that job till this day.

I am very active in political circles and very popular with the women. In 1938 I was asked to manage the Polish Falcons' camp in Somerville, New Jersey. I left the job I held at the time and accepted this position, not realizing that it was a summer job. After the season was over, I was out of work for three days. Then I was asked to work as the custodian of the Polish Falcon Club at 280 New York Avenue, Newark, in which we are now located. In this building, we rent halls for various affairs, such as weddings, parties, meetings, etc. I have seen many different types of people. I also have to be a bartender. One must know how to treat different types of people. At times it is very boring, and yet one must contend with this. I now live in East Orange with my wife and sister and brother-in-law.

The Polish people today are more patriotic than in the years past. Always being very thrifty and good sports, it seems they have changed considerably due to the crisis of war. They do not blame the war on the German people, even though they fought with them many times. This blame is put on the heads of the German and Polish governments. I feel that the people have been sold out. Do not quote me on this. They were always good warriors and still are, and I believe Poland will rise again, just as strong as she has been before. And if they do, they will prepare themselves more strongly for such events as these.

Sinch O'Har

Saw Poland under German Rule

I was born March 30, 1908, in Brooklyn, New York. In the spring of 1911, I went with my parents to Switzerland. I stayed there a year. Then I went over to Poland, in the province of Poznań, at that time under German occupation, and stayed there till 1928.

I went to school the usual way, as did everybody else. I finished gymnasium—equivalent to high school—and I have a college education. During the war, my father, being an American citizen, had to report to the city hall twice a day. At that time the German government threatened to confiscate my parents' property. With the help of the Spanish consul, who took care of American citizens, they didn't confiscate it. I did some extensive traveling in Europe, visiting Germany, Denmark, England, France, Sweden.

What else would you like to know? I can say this: I saw Poland under German rule, as an oppressed nation, and then as a free country. I like the countryside—customs—and it took some time, of course, to change them. I would call them hidden frontiers that existed between the people. The people from south Poland would live differently than from those in the west or east. This was eliminated when Poland was united.

When I returned to the United States, I attended the Newark Technical School and New York University. I think this is not important. I studied various subjects—architecture, then I switched to journalism. Frankly, my life was not exciting, and there is nothing to tell.

Sinch O'Har
October 23, 1939

Early Polish Life in Newark

Many Poles worked in Balbach's Refinery and Smelting Works and in the Public Service Gas Company. Foundries, hat factories, tailoring concerns, shoe companies, and tanneries also employed them. The respondent himself worked for Freed's tailor shop and for the Johnson and Murphy Shoe Company.[20] The Poles worked in the first union hat shop—the Whitehouse Hat Factory on Union and Market streets. A Pole by the name of Boczar had a tailor shop on Bergen and Fifteenth avenues. One of the early unions was the Tanners' Association at Twenty-eight South Orange Avenue. The hall was bought from Umbach about 1900. Many of its officers and members were Poles.

The Poles were principally Roman Catholic. If they had a dollar to give, they gave it to the church. They didn't have the processions and showy displays that the Italian people had on saints' days. Weddings were the most celebrated events in the church, and the respondent says there were plenty of them, sometimes ten or twelve on Sunday. It used to be the custom for the bride to go from door to door to invite neighbors to her wedding. To the prospective guest, she would first bow daintily and then invite him or her to be at the affair. It was common for owners of saloons with dance halls to give the use of the hall free to couples about to be married. This was a means of attracting business.

John the Baptist Day was the day when the Poles used to go to the lake to go swimming. This day inaugurated the beginning of the season when it was supposed to be safe to go swimming.

In the old days, many funerals would be postponed until Sunday, when they would have a band at the cemetery. If the deceased was a member of a society, all the members of his organization had to be there. If they were absent, they were fined. This applied to those who might be living in the Ironbound district and had to be present at St. Stanislaus Church on Belmont Avenue. It was not customary for the Poles to encircle the house of the deceased before the burial. They went straight from the church to the cemetery. The burial ground for the old Polish residents was the Holy Sepulcher Cemetery.

For recreation, the Poles held dances and conducted dramatics. Those affairs demonstrated their great love of music. The dramatics were conducted by the Lutnia and Graza Woslsce dramatic clubs. They had many of their shows at Krueger's Auditorium. Caledonia Park and Seifitz Park were the popular places for Polish affairs. Seifitz Park, on the corner of Morris and Springfield avenues, was probably the most commonly used because it was least expensive to rent.

The first Poles came from Prussia, and many were political refugees. Many had served by compulsion in the German army and were eager to live in a land which had more freedom. They would come here alone, get a job, and then send for members of their families. In the late 1890s and the early 1900s, there were more Polish women than Polish men in Newark. Men were in demand by the women, who worked as servants in the wealthy homes. The Polish girls would seek their men in the saloons and dance halls. They would meet a likeable young man, whom they would call a "greenie." They would go as far as to propose marriage to the man they thought was "the one." Very often, if the marriage was arranged, the girl would entrust her savings to her future husband. It was not unseldom that "the one" would vanish with the money a few days before the marriage ceremony. The respondent told about one young man, who had a servant girl's savings in his pocket and was just about to have the marriage ceremony performed, when he asked to be excused for a few minutes to get cigarettes. "He never showed up again and the girl is probably still waiting," said the respondent.

In the early days, both the husband and the wife worked. Sometimes it was only the wife. Some of the young Polish men had an inclination to loaf and to let the wife assume all the responsibilities of making a living and paying expenses. It was not uncommon for a woman to use all her savings for the purchase of furniture for the establishment of a home. Many Polish young men and young women remained in poverty by keeping up their family duties of supporting members of their families living in Poland.

The respondent, whose family was poor, said that, in addition to his father and mother, four boarders were kept. They only had three rooms for these seven people. The respondent says he remembers one boarding-house which consisted of only three rooms and which housed twenty-three people. One-half of the boarders worked nights, and the other half, days. The men of the night shift occupied the beds in the daytime that the men in the day shift slept on at night. Many houses, originally designed to house only one family, housed five families. In order to make use of as much room as possible, the wooden frames of beds were hinged to the walls. Such beds had mattresses of straw and a few cheap blankets. The beds were put down only when a boarder arrived home to go to sleep.

The burden of taking care of the boarders fell on the woman of the house, who washed their clothes and cooked their meals. Each boarder had a grocery book of order slips. Each day, he would put in an order for the food he wanted for dinner. Each day, such women could be seen tramping to the nearest storekeeper with a pile of these books and returning with food. The food was divided into the portions ordered by the boarders. Strings or paper tags with names were attached to portions, which were later cooked. The strings or the tags identified the portion of each boarder. On payday, each boarder paid the accumulated amount of the slips to the storekeeper.

Because of the absence of sanitary conditions in Polish sections, they had a high mortality rate. This was especially true among the children. In the early 1900s, the respondent, who is an undertaker, declared that he used to bury on average fifteen Polish children a week. Today, he seldom buries more than one Polish child a week. In this period in the development of Newark industry, immigrants were coming over here in droves, and no effort was made to improve their ugly surroundings. New homes, which should have been provided for them, were never built.

Poverty was so widespread among the early Poles that they had to send their children to work at the early ages of fourteen and fifteen, in order to help support the family. If the Poles had been better off, they would have preferred to have their children better educated. Despite their hard struggles, many Poles managed to save enough money through their building and loan association to buy homes in suburban areas. Many of them live as well and in as much style as native-born Americans.

Ernest Pentz

Weddings in Poland and America

The wealthier classes of Poles in New Jersey followed the native Polish custom in their marriage ceremonies and celebrations. There is quite a difference between the Polish wedding customs and the American customs. In the present reformed weddings, the father brings the daughter to the altar, kisses the bride, and then the groom takes over. There are no intermediaries used in America in regards to a Polish wedding. The parents supervise the marriages of their children to some extent, but leave a great deal to the best man. In some sections of Poland, the marriage age of the bride ranged from twenty-four to twenty-seven and the groom from twenty-five to twenty-eight years. In America, the average marriage age of the Poles is three years younger.

In Poland, the parents did not give their daughters any form of dowry; but in America, as a general rule, the girl's parents do help out a great deal in furnishing a home for the newlyweds. In some cases, it is known in Newark that Polish weddings lasted more than a day, but this very seldom happened in Poland. Almost every Pole gets married in a church, even those not connected with the church. It very rarely occurs that a Pole does not have his wedding ceremony in a church.

When a couple in Poland keep company and they profess love for each other, the girl's parents arrange to send an elderly man to the parents of the young man to get their consent to the marriage, to check up on his background, and to find out the type of family he comes from and his qualities as a man. The boy's parents send an intermediary to the girl's parents to find out the same, and they then arrange plans for an engagement celebration and dates for the engagement and the wedding. The engagement party is a very large and beautiful affair with all the friends and relatives present. At this affair, they announce the date of the wedding.

Three weeks before the wedding, the date is formally announced in the church, and all are invited to the ceremony. The best man and his assistant arrange all the affairs in regards to the wedding. After the wedding announcement in the church, the best man and his assistant call on the relatives of the couple and the guests and invite them to the wedding in the name of the groom. The wedding ceremony must follow the rules of the church, and very seldom does a Pole break from this custom.

Before the wedding ceremony, the best man, the groom, ushers, and bridesmaids call at the home of the bride. An elderly man, a friend of the bride, makes a speech and then calls on the parents of the bride for their blessings before leaving for the church. The groom then places a beautiful headpiece with rosary beads on the bride's head. The best man and ushers then leave the bride's home for the church on horseback, and the bride and bridesmaids ride in a large, open carriage. This cavalcade rides through the streets slowly and is greeted by all their friends en route to church. It is unheard of that the couple is not blessed before entering the church.

The priest conducts the marriage ceremony, with the same marriage vows that we have in this country today. After the ceremony, they all leave for the home of the bride, and a large and elaborate affair is held. On entering the home of the bride after the church ceremony, the parents of the bride offer the guests who enter the home bread and salt as a sign of love and affection, best wishes and prosperity, health and happiness. Very ancient songs are sung; some of the songs are from biblical days. There is a large dinner, and plenty of liquor is served to the guests. After dinner, they dance for many hours, and the bride has a dance with all the male guests and receives their gifts. After the dance, the groom removes the headpiece from his wife's head, and again the parents of the bride offer their blessings. The wealthy newlyweds of Poland went on a honeymoon.

Murray Koch
January 22, 1941

he histories of the Lithuanians, Russians, and Ukrainians show the dynamic nature of ethnic identity in the United States. Until 1899, the United States listed immigrants according to their country of origin. Thus, the nineteenth-century designation of Russian included a number of different ethnic groups from within the Russian empire, including the Russians themselves (formerly known as Great Russians), the Byelorussians (or White Russians), the Ukrainians (formerly called Little Russians, a term they

Lithuanians, Russians, and Ukrainians

today intensely dislike), the Poles, the Lithuanians, and the Jews. In fact, it is estimated that 44 percent of the "Russian" immigrants from 1899 to 1910 were Jews, 27 percent were Poles, and only 4 percent were Russian—and included in that 4 percent were Byelorussians and Ukrainians.[1] In the period between 1910 and 1930, 58 percent of the immigrants from Russia were Jews, and only 17 percent were Russians, again including Byelorussians and Ukrainians under the term Russian.[2]

Because eastern Europe had a long history of conquest and conflict, resulting in submerged and reemerged nationalities, the matter of ethnic identity is complicated. The name "Ukrainian" was not commonly used by Ukrainians themselves until the second quarter of the twentieth century.[3] Yet the Ukrainians hark back as a people to the Kievan state, which under Vladimir the Great (980–1015) extended from the Volga River, in what is today the Soviet Union, to the San River, in what is today eastern Poland. In 1240 the Mongols captured Kiev, and over the following centuries the Ukrainians were subjugated in turn by the Lithuanians, the Poles, and the Russians.

The Grand Duchy of Lithuania, with its medieval capital in Vilnius, reached its pcak of power in the fourteenth century, when it extended from the Baltic Sea to the Black Sea, including under its rule the Poles, the Byelorussians, and the Ukrainians. In 1386 the Lithuanian grand duke married a Polish queen, thus unofficially uniting the two countries. In 1569 the unification was made official in the face of their common enemies, Russia and Germany. There followed centuries of acculturation of Lithuania to Polish culture. This long history of unification of Poland and Lithuania has resulted in both Poles and Lithuanians in the United States claiming some of the same heroes, notably Thaddeus Kosciuszko, who fought both in the American Revolution and in the unsuccessful revolt against Russia in 1794, and his private secretary, Julian Niemcewicz, who married into the Kean family and lived for a while in Elizabeth, New Jersey.[4]

During the seventeenth century, there was a series of Polish-Ukrainian wars. In 1649, the Ukrainian Cossacks, under Bohdan Khmelnitzky, allied with the Tartars to defeat the Polish army. The period is remembered by Ukrainians as a restoration of Ukrainian independence; but the Poles and Jews remember it as a reign of terror in which thousands were killed. In 1667, the Ukraine was divided, with Russia taking the part east of the Dnieper River and Poland taking the part west of the Dnieper. With the partitioning of Poland in the late eighteenth century, the former Ukrainian provinces of Galicia (in southern Poland today), Bukovina (in Rumania today), and Ruthenia (in Czechoslovakia today) became part of Austria-Hungary, and Russia retained the eastern part of the Ukraine. Lithuania and Byelorussia became incorporated into the northwest region of Russia in several administrative provinces (*guberniyas*), including Vilna, Minsk, Vitebsk, and Smolensk.

In the nineteenth century, there was a resurgence of Ukrainian nationalism among writers such as Taras Shevchenko (1814–1861). In response, Russia suppressed the Ukrainian language and banned the publication of Ukrainian books. In Lithuania, Tsar Nicholas I embarked upon a policy of russification. Lithuanian monasteries were closed, Russian law replaced Lithuanian law, and the printing of books in the Lithuanian language was banned. A similar policy was followed in Byelorussia.

After World War I, there was a brief period of independence for these submerged nationalities. In January 1918, an independent Ukrainian republic was declared; in February of the same year, Lithuania declared its independence; and in March, Byelorussia did the same. There followed a civil war in Russia between the Red Army (Bolsheviks) and the White Army (not to be confused with the White Russians) and a war between Russia and Poland over the possession of East Galicia, which Russia lost. In 1920, the eastern Ukraine was incorporated into the Soviet Union as the Ukrainian Soviet Socialist Republic. In 1921, Byelorussia was divided up between Poland, Lithuania, Latvia, and the Soviet Union (both as the Byelorussian Soviet Socialist Republic and as part of the Russian Soviet Federated Socialist Republic). Lithuania retained its independence between the two world wars only to be annexed by the Soviet Union during World War II.

This long history resulted in long-standing hostilities between Ukrainians and Poles and between Poles and Lithuanians, which were brought by these groups to America. It has also complicated their ethnic identities in the United States. Many of the so-called Russians who came to the United States prior to 1910 were either from Galicia or Byelorussia; most of them were peasants and unskilled laborers. Some Galicians adopted a Russian identity, others adopted a Ukrainian identity, and still others adopted a separate Ruthenian identity (associating themselves with other people from the Carpathian Mountains in eastern Czechoslovakia, southern Poland, and western Russia). The term "Ruthenian" was used to include people from Galicia, Hungary, and Bukovina; but between 1890 and 1916 there developed differences between the Galicians, who were willing to accept a Ukrainian identity, and the Ruthenians, who adopted a separate Carpatho-Russian identity. Strangely, the Carpatho-Russian identity has disappeared in Europe, but has been maintained in the United States. By the same token, some of the Cossacks (who were a peasant military service class) adopted a Ukrainian identity, but others retained a separate Cossack identity in the United States.[5]

Religion was another cause for changes in ethnic identity. In the nineteenth century, the Russian Orthodox church included both Ukrainian and Carpatho-Russian immigrants. Belonging to a Russian Orthodox parish often resulted in the immigrants thinking of themselves as Russian. It was not until the 1920s that a separate Ukrainian Orthodox church was founded, reflecting the emergence of a Ukrainian identity. Other Ukrainians, especially those from Galicia, Ruthenia, and Bukovina, were members of what was called the Greek Catholic church. This church was under the jurisdiction of the Roman Catholic church, but it followed the eastern, or Byzantine, rite, which meant, for example, that their priests were allowed to marry. This resulted in some tension between Roman Catholics and Greek Catholics, especially because the Roman Catholics pressured the Greek Catholics to conform to their ways. Some Greek Catholics, especially some of the Ruthenians, joined Roman Catholic parishes, especially those with Slovak populations, and thereby became Slovaks. Other eastern rite Catholics abandoned Catholicism altogether and joined Russian Orthodox parishes, thereby becoming Russians. Finally, in 1916, the Vatican allowed for separate administrations for the Ukrainian Catholic and the Ruthenian Catholic churches, which in essence represented the split of Ukrainians into two ethnic identities.[6]

The Oldest Lithuanian in Newark

In 1887, seventeen Lithuanians arrived in Newark. They settled in the district of Prince and West Kinney streets. Mr. Vincent Ambroze was one of them. This group of Lithuanians found work, and, as soon as they accumulated a little money, they sent some of it to relatives or friends in Lithuania to enable them to purchase passage to America. Many of the Lithuanians who had no friends in this country worked their way over here on ships or by leaving their country and earning enough in such countries as Germany or England to buy passage to America.

When Mr. Ambroze arrived in Newark, the house in the vicinity of West Kinney and Prince streets, Newark, had none of the modern improvements such as exist in many of the newer homes of today. Houses in those days had no heating systems, no toilets, no gas or electricity; neither were there hot and cold water systems. Many of the houses remain in that vicinity. The average pay for workers in those days was about eight to ten dollars a week, and there was no eight-hour day.

In 1887, if anyone lived in the vicinity of the streets already mentioned, people would say that he was living up on "the Hill." Near this district quite a number of hat factories existed, and in these factories many Lithuanians became employed. In the 1890s and early 1900s, the majority of the Lithuanians were in the hat business.

Mr. Ambroze moved later to the Ironbound district, in the vicinity of Ferry and Van Buren streets. He first engaged in the selling of shoes and miscellaneous merchandise. When he moved to the Ironbound district, he still engaged in business. From selling shoes, he changed to the real estate business. In or about 1900, he became court interpreter in the Second Criminal Court of Newark on 136 Van Buren Street. In 1908, he became the first Lithuanian to hold a political office. He was elected in that year to the office of justice of peace in the Fifth Ward and was reelected many times thereafter. He served as court interpreter for thirty years. He is now on a pension from the city.

Mr. Ambroze said that the early Lithuanians not only worked in the hat industry, but many worked on the docks in Hoboken and Jersey City. Many of these dock workers had to seek new employment in 1890 because of a strike against the poor labor conditions. These former dockworkers found work in the Balbach Smelting and Refining Company. The pay at Balbach's at that time was one dollar and five cents a day. The life of a worker in Balbach's was very short because of acid and gas fumes resulting from the process of smelting. At that time, there was no protection by law or any other way of correcting this situation. Mr. Ambroze commented that the Lithuanians stood up quite well under the conditions that they worked.

Another industry in which many Lithuanians worked was the leather industry. They tanned leather and helped in the manufacture of shoes. He cited the case of one Lithuanian who has been employed by the Johnson-Murphy Shoe Company for fifty years. "Today," he says, "the majority of Lithuanians are skilled or unskilled manual workers."

I inquired from Mr. Ambroze if many of the Lithuanians appeared very often in the criminal court on criminal charges. He replied that very few were arraigned on any serious criminal charges. On the whole, they were a peaceful people.

The Lithuanians have always been to the forefront in civic activities. They have always fought for the improvement of conditions in their neighborhood. In 1916, when Newark celebrated its 250th anniversary, the Lithuanians participated actively. When we joined in active participation of the world war, the Lithuanians raised large subscriptions for Liberty Bonds, and many Lithuanian youths served in the American Expeditionary Forces. Two years ago, they took active part in the celebration of the granting of a charter to the city of Newark.

At the end of our conversation, Mr. Ambroze informed me that one of the outstanding Lithuanians in Newark was Captain Stephen Darius, an American aviator who lost his life when his plane crashed in Germany. Captain Darius was born in Lithuania. He came to this country as a small boy and attended the Newark public schools. He lived on Jackson Street. He served in the United States Aviation Corps during the world war and attained the rank of captain. He joined the corps in Chicago at the beginning of the war.

In 1932, the Lithuanians in the United States raised money for Stephen Darius and Stanislaus Girends to buy an airplane for them to fly from New York City to Kaunas, the capital of Lithuania.[7] The machine that was brought was an old model completely reconditioned. When they asked the aeronautical authorities for a permit to fly to Lithuania, the permit was refused, but they attempted their flight anyway.

They cracked up in Germany, but many people in Europe contended a great deal of mystery surrounded their fatal mishap. The September issue of the magazine *Popular Aviation* contained an article that implied that the plane that they flew on July 15, 1933, from Bennett Field and that crashed in Germany on July 17, 1933, did so, not because of bad weather or lack of gasoline, but because of rifle shots fired by German riflemen. European nations cried that the men had been shot down. However, the whole affair was whitewashed.

At the end of our last interview, Mr. Ambroze told me that his daughter, Stella Ambroze, was the first Lithuanian to become a teacher in Newark. Today, there are over twelve Lithuanian women who teach school.

Mr. Ambroze told me about one of the judges who served in the court where he was interpreter. The judge was a partner in a brewery. He would always ask any drunk who appeared before him what did he get drunk on—beer or whiskey. If the defendant said it was beer, he would always get a suspended sentence. If he said that whiskey got him drunk, the judge would fine him ten dollars. Evidently, the judge was partial to his own business interests.

Ernest Pentz

Lithuanian Was Prohibited

Mr. Andrew Ziugzda owns one of the largest, single-proprietor bakeries in Newark. Thirteen people work for him, and he has four trucks which deliver his baked goods. At the bakery he has a store, where he sells his goods retail. The rest of the baked goods are sold to the city and Essex County institutions. He began his business in 1912, and it has grown in size since.

Mr. Vincent Ambroze introduced me to Mr. Ziugzda when I was in Mr. Ambroze's store, a steamship agency. Mr. Ziugzda walked me over to his bakery. He told me that he came to this country in 1901 and settled in the Ironbound. While we walked, he showed quite a number of corner buildings owned by Lithuanians. He said that in 1929 or 1930 quite a number of Lithuanians owned more property than they did today. In those days before the depression, the Lithuanians enjoyed quite a bit of prosperity. Today, many Lithuanians have lost their homes and property because of the depression; and quite a number, who had been well-off, now belong to the poorer classes. He declared that, when he came to this section of Newark in 1902, the streets were unpaved, and many of the houses and buildings standing today had not yet been built. The settlement of the Lithuanians in that district was a boon to building and to the community. I took particular notice that all the buildings owned by the Lithuanians had saloons on the ground floor. I learned during the conversation that many Lithuanians go into the saloon business. I observed that the majority of saloons in the Ironbound district were owned by or run by Lithuanians.

Mr. Ziugzda showed me around his bakery and explained the steps necessary in making and baking bread and other baked goods. He showed me his modest library of books printed in Lithuanian, books which he hopes someday to give to the public library here or to give to Lithuanians in Lithuania. He took me into the cellar of his shop and showed me an interesting collection of Lithuanian newspapers dating from 1900 to the present year, 1939. He explained to me that the Lithuanian language was prohibited in 1900, when Lithuania was part of Russia. Despite the ban, the Lithuanians secretly had their newspapers printed in East Prussia and smuggled into Lithuania, where they were read in secret. The Lithuanians also had secret schools, where they were taught the language and the patriotic spirit of Lithuania was kept alive. He showed me copies of the newspaper *Varpas* (The Bell) printed in East Prussia and smuggled into Lithuania. They were bound copies printed in 1900. He also showed me bound copies of the newspaper *Ukininkas* (the Lithuanian national newspaper), printed in 1901 and 1902, which he used to receive from Lithuania. This was another secret paper printed by the Lithuanians. He declared that many of the Russian policemen knew that the Lithuanian papers were being smuggled into Lithuania and that the Lithuanians were conducting secret private schools, but they did nothing about it.

Mr. Ziugzda showed me interesting collections of newspapers from Lithuania, in which he has preserved bound copies since 1900. The most interesting of these were *Kala* (Friend), *Ameriickos Lieteiviu Dienrastis*, and the newspaper *Vilnius*. The two were published during the world war. The *Vilnius* was suppressed in 1938 by the Polish government. Today the government only permits the paper to be sold during one or two weeks. The publisher must change the paper's name at each interval.

The copies of the paper I saw were filled with white squares where the government censors had deleted material. This was the first example of censorship that I had ever seen. Mr. Ziugzda's newspapers fill two trunks. The official paper of Lithuania is *Lietuvos Aidas*.

Mr. Ziugzda also showed me the new *Lithuanian Encyclopedia*, recently published in Lithuania. It consisted of six large volumes on the same quality paper as the *Encyclopaedia Britannica* and excellently printed. The books all had leather covers. It was through Mr. Ziugzda that I was able to meet and to know Dr. Kaskeucius.

Ernest Pentz

Not the Hyphenated-American Type

Doctor J. Kaskeucius has lived in this country since 1911, and, until a few years ago, he was a resident in the Ironbound district. He learned his profession in Lithuania, and he is one of the country's authorities on Lithuanians in America. He is a man in his early fifties and an energetic and enthusiastic talker. His avocation is writing. He contributes a daily column on health to one of the leading Lithuanian newspapers. He has translated Upton Sinclair's book *Oil* into Lithuanian, Heckel's *Wonders of the Universe* from German into Lithuanian, and M. Ilin's *Men and Mountains* from Russian into Lithuanian.

I asked the doctor questions about the early struggles of the Lithuanians in Newark, their activities in general, their general character, factions among themselves, and the accomplishments of individual Lithuanians.

The doctor said that the Lithuanians came over here as farmers and had to adapt themselves to industrial work. In the different factories where they first worked, they were often ridiculed by workers who would call them "Polacks." They overcame the early discriminations against them by their very high character. On any job, they worked hard and efficiently. They have the reputation of never leaving a job unfinished. From interviews which I have had with other nationalities, I can say that they all spoke very highly of the character of Lithuanians. The doctor also emphasized that Lithuanians have never been known to scab on their fellow worker.

Up to ten years ago, there were two factions among the Lithuanians: the Catholics and the Free Thinkers. They never had any economic differences, but they had great antagonisms between them on matters of religion. Today, no such antagonisms exist. These groups now have many things in common—mainly the fight for democracy in their own country and in this country—and they unite on all common issues. Politically, the Lithuanians are Democrats, mostly of the New Deal variety. There are exceptions, of course. I have spoken with a few Lithuanian businessmen who are not entirely with Roosevelt or who are skeptical of the accomplishments of the present administration. The doctor also emphasized that the Lithuanians are not of the hyphenated American type. They place their American citizenship far higher than any love that they might have for their mother country.

In our conversation on the culture of the Lithuanians in Newark, he said that their cultural level was much higher now than it was ten or twenty years ago. Like the Italians and the Jews, they encourage their children to take all the possible advantages of the free education offered to American children. Lithuanian youths show considerable ambition and make use of their spare time by going to night schools. Lithuanians today are making their mark in the arts, in the professions, and in business.

The doctor brought up the subject of music. He declared that quite a large number of his countrymen are good musicians. They love singing and have their own choral groups. They are especially fond of picnics and dancing. In the summertime on weekends, Lithuanians can always be found at those picnics. In the wintertime, they can be found in their own dance halls, where they have singing and dramatics. The choir they have in Newark is called the Sietyno Chorus.

The doctor pointed out another characteristic of the Lithuanians, which I myself observed in my association with many of them. This is their kindly hospitality. Other national groups have also observed this characteristic. They put into practice their proverb "Stranger in the house, God in the house."

The doctor said that his daughter is an actress, a ballet dancer, in Hollywood. His son aspires to be a dramatic actor. He said that many of the Lithuanians are actors in Hollywood. He emphasized that Lithuanian artists and professionals came from common working people. Anna Kaska, who sings in the Metropolitan, is a self-made artist whose father was a tailor. She came from Brooklyn. Miss Radonai who use to go under the stage name of Helen Smith is a famous toe-dancer. She was born in Newark. Her mother was a waitress and her father an agent for the Prudential Insurance Company. She married a London actor and now lives in England.

Ernest Pentz

Stories about Lithuanians

Reverend Kelmelis, local Lithuanian Catholic priest, told me about his cousin, who came to this country more than fifty years ago. This cousin arrived in New York City shabbily dressed, with no shoes, and barely enough money to sustain himself. He had to walk to Plymouth, Pennsylvania, where a job was waiting for him. His first job in Plymouth was in a shoe factory. Later on, he opened his own factory and established a good and thriving business. At his death, he was a wealthy man.

On May 11, I interviewed a second-generation Lithuanian who moved with her husband to Newark. Her husband, who was also Lithuanian, was transferred from a factory in New Haven to a factory in this city. She related to me the early experiences in this country of her father, who is now seventy years of age. He came to this country at the tender age of fifteen. He had been inducted into the Russian army at the age of fourteen, but he escaped from the country on a boat bound for the United States. He arrived here wearing his Russian uniform. From New York City he found his way to New Haven, where he had some relatives and friends. Not long afterwards, he found employment with the Corbin Lock and Cabinet Company. Today, he is still employed by that company. The company has offered to give him a pension, but he has refused to accept it. He would prefer to keep right on working until he dies. This man's history is the history of many Lithuanians who have come to this country.

Ernest Pentz

A Model Family Man

A Russian male, about forty-five

I was in the world war in 1914, when Russia declared war on Germany. With all the chances for losing my life, I considered myself lucky to have come out of it without a scratch.

Shortly after the Brest-Litovsk Treaty, when I quit military service, I married and settled down in Orel. Then came the revolution, and I did not like it.[8] I managed to get enough money to come here in 1918, and here I am since.

Life in America was at first like a paradise to me—peace, democracy, nobody to bother you. I went to work as a laborer until I picked up enough of the language to go to work as a carpenter. That was my trade in the old country.

In 1920, came my first boy. Life took on a different color. I had something to live and to work for. Of course, I never earned very much money, as money goes in this country, but I always managed to keep my family and myself in fairly decent conditions.

In 1922, I knew enough of the language and of the American ways of doing carpentry work to join the carpenters' union. This was a great help to me more than once when I was out of a job. Strange, I managed to have at least a part-time job right along, all the way through this depression period. Only once, I did not work for almost four months.

That was hell. I don't know how I ever managed through that period, but I will never forget it. My family and I went hungry many a day. I had to move several times because I did not have rent money enough. In four months, I came down from a beautiful four-room apartment to one large furnished room, in which the four of us had to live on six dollars a week. It was a light-housekeeping room up on Belmont Avenue. Just my luck, pretty soon the union found me a part-time job, and things again began to get lively for me. We took a two-room apartment in the North Newark section. For the last four years, I had a more-or-less steady job. I bet if I did not belong to the union, I would be in the grave by this time, and maybe my whole family with me.

My kids—two boys—are now all right. Johnny graduated public school last year and is now in the first year of high school. Little Benny will graduate public school the end of this school year, and he'll go to high school then, too.

I am not an optimist by nature, but I'll tell you: a good woman can make a man, just as surely as a bad one can break him. I have a wonderful woman, and her whole life is her children. She is a little better educated than I am, and she is a wonderful help to the boys. There is nothing she would not do for them.

I don't know what more I can tell you. My life is very simple, I suppose. You may call me a model family man. I love my wife, and I love my children. My whole concern is with them.

Would I want to go back to Russia? Not on a bet. I am perfectly satisfied here. I would probably get lost in Russia, if I ever got there. My American citizenship means a real thing to me. I would not exchange it for anything in the world. Good old USA is good enough for me.

Something unusual or interesting in my life? I am afraid I wouldn't know what to say. Perhaps my coming to America was the most interesting event in my life and the most exciting event. My wife and I were facing an uncertain future. We did not know anybody in the United States. But, little by little, we got acquainted with some Russians in Philadelphia, where we first landed. About two years after, when I began to speak the American tongue enough to get around on my own, we came to New York City, but we did not live there very long. That city has always been a confusion to me—too large to understand, too much to itself to be sociable and human. It is like a gigantic machine. Men are a little better than robots; women, frail and precarious. Their tempo of working and of living is amazing.

One Russian friend we knew in Philadelphia came to Newark. We corresponded with him for some time. Then, we too decided to move to Newark, and here we stayed since 1924. Of course, I know New York City now a little bit better. I am not afraid of it. But Newark is big enough for me. My family got so used to this city, I think it would break their heart if we moved now to any other city.

You will excuse me now. I'll have to go to work. I hope I meet you again and tell you more about my life, if you want to. And I'm always glad to meet Russians around here. There are so few of them around here for a large city like Newark.

A. Basil Wheeler

A Visit to a Ukrainian Priest

During our research on the Ukrainian people in the Third Ward, we were informed at the Ukrainian Center in the ward that if we were to visit a certain Ukrainian Catholic priest and told him of our purpose, he would gladly assist us. We thereupon visited the good Father and were ushered by his maid into a gloomy-looking room, heavily curtained, with many religious symbols and paintings littering the walls. There was one frieze of Christ covered over with scarlet red paint, smeared with indiscriminate taste. The room was extraordinarily quiet and serene. This may have been due to the complete exclusion of the outer world, an effect brought about by the muffled windows. By all appearances, it was a deliberate effect. We seated ourselves in a large, plush chair, and soon the Father entered. He peered at us as though he condescended to see us. When we introduced ourselves, he extended a limp hand, which we were compelled to seize. He was completely apathetic and waited as though to be served. I've never before witnessed such smugness and superiority in clerical garb. He didn't utter a word, and we began to state our business. He listened to us much in the manner of a very high prelate.

We explained the nature of our visit, and he immediately demanded credentials. He spoke in Ukrainian. We explained we did not understand, and he became very frigid. "What are you?" he asked. His tone was most unfriendly. We said we were Polish and this was obviously a mistake. It made him very unhappy to hear us say this. "What is your business?" he asked. We had to go through the entire routine once more. We read him some of the questions to reassure him. For a few moments he seemed to weaken, and he showed some concrete interest for the first time. The questions we read to him dealt with prejudice, education, and jobs, etc. He told us that Polish employers refused to hire Ukrainian help. We knew then why he resented our alleged nationality. He told us, furthermore, that since we were from WPA, he would require credentials. "WPA," he said, "is run by the Jews," and unless we brought him credentials, undersigned by some reliable person (read Christain), to all intent and purpose the survey might be an attempt on the part of the WPA Jews to attack his people. We received this information graciously and left. As we walked down the steps, we encountered a ragged and pitiful individual, walking into the Father's apartment. He stepped aside when he saw us, and tipped his hat, mumbling incoherent amenities in a very humble and obsequious way. I was appalled for a moment at such servility. I was able to understand, however, the priest's resentment at our apparent ease and utter lack of awe and mystification in his most august presence. He was obviously unused to people who did not scrape and bow. To have seen such a thing in America for some naive reason was a juxtaposition of European custom that nonplused me and left me strangely disturbed. My companion explained to me that the whole occurrence was commonplace.

Irving Zuckerman
November 21, 1939

One Round of Hell after Another

Yes, I would love to live like some people do—get married, have a nice home, get everything I need. But how can a man do that without an assured employment or income? It just cannot be done. I live in a house not fit for rats to live in. I am obliged to eat the cheapest food, which is never quality food. As you see, I am wearing rags. And my future? Only an undertaker can tell. I can't think of amusement or movies because I never have any money. When I have it, there are bills to pay—more bills than I can pay. And so it goes, all the year round. The only time I get a square meal is when I get something extra to do. A friend of my father's is running a small garage and repair shop up on Clinton Avenue. Occasionally, when I am out of work, he gives me odds and ends to do. Since my father and mother don't know what I get paid here, I spend a little on myself in order to put something under my belt. Imagine this damnable situation. I have to lie to my father and mother in order to catch up with my famished condition. I tell you, life for me is

one round of hell after another. I'm afraid I can't tell you much more
that would be of any interest to you.

A. Basil Wheeler

The Greatest Regret in My Life

A Ukrainian male, age thirty-eight

My parents came here over forty years ago, so I cannot tell you much
about the old country. I was born here.

The most important event in my life? Maybe it was the day I graduated from high school. My mother and father wanted me to go to college; I wanted to go to work. What a fool I was! I thought my parents
could not afford to send me through college, so I decided I would help
my dad by going to work. But whatever the difficulties, I realize now
what a fool I was. After all, if I had a college education, my life would
have been quite different.

My father wanted me to be some professional—a doctor, lawyer, or
an engineer. I had a leaning towards medicine. But look at me now—
hardly better than a plain laborer. I do odds and ends in the building
trades, but this work is seasonal and piecework. I never earned more
than a thousand dollars a year.

That is the greatest regret in my life. I am a misfit. I thought and
dreamed of becoming many things. I drifted from one job to another
and never mastered any worthwhile trade or business to call it my line.
I am a creature of circumstances. I have to take whatever I can get, and
nowadays the getting is very poor.

I remained single because I never could tolerate the idea of being
married on my meager income. I suppose I'll die a bachelor, although
my mother always tells me I should marry anyway—that it would
make my life happier. But what kind of a happiness could a man have
on the prospects I have—or rather haven't?

Somehow, I feel life has cheated me out of a possible good living. I
am not sure it was all my fault. Nor was it the fault of my parents. It
seems to me it just had to be that way. Often I tried to make something
of myself, but there isn't any use. I just can't make a go of it.

It seems to me I am living only to die and perish from this miserable
existence. Probably my only excuse for living is my mother. My father
died a few years ago; and ever since, I felt that my life will never be my
own.

A. Basil Wheeler

Where's *Svoboda* for People Like Me?

Ukrainian male, age twenty-six

I was born in this country. I know little about Ukraine or the Ukrainian people as they live in the old country. So, about that I can tell you nothing.

In the United States, I do know my people. I mix with them in church, in clubrooms, in homes. I have many friends. Most of them are Ukrainians, and a few are Russians, Ruthenes, and Galicians.

In this country my people are clannish. They stick together. They attend their own churches. They mix very little with the American population, except on the job. They celebrate their own holidays. One holiday celebrated here by all Ukrainians is Shevchenko's Memorial Days on February 25 and 26. The celebration is generally memorialized by festivals and dances held by different organizations.

About myself? What can I tell you that would be of interest or importance to you? Let me see. After I graduated from the Central High, I went to work as an apprentice to a molder in one of the iron and bronze works in Irvington. At the time, my parents lived in Irvington. I learned the art of making many different things out of iron and copper. I am now a full-fledged molder and make pretty good money, when I work. The trouble is I do not get much work—on the average about six months out of a year. I have to help out my parents besides myself. But how can I do that when I am never sure of my job? My folks cannot get relief because I am supposed to be working. And I am not working enough in the year to help them all year round. There you are. I am always on the run, getting nowhere.

We who are born in this country, of course, are different from those born in the old country. We feel this country is our home. The nationalist group among our people, as you know, is the only group that harps upon the "old country problems." But I am little interested in that. I have problems enough right here, and I wish somebody would tell me how to solve them. Some of my friends belong to the Ukrainian National Association and want me to join it. But not me. I think it's a waste of time to belong to this organization. All they talk about is "our Ukraine." But where in hell is Ukraine? I can't find it on any map, except as a southern district in the Soviet Russia. No, I am too much of an American to be interested in that stuff. They publish *Svoboda*, but where's *svoboda* [literally, "liberty"] for people like me?

A. Basil Wheeler

Unlike Newark, Paterson was founded to be an industrial center. In 1791, with the encouragement of Secretary of Treasury Alexander Hamilton, the state of New Jersey incorporated the Society for the Establishment of Useful Manufactures (known as the SUM) to establish an industrial city at the falls of the Passaic River. The city was named after William Paterson, the governor of New Jersey at the time. The SUM hired the French engineer Pierre L'Enfant to design a system of water raceways to power

---

Dutch

---

the factories. The first cotton-spinning mill was opened in 1794, but by 1776 the SUM's manufacturing efforts had failed.[1]

Cotton manufacturing continued in Paterson until 1837, but by then it was eclipsed by the locomotive, machinery, and machine-tool industries. In 1839 the city's first silk weaving mill was started, which attracted the attention of English silk manufacturer John Ryle, who relocated to Paterson. By 1890, Paterson was being called the "Lyons of America," having established itself as a center for the manufacture of silk ribbon and broad silk.[2] But Paterson was an anomoly, according to historian Steve Golin, because not only did it rely on immigrant workers, but the peculiar nature of the silk industry required highly skilled workers.[3]

The first immigrants in Paterson were skilled workers recruited by the SUM in England, Scotland, and France. Metalworkers from Sheffield and Birmingham were attracted to Paterson in the early nineteenth century, as were textile workers from Manchester. John Ryle was from the English silk manufacturing center of Macclesfield, and between 1870 and 1893, approximately fifteen thousand silk workers came from that town. In 1880 about two-thirds of Paterson's silk weavers were foreign-born, and about 20 percent of all the silk weavers in Paterson were English. Most of the rest were Swiss, German, and Scottish.[4]

In the last two decades of the nineteenth century, the immigrant population of Paterson began to change. Northern Italians, especially skilled weavers from Piedmont and dyers from Lombardy, began to come to Paterson in the 1880s. After 1890, unskilled dyers' helpers came from southern Italy. Around the turn-of-the-century, Polish Jewish broad-silk weavers, especially from the textile centers of Łódź and Białystok, began to come to Paterson.[5] By the 1930s the foreign-born were about one-third of the population of Paterson. The major ethnic groups in the city were the Italians, Jews, Syrians, Poles, Germans, Russians, and Irish.[6] There was also a large Dutch population living across the Passaic River in the streetcar suburb of Prospect Park.

Unlike the nineteenth-century Irish emigration, in which one-third to one-half of the rural population left the country, the Dutch emigration was relatively moderate. Until the 1890s nearly 90 percent of the Dutch emigrants came to the United States. More than three-quarters of them came as families, indicating a desire to stay. They were primarily from rural areas of the Netherlands, especially the northern provinces of Friesland and Groningen and the coastal province of Zeeland. They settled primarily in Michigan, where many of them went into farming. In the twentieth century the emigration pattern shifted somewhat from the provinces to the cities, with many Dutch immigrants coming from cities such as Amsterdam and Dordrecht. This coincided with a belated industrialization of the Dutch economy after 1900.[7]

In numbers the nineteenth-century Dutch immigration to northern New Jersey was a secondary settlement compared to the Midwest. Also, unlike the Dutch in the Midwest, those who came to New Jersey during this time settled in and near the city of Paterson and worked in the city's textile factories. In 1920 there were 12,737 Dutch living in New Jersey, and 60 percent of them lived in Passaic County, in which Paterson is located. Of the 126 heads of families who left the Netherlands between 1847 and 1877 listing New Jersey as their destination, one-half were workmen. Only four were listed as "well-to-do," seventy-three as "less-well-to-do," and forty-eight as "indigent." Two-thirds were under the age of fifty, a third of them in their twenties. And one-half had children with them.[8]

Many of the Dutch in the Paterson area actually settled across the river in Prospect Park, which was situated on a hill overlooking Paterson. Development began on tracts of land owned by Jersey-Dutch farmers Cornelius P. Hopper and Gerrit Planten. Most of the homes were two-family structures, which produced income for their own occupants. Originally part of Manchester Township, the borough of Prospect Park was incorporated in 1910. In 1914 a trolley line was built along Goffle Road connecting Paterson, Prospect Park, Hawthorne, and

Ridgewood. In 1923 bus service began along Haledon Avenue. By 1930 Prospect Park had a population of 5,509, of which 1,981 were foreign-born and 2,754 had foreign or mixed parentage. Known locally as Little Holland, a majority of the population was Dutch. From the turn of the century until 1940 a Dutch language newspaper, *Het Oosten*, was published in town.[9]

Prospect Park played a role in the Paterson strike of 1913. Many of its residents were employed in the dye shops, where the strike began. During the strike, police deputies patrolled the streets of Prospect Park. A group of them were stationed at the Sixth Avenue Bridge to Paterson to prevent strikers from molesting nonstrikers. The strikers gathered on an open lot owned by a man named Muh, where there occurred a clash between the strikers and the police. It became known as the Battle of Muh's Hill.[10]

Lini De Vries, who grew up in Prospect Park, gives a vivid description of life in Prospect Park in her memoir, *Up from the Cellar*. Her maiden name was Moerkerk. While she had mixed Dutch and Jewish parentage, she was raised in the Dutch Reformed Church. Her mother wouldn't allow her to speak English at home. Her father spoke English, but could barely read and write it. At the age of twelve, she started work in a silk mill in Prospect Park. Her mother lied about her age to get her the job. She worked initially as a "bobbin girl," carrying the filled bobbins from the winders to the warpers and the empty bobbins back. She wrote about her shame at being a "mill dolly."

Later, she became a quill winder in a cotton mill in the neighboring town of Haledon. In this job, she threaded the cotton from the bobbin to the quills attached to the loom. Here she came in contact with Syrian, Armenian, Italian, Polish, and Irish workers. This was the first time she was exposed to Catholics. Then she found work as a winder in a mill in Paterson, where she witnessed the death of a co-worker, who was scalped by a machine belt. She also worked in a silk ribbon mill. "At lunchtime," she wrote, "I was apt to share Polish sausage, Italian spaghetti, filled flaky Syrian pastry or stuffed grape leaves, in exchange for some Dutch cheese pastry filled with *comino* seeds." She lived for a time at the YWCA Boarding Home for Working Girls on the affluent Eastside of Paterson. "This side, the Eastside," she wrote, "meant tennis courts, children who could go to high school and college, and bosses' sons who thought we of the other side could be 'made.' That didn't matter too much as long as I could see fresh white curtains gently moving in the window, hear birds sing, not see smokestacks of the mills, and feel free of filthy words heaped on my head."[11]

Stricken with USA Fever

My interviewee has a real fine personality. He is six feet tall, has a thick mop of gray hair, wears glasses, walks as straight as a die, and is a real good dresser. He is a good-looking man with a friendly, good-natured disposition.

My father was born in Stellendam, Holland, in 1837, of very humble parents. My mother was born in the same place in 1840, also of poor parents. My grandfather had a small farm; and, during the summer season, he worked for other farmers to make a little extra money. My grandmother and her children worked their own land. They had a few chickens, a cow, and a couple of pigs, which they butchered in the fall for use in the long winter months.

My grandparents did not have much education. They could go to school only in the winter; and then, when the weather was bad, they stayed home. As soon as spring came, there was no more school. That was the same for everybody else. All children from the outskirts of every little town had the same experience, no matter how young. Everybody had to till their own land, because the head of the family had to work for others. What little money he earned was necessary to buy the things they could not raise themselves—like spices, shoes, clothes, and other wearing apparel.

At that time, there was a lot of talk and agitation about the United States and the opportunities there. Several families had gone out there before and sent back news in glowing terms. This was how my grandfather became stricken with USA Fever and decided that, if he could raise enough money, he would go also. Once there, he was assured, his worries would be over.

He stayed another season, saved every penny he could, and, when next spring came, he found a buyer for the whole caboodle—a young married couple who were glad to take over everything—chickens and cow and furniture. There was a little left after passage was paid. My father was then twelve years old. It was a most eventful voyage—a small sailing ship with a big load, and just our family as the only passengers. The weather was terrible, with everyone on their knees several times, praying to God to be saved. After much anguish and suffering, and eighty-nine days on the big ocean, they landed safely in the USA.

A man and his son, who was a friend of one of my grandfather's friends in Paterson, was waiting for them with a large, covered wagon, wherein everything was loaded. And the family went on their next journey—this time in the United States. It did not take them long before they arrived on the Preakness farm.

After he worked for the farmer all that summer, my father was offered a job in a Paterson mill through new friends and gladly took the job. After a few weeks, they rented a little place in Paterson, and the family of six moved to the city. They thanked the good farmer and his charitable wife for their kindness. They kept up the friendliest relations, after they moved until their last days. After a couple of years, the family moved to Passaic, where my grandfather obtained a better job in a woolen mill. All the four children were graduated in the Passaic public schools.

Of my mother's background, I do not know much. She came to America with her parents from a different section of Holland when seven years old. Her parents also settled in Passaic, and she too was educated in Passaic public schools.

When my father was eighteen years old, he got a job in Passaic for a cabinetmaker—a first-class mechanic. He worked for him for five years, starting at one dollar per week and his dinner. After five years of learning the trade, he was raised to twelve dollars because he was a hard and conscientious worker. He soon became an expert himself.

My father and mother went to the same church and got to know each other there. There was very little amusement outside of the church that Holland parents approved of. So that was the only fun there was. They were never left alone, and, when they went for a walk or went out together anywhere, there was always somebody with them. They did not see each other during the week. They lived quite a distance away from each other, so Sunday was the only time to be in one another's company. This went on for a couple of years, when they announced their engagement with all concerned in full agreement. A little while after, they got married. They were then both twenty-five years old. My father had a good job and his wife, who was employed in the mill, kept hers. They had no worries for a couple of years. They moved to bigger quarters when they expected an increase in the family. Their new place was in his in-law's immediate neighborhood. When the baby came, his mother-in-law and his own mother were there to care for his wife. After that, they had six more children, all delivered by either other mothers or a midwife, and never an instrument used. A little after the birth of their first child, my father took a job in Paterson, where he was offered a better salary. So they moved to Paterson and rented a floor somewhere, where Prospect Park is now, and there I was born in 1867.

Our family prospered and increased. Father bought a home of his own. We all went to school in Paterson when we were old enough. We all had a carefree youth, regulated strictly by our parents' religious ideals—church on Sunday mornings; Sunday school in the afternoon; after supper, services, after which we had entertainment and fun among ourselves; and early to bed. Seldom on a Sunday night was there a light to be seen burning in our neighborhood after nine o'clock.

Every one of us was allowed to choose his own trade. I went to work in a Paterson office after graduation. After a couple of years of bookkeeping, I was offered a job in a coal dealer's office, supplying a big percentage of the Holland population. Everybody was well acquainted with my whole family, so I became a very popular figure with the trade. I was the only boy in my family who wanted to mix with others. I joined different organizations and went in for a bit of politics.

Since then, I did not spend much of my time at home anymore. Every evening, I went to this or that meeting of this or that society. I served on all kinds of committees and had a very busy life for a while. I went to suppers, receptions, and dances. My parents were all against it, wanted me to adhere to all the old family customs, but I would not listen. I was not doing anything wrong. Besides, I clung reverently to all my Christian teachings and would not miss my church services for anything in the world. For women, I did not have time, until one evening I came home early and found we had company—a friend of my Dad, his wife, and daughter. I was to go to a meeting, but that night—I don't know why—I stayed home with the company. We all had an enjoyable evening, especially me. We were having a dance the next week in one organization I belonged to; and before our company went home, the young lady, with her parents' permission—she was then twenty-three years old—promised to accompany me to the dance. Well, I had fallen. And how!

That dance was the beginning of the end of my bachelor days. I did not give up all of my social activities. Not quite. I kept my membership in all of them and did not have to tell my friends why I missed some of the meetings lately. They all knew the worst. Well, my lady friend was a good sport and did not object to my keeping up of my social life. She herself liked it, too, and went with me, whenever she was permitted to do so.

To make it short, two years after the lucky evening, we were married. I had so many friends that I could not expect an ordinary wedding feast. Against the objections of both sides, I hired a hall to accommodate all my good friends. To this day, I have never regretted it. Shortly after, I left my good job and embarked in the coal business myself. I succeeded right from the very beginning. We were both twenty-five years old when we married. We raised four children. All received a good education. Everyone but the youngest son married within his or her national origin. The youngest boy married a Belgian girl, which is just about the same as us. They speak the same language.

I, myself, went in for a little politics. I was elected into office several times. I enjoyed the confidence of all my many friends. I have prosperous business, with two of my sons as my prospective successors. I am now seventy-three years young and in good health. I gave up most of my political ambitions, and I try to take life a little bit easier. My children's beliefs, ambitions, and activities do not concern me much. They are ideal citizens, and I don't interfere with any of their ideas. We are all peace-loving, democratic, and against any and all dictatorship in our own United States. Our church activities are no different than they were one hundred years ago, and my children adhere to it too. In case of death in the family, we have a simple service in the church, a family gathering, and we mourn our dear deceased for a full year. I do not worry about death myself, for I know it is the only thing in this world which is the same for the rich and the poor alike.

Arthur Vermeire
February 23, 1940

Pork One Day, Pig the Next

My interviewee is now seventy years old, stands upright, is very well preserved for his age, reads without the use of glasses, and has still a thick, gray shock of hair. He is good and healthy, has a friendly disposition, and in all is a real old gentleman.

My ancestors were all very poor, uneducated, farm laborers in Holland. My father and mother both were from around Maastricht, in the province of Limburg, around the banks of the river Maas. My father was born in a little stone house near the river, and so were his nine brothers and sisters. He used to work his little plot in back of the house to raise enough to supply us for the winter—potatoes and all kinds of vegetables that my mother could can or jar in the fall of the year.

We used to have fat hog ready around the first week of November. My father butchered it, and from the blood my mother made bloodwurst. All the insides—like the heart, lungs, and the liver—were eaten first. The intestines were cleaned and prepared for sausages, and the head made into headcheese. My mother used to put it in shallow stone pots and cover them with fat to keep the air out. We could keep it for weeks. The other meat was put in salt brine in large, deep, wooden tubs and put away in our deep, cool cellar till it was ready to eat. It was then taken out and hung up to dry. How we used to smack our lips when mother cut us a couple of thick slices of homemade rye bread and a slice of the new, fat, salt pork between them!

Now, in the good old USA we have two or three kinds of meat every day, but in those days it was pork one day, pig the next, and then a little bit of hog for the whole winter. And nobody complained because we were glad to have that once a day. All of us children wore wooden shoes, which we wore only on Sunday to go to church. Sometimes we had our shoes so long that our feet outgrew them, and the next brother had to wear them on Sunday. The same thing went for our Sunday clothes. As soon as we came back from church, off they came and back into the alcove.

My mother used to have some job. Between us kids and the wash and the housework and the meals, she was never done. I never, in all my days, saw my mother in bed. She was first getting up and last to go to bed. There was a lot to be done while we were sleeping—washing our clothes and darning our socks, sewing on buttons every day almost, and never a complaint.

My father took odd jobs in the city for the winter months and made a little money to buy a little clothing and some things we could not raise ourselves. Sometimes in the summertime he could catch a few days' pay by helping to unload all kinds of freight from ships that stopped at the docks. And so we got along. All us children went to school in the city—a walk of about two miles—until we could read and write. Then we had to stay home and see what we could do to help. Some of us went to work on the big farms near us. A couple of the girls went to work for businesspeople in the city.

I worked on the farm first, then got a job in the city, and from one job to another, and I learned a little bit of everything. One day, I had a chance to work on a ship. I took the job and made a few trips to Rotterdam. Something went wrong there on my last trip, and we stayed there a few days. In the meantime, I looked around the dock and got acquainted with a young sailor from a large freighter. He took me on the ship and showed me around. I was so impressed. I told him I would like to work on a boat like that too, and, before I knew it, I was hired. I went to my own little ship, sneaked into my cabin after supper, and got my belongings off. My friend helped me carry them to my new quarters, and the next morning we were off to the USA—Boston, to be exact.

The work was hard. I had to help around in the kitchen and give a hand wherever needed, but what did I care? I was seventeen years old then and used to hard work. We arrived in America in due time; and having finished my work, my new friend and I went on shore for a few hours. I had so much to look at. Time went so fast. We just about got back in time to retire. I wrote a letter to my parents in Holland from Boston and told them all about my first trip to the United States. I wanted to reassure my good mother of my well being. I knew she worried much when she found out from my old shipper that I had run away—God knows where to.

Well, I liked my new job, and my boss liked me. I worked for the company for three years. The last time I arrived in Rotterdam, I took the first train home to say goodbye to my parents, who I loved with all my heart. I told them and my brothers and sisters and other members of the family how I made up my mind to stay in the United States on my next arrival.

I was born in Holland in 1869 and made my permanent home here in the USA in 1899—just thirty years later. My sailor friend and I lived together for about six months, when a man he knew invited him to Paterson, New Jersey, where, he said, there was plenty of work for anybody. We all went to Paterson and been here ever since.

I worked at several jobs in the mills and made good money. I made new friends every day among them Hollanders, who came from nearby where I came from. We used to sit down in the beer parlor—three or four of us—and talk of the old humdrum life we used to live in the old country—how people have to work there all their lives for just enough to eat, to have clothing, and to raise big families. For what? Slavery! How lucky we thought we were being in the United States, where we could eat all we wanted and think all we could—sometimes a bit too much—but nobody cared. And there was always more money the next Saturday.

I used to send home a little money whenever I thought of it. Sometimes I forgot for a while, but I used to catch up the next time. I was so happy when the folks wrote me what they did with the five-dollar money order they received from me. Then, through one of my cronies, I obtained a job in a locomotive shop. That was all new to me. But I caught on pretty quick, and, after a while, I became quite efficient and was earning good salaries.

I was boarding with a Holland family at that time, and through them got acquainted with the daughter of one of my neighbors, who was also from Holland origin. She came over with her parents when she was a little girl. Her father was a silk weaver. I was never much of a lady's man. I had all the fun I wanted with boy friends—mostly playing cards and all other kinds of indoor games and drinking beer. That was my sport. Little by little, this young lady cut down that sport, and it was not long before she took up all of my spare time. I did not see much of the old gang anymore. We went out for long walks on Sundays after church, I spent my evenings at her home, and I abided by all the rules of the game. Her parents had very definite and very strict ideas, and were, like most Hollanders, very good Christians. Soon after, we decided to get married. I was then twenty-seven years old and my wife twenty-five. We stayed at her house for a while, until something suitable turned up.

My wife worked in one of the Paterson silk mills for the next year, until the first baby came along, and then six more—seven altogether. From then on, we rented our own little house, and we had our hands full. My wife was a healthy, strong woman and brought all her children into the world without any trouble, with a Holland midwife and her mother in attendance, with never an instrument used—all healthy children, all of them alive and well today. As time went by, they went to the Paterson public schools, and all graduated from high school.

At home, everyone observed all the rules of their Dutch upbringing, but were otherwise very broad with their American-born playmates. Also, on Sunday, they went to all the Sunday services with us, just as before. And until they went out on their own, we never had any difficulty about their different ideas, national or political. I never interfered. Most of our common amusements we got through church affiliations. We became friendly with each other after services, we played all sorts of games, produced plays among us, and had some real enjoyable Sunday evenings.

The children, being with us all the time, grew up the same way, with little differences of ideas and aspirations, and grew up to be most satisfied, contented citizens. When I was fifty years old, I quit my job in the locomotive works and took an easier one as caretaker of a public building. I kept this job for fifteen years and got to know a lot of interesting and prominent people. I liked my new job very much. It was like taking a vacation after a life of hard work. All I had to do was see that the other men kept the halls and rooms clean and kept the place warm in the winter. As I said before, I did this for fifteen years altogether. My superiors had become good friends in those years and were very reluctant to let me go. But after a little talk, they realized I had done enough work and deserved a real layoff.

My life partner died a few years ago, and right after that I was injured by a bus. I lay in the hospital for three months with my two legs broken. I was a very lucky man because I have regained their use and I am as good as ever again. I got a substantial settlement from the bus company, and I am now spending my time with my children. The all love Dad and Grandpa, and there soon will be four generations in the family. I just hope I live a little while longer, with God's good grace.

I am a happy old man, surrounded by my own family and loved by them all, with my grandchildren my best friends.

Oh yes, if and when we have a death in the family, we have a regular church service, simple, with a gathering of all relatives. The close ones wear mourning for a full year.

February 27, 1940

A Hollander's Mainstay

My interviewee is a medium-built, good-looking, gray-headed old gentleman. He wears glasses and walks as straight as a die. He is very active for his years and of a very friendly disposition.

Father was born in St. Peter, province of Zeeland, Holland; Mother in Ouddorp, on the island of Flakkee, Holland. He came to the United States when he was very young—only ten years old—with his father, who was an undertaker. He was from a prominent and well-to-do family. He finished grammar school in Holland. He was very religious and led an exemplary life. Mother died, and Father got married again. He had twenty-two children by his two spouses. Several were stillbirths, and others, including me, were all born the natural, healthy way with doctors and, in some early cases, midwives in attendance. My parents were very lovable people and very well liked.

My father considered times in Holland normal enough, but he wanted to come to the United States to be a pioneer at his business. Not many people emigrated in those days. I worked with my father at his business in Paterson with more of my brothers, who all learned the undertaking business. In later years, all of us established ourselves in our own businesses in Paterson.

I was born in 1869 in Paterson. I married my first sweetheart in 1904, after a two-year courtship under the watchful eyes of Father and Mother. I have but one daughter, who helps me in business. I own my own home.

My father tells me my mother was twelve years of age when she came here. He remembers it took him and his parents ninety-five days to cross the Atlantic in a small windjammer. And what a trip! He became a very prominent citizen. He served in Paterson as coroner and also as tax commissioner.

We always lived in Paterson and were always a happy family, married with men and girls of our own national origin. If any of us leaves this earthly life, we bury them with a simple religious ceremony and a general family gathering. I love democracy, hate despotism and dictatorship, and mind my own business as much as possible. I am in good health, and I get all my recreation in my own family circle.

I remember my father saying how poor the people were over in Holland. Most of them worked in the surrounding farms for just a little more than three meals a day. They had a little piece of land they rented and farmed for their own use, and they had to work that either in the early morning or after their regular day's work was done. They lived in small stone houses with just a stove, a table, a few chairs, a chest of drawers, and bedding, mostly homemade, to sleep in. They had a few chickens and killed a fat pig every year, which gave them meat, lard, and salt pork that hung up at the ceiling. They made their own bread from rye and oats they grew and took to the nearest windmill owner to grind into flour. The children would go fishing and dig clams on the shore, and so they existed.

My grandfather was a respected man back home. He was the only undertaker in the village, and, even if he did not make much money, they were better off than most other people and considered a better class. They lived in a large brick house of nine rooms, right across the street from the church, with good solid furniture and good beds and the necessary conveniences to keep us comfortable; a good seed plot in back of the house, where they raised all kinds of vegetables; and an orchard with fruit trees.

They used to help Grandmother in the fall to put all the fruit and vegetables in glasses for winter use. They always had enough, or more than they needed, from one fall to the other. They also salted their own pork meat, which they put in large stone crocks, and made sausages, bacon, and headcheese, which they kept in a deep earthen cellar as cold as an icebox. They had a cow and chickens and always had a generous supply of fresh butter, milk, and eggs.

Then my grandfather decided, after long conferences with Grandmother, to come to the United States. It took over a year before she was ready, and the townfolk gave them a rousing farewell party, with the new village undertaker established in his place. They departed full of hope and determination—Grandfather, Grandmother, and nine children. After a journey of ninety-five long and dreary days, tossed about by terrific storms and bad weather, they arrived here and came right to

Paterson, New Jersey, on top of a hill, which is Prospect Park now. The Hollanders there had formed somewhat of a colony. For them all, it was hard to believe at first that they were in a different country. There was a grocery store, a butcher, a baker—in short, every kind of business where a housewife could go and buy something she needed for her home.

Well, the nearest undertaker was down the hill in Paterson, so my grandfather just put out his shingle, and our Holland neighbors took us right into the fold. That was my grandfather's big break. They had a little farmland in the back. The boys and an older sister and my father in between jobs went to work on it and raised all the potatoes we needed and a good supply of vegetables, which were canned in the old-fashioned way. At the passing of the first year, they were all happy and content.

The population increased more and more, and so did the business. Three of the boys were learning the business now and were a big help. The girls started to help Grandmother a little now, and so things went very smooth. On Sundays, they went to church in the morning and again in the afternoon. After the services they came together in the back of the church and talked and entertained each other. In that way, my father met my mother, the eldest daughter of a carpenter.

For the first years, they saw each other only on Sundays in the back of the church. Then, when it began to look serious, my mother was invited home, and she was accepted in the family circle. They used to go for a walk once in a while, with my father's sister as chaperone. Most of their get-togethers were either at my father's home or my mother's. Public amusements were scarce and mostly taboo for religious Hollanders. From then on, one after the other married within their own national origin, were educated in American schools, and gradually accepted the American standard of living.

The church is a Hollander's mainstay—his principal way of coming together and entertainment. Very few people bother with politics. It doesn't interest most of them. They are a peace-loving, great democratic people.

February 1940

American-born Partners

My interviewee is a big, heavy-set man, six feet tall. He looks good and healthy, wears glasses, and has a pleasing, friendly personality. He is sixty-five years old.

My father came from a very humble family in Helder, North Holland. He was born in 1848. He was a common laborer in a large sugar plant three miles from his home. He walked that distance to and from work every day, as far back as I remember. No matter what the weather, through rain, snow, and ice, he plodded to work. On very bad mornings, when it snowed, he used to go one hour earlier to be sure he was on time—six o'clock. From the fifteenth of October until the end of March, we did not see our father while it was daytime.

In the springtime, we all had to help cultivate the little plot we had some distance away. If we were to have bread and potatoes or some other vegetables for the long winter months, my mother used to put them up in jars—as much as we could raise. And so, with a few chickens, a couple of milk goats, and a fat pig we killed every fall, we used to get along very good. We did not know any better. I often think of those days now and of my poor father and his superhuman courage.

My mother, too, was nothing but a slave. She worked for well-to-do farmers since she was ten years old—the first five years for twenty-five guldens per year to help in the kitchen, feed the other help, tend to the chickens, and keep the house clean. And they mean clean in Holland. That meant twenty-five guldens for her parents, and they had one less mouth to feed.

The only pleasure these poor people had was on Sunday, when they all went to church twice a day. They dolled up in their best clothes for the day, and, after evening services, they came together and enjoyed such fun as they could create themselves. On such an occasion, my father met my mother. As for courtship, it was always the same. They met only on Sundays and holidays for a little while. Then, in the early evening, he took her home, accompanied by other members of her family, because it was a long and very dark walk.

When my father received his full man's wages at the mill, they got married, rented a little stone house on the outskirts of the town, and started to raise their own little family. It was not so hard in the beginning. It was mother's job to take care of the garden in the spring. Planting had to be done in daylight, and my father had to leave the house at five, when it was still dark. Then the children came. In the summer season, Mother had to drag them along to the field till late in the afternoon, when she went home to cook the humble meal for supper. And so the years went by—the same existence. They did not ask for pleasures. They had that home. They did not know any better.

My older brother got a job with my father at the sugar mill. My two sisters later went to work in the city for well-to-do city people. One sister later married a good tradesman and got away from the dull and poor farm life. I went to work for the town printing shop when I was thirteen years old. After I graduated from grammar school, I had to do all the errands, clean up, sweep, and do all odd jobs around the shop. I learned the business from the ground floor and became an expert printer.

I was born in Helder too, in 1875. In 1895, I got my printer's diploma and helped to print the town's little newspaper—just a double sheet, about twenty inches wide and twenty-eight inches long. It was called *Het Volksblad*. Being a real educated man and a good editor, my boss got his paper in many a home for miles around the countryside.

As I said before, I had two sisters and one brother. All of us were born in the same little brick house. Just a few days before the blessed event was expected, my grandmother would arrive and take charge. She did all the housework, delivered the baby, took care of Mother, and stayed a couple of weeks more before going home again. She delivered all of us the same way, without the slightest trouble or nervousness. You know, we could not afford anything like a doctor in those days. In my case, the doctor would not improve on my grandma, to say the least.

We lived on the outskirts of town, and I had about a two-mile walk to school. My father having a steady year-round job, we went to school every day, without an absence, until all of us graduated from grammar school, which was quite an education around our district. Every child was not as lucky as us. Some days the class was only half filled, the children staying home for some reason or other. So it was that very few of them ever graduated and could just about read and write.

Every little town in Holland had its main street, with its usual marketplace in front of the church. The street extended about a quarter of a mile on each side of the church and was made up of the different business people of the town—the undertaker, the hardware store, the baker, the butcher, the tailor, the blacksmith, the beer saloon with the dance hall, a few more combination grocery-beer stores, a few private homes of retired farmers. That comprised the heart of the town. Some of the bigger towns also had a hostelry, where travelers could be accommodated for the night.

The actual farms were outside the town and were pretty well scattered around. Likewise were little settlements of small brick houses, occupied by farm help and other laboring people, who led, as a rule, a very meager existence. Still, they were of a robust build and apparently very healthy.

The small farmers' tools are, even today, very old fashioned. They don't use any labor-saving devices. There is no money to buy these modern implements. The larger, more prosperous farmers are using more and more the modern methods of farming. It saves them time and labor and raises their living standards no end.

Around 1897, a couple of our townspeople sold out everything they had and came to Paterson, U.S.A. One of the boys was a good friend of mine. When he said goodbye to me, he promised he would not forget me and would write regularly. He kept his promise after they settled down in their promised land. It did not take them long before they were all working at something or other. They wrote me about how the section where they lived was comprised of all Hollanders, which they called "Little Holland." It had Holland stores and everything just about like home. With every letter I received I became more interested. A little after my twenty-fourth birthday, I had made up my mind. I was still single. I knew a good trade. My boss supplied me with a wonderful reference, even though he was very sorry to lose me. And after saying goodbye to my parents and brother and sisters, I came to Paterson to join my friends.

When I arrived, I found they had done quite a bit of advance advertising about me. Before I knew it, I was working in a downtown printing shop for ten dollars a week. At the end of the first week, on a Saturday, my new boss called me aside and told me that he had just tried me out for a week and that he would raise my pay to the full wage of fifteen dollars. No need to tell you how happy I was. I was earning three times as much as I did back home, and that only the second week in the United States. My boss also was a Hollander, and we became real pals. I liked my job. I boarded with a Holland family—a mother, father, three sons, and two daughters. I fell in love at first sight with the oldest daughter, but I kept it secret for a long time. I went to church on Sunday with the family and spent a lot of time with my prospective bride. I could see her actions betrayed her feelings toward me. One evening, coming home from church, we lagged a little in the rear. With a terrible effort on my part, I popped the question. Well, from then on I figured the quicker the better because we lived under the same roof. We set a date for the wedding day. We were openly engaged.

I was then unanimously accepted in the family. Three months later we got married, two years after I arrived in 1901. We stayed with my in-laws just as before. They cooked for us, and we paid board. My wife did not have anything much to do, and she got sick of it. She went out and got a job in a Paterson silk mill. Our expenses did not amount to much, so we were able to save quite some money out of both our pays. We were very happy.

I was twenty-six years old when I got married, and my wife twenty-five. She bore me two children—one boy and one girl. Both were born in the natural way and with an expert Holland midwife in attendance. My wife was afraid of doctors. When the time came just before the baby was born, we moved into a four-room apartment not far from my in-laws.

The children grew up healthy and strong. When old enough, they went to school in Paterson. I was still working at my printing job, but, by this time, I was very well-acquainted with the trade and had a lot of friends. I had saved a little money, and, after talking it over with the missus, I decided to start in for myself. I was then thirty-five years old. I built up a prosperous business, and am still at it today. Both my children graduated from high school, and both are married.

My son did not want to be a printer, so he went to work for a large concern in New York City and today enjoys a good position. My daughter too is happily married to a professional man. They both chose American-born partners and are very happy. My son in-law's ancestors are Irish, and my daughter-in-law's are German. We never had any difficulty about American ideas. The same with the children. We never interfere. They do anything they want to do according to their own desires. When death occurs in the family, we have a simple church service. The whole family comes together, and the immediate relatives wear mourning for a year. I do not know my children's attitude towards our own church. They are both intermarried, and we don't consider it wise to question it. Both my in-laws' children are Catholic, and I am sure neither of them will intermarry another.

About politics, I do not bother with them. I haven't got time anyway. I love peace and democracy and hate dictatorship. We come from a healthy family. I don't remember having had any serious sickness outside of a common cold or children's diseases. We try to keep healthy by eating simple, substantial meals and find our own amusement in our own family circle.

Arthur Vermeire

We Never Complained

My interviewee is a fine-appearing man, close to six feet tall, well-built, with a luxurious crop of hair. He is middle-aged and very friendly.

My father and his ancestors were born in the township of Filippine, province of Zeeland, Holland, in 1865. I don't remember anyone in our family having a special trade. They had their own little farm, where they raised everything they needed for the winter. They had a few chickens, a couple of milk goats, a few pigs, and some rabbits. So there was always some kind of meat on Sunday. During the week, it was salt pork sandwiches, homemade rye bread, and mashed or fried potatoes. Sometimes Mother would bake a white raisin bread for Sunday. That was something real special for all of us. When my father could get a day's work, he took it every chance he had. He needed the cash to buy things he could not raise on the farm, like rice, salt, sugar, spices, coffee, and things to wear, such as shoes for Mother and Father. They did not buy them very often. All us kids used to wear wooden shoes. They were dry and warm in the winter and, above all, very cheap.

Education was a luxury. We went to school when there was nothing else to do—mostly in the winter. As soon as we were able to read and write, it was all over, and to work we went. A great many of our neighbors were totally illiterate. They could not sign their own names. In some sections, the school was so far away that the children could not walk that distance, especially in the winter. When we were at home, we all helped around the farm to feed the hogs and the chickens, clean the barn, milk the goats, and feed the rabbits. We would go to town on Friday with my father to help him with the handcart, loaded with whatever he had to sell at the marketplace—sometimes a dozen dressed rabbits or a few bags of potatoes. Every one of us wanted to go to the town because we all liked our father very much. He was so good and jolly and patient. And so was Mother. She was always on the go from morning until night, always seeing to it we had on clean clothes and our stomachs were full. That's why we were a healthy family. Our neighbors were the same, clean at all times, just as if everybody was running a race with each other for cleanliness.

The whole surrounding population was all of the same type. Everybody produced as much as possible in the summer, and in the fall they all sold their surplus at the marketplace, a little at a time, every Friday. Some had to carry it, but most everyone had a pushcart or a low wagon with two wheels, pulled by two or three big, trained dogs. Twice a week, my father peddled. On Monday, he got a load of coal and went to town to sell it to poor people who could not buy much. On Thursday, we went to the beach and dug a load of clams and sold them in town. Every week, we argued about who would go for coal or go to the beach with Father. And so the days passed, year in and year out. We never complained; we did not know any better. As far as I remember, there was no change in the way everybody worked. There was no machinery yet; everything was done by hand. Only the well-to-do farmers could afford horses and wagons and some new mechanical devices sold to the farmers in those days.

It was around 1885. My father was twenty years old. He received word from a friend of his, whose people had come to the United States the previous year, telling him about the opportunities there and how he worked in the mill and made good wages—more than anything he could dream about in the old country. A couple more of these letters settled everything. After arranging with his friend for his passage across, he said goodbye to his parents and brothers and sisters and to his recent sweetheart of a few months. He came over with about twenty more Hollanders he met at the pier, all of them going to some relative across the ocean, full of hope and dreams. After an uneventful trip of nearly two months, they arrived in New York, safe and healthy. My father proceeded to his final destination—Paterson.

When he arrived at the station, he gave the address of his friend to a messenger boy, who took him there promptly. He was well received, had a good, old-fashioned supper, and, after many questions and talk about their old neighbors in the old country, he went to bed the first time in America for a refreshing sleep. The next morning, after breakfast, when the others had gone to work, my father sat down and wrote a big letter home to tell the folks all about the voyage and of his safe arrival. He also told his sweetheart how he was going to send for her, just as soon as he got a job and saved enough to have her come over to join him.

He did not have to wait long for a job. After a couple of days rest, his friend took him along to the mill. He was promised work as soon as he could learn silk weaving. Being a bright young fellow, it did not take his friend long to teach him as much as he knew about the business. After a few weeks, he started at his own loom as a weaver. He became more efficient as time passed, and it was not very long before his old-country sweetheart got permission from her parents to join her Dick in the far-off United States, on condition they get married right away.

The passage was arranged, and she came to the Land of Promise. Everything was in readiness when she arrived, after quite an exciting crossing of forty days. They were united in marriage the next day by a Holland person. They lived at my father's boarding house for a while, until they were able to rent a little place of their own and buy the needed furniture to start housekeeping. My mother liked it here in America from the very first day. She missed her family very much at first, but soon made up her mind that she had made her choice. After a few weeks, she met the whole lot of new Holland people after church services on Sundays and had made many new friends. Having nothing to do at home, she was soon looking for a job and found one soon in a winding mill.[12] One of her newly made friends took her down, and she learned winding and soon brought home her first American pay.

From then on, they were able to save quite some money. They had very little expenses, and they were very saving. My father was now very interested in learning to be a loomfixer.[13] He seemed to be very mechanically minded. When I came along four years later, in 1891, my dad had a good job and a steady one.

We belonged to the First Holland Reformed Church. We went regularly every Sunday to services in the morning and to evening services after supper. We made many friends. Visiting them and visa versa was our best and only entertainment, and we derived a lot of satisfaction out of it. In the course of time, four more brothers and three sisters were born in the natural way. We had a good, intelligent midwife and neighborhood friends, who took care of my mother. She did not believe in doctors; she was very much afraid of them. Eventually, we all went to the Paterson public schools, and all of us finished grammar school. Most of us learned a trade. One entered business, and I learned to be a carpenter. I worked steady at my trade for many years. I worked for a big contractor in Paterson, and I worked myself up to an important position in the company.

At twenty-five, I met my present wife, a daughter of one of my foremen, also a Hollander. We became fast friends, and I was invited to his home one night to meet his family. I was introduced to the young lady, and after a very enjoyable evening, I went home with a promise of a return visit. I wanted them first to meet my family, too. They came the very next week. I introduced them to my whole family, and that was the start of the finish of my bachelor life. We kept seeing each other once or twice a week, always at her home, where she helped her mother with the housework. Her two older sisters were already married to good providers. They were very happy and doing fine.

My girl's parents had a very nice home of their own, tastily furnished with all the latest comforts. It was also much too big now, there being only three in the family. But her mother dropped a hint and said she hoped that, if her daughter got married, she would stay with them.

We used to go out for a walk once a week. The other times, I would see her at home, evenings and then again on Sundays. We would attend services together. That is the way it went for nearly three years, when we decided to get married. So we did the month of June 1919. Both our families got together, and we celebrated with a very delicious wedding dinner. In the early evening, we took a train for good old Niagara Falls. We stayed at a hotel there for a week and really enjoyed ourselves.

The weather was beautifully warm. Nothing but loaf and do as we pleased, just by ourselves. Well, this was different. The happy days went by only too swiftly, and it was Saturday morning before we knew it. We had to start packing again for the return trip home and life together. A little after dinner we were on our way back to Paterson, where we arrived late Sunday afternoon. By the time we had eaten supper and unpacked our grips, we were tired enough to go to bed for a good night's rest. I had to go back to work in the morning.

As my mother-in-law suggested some time before, we stayed with them and got along fine with each other. We are still living together, and all of us are in perfect health. Three years after our marriage, a son was born to us, the only child we had. He was born at home in a normal way, with a doctor and my mother-in-law in attendance. He was a healthy baby of eight and a half pounds. My father-in-law met with an accident on the job. He fell off a platform and hurt himself. He was home for a few weeks and went back to work again, but never felt right after. A year later, he retired from work, but not before he put me in his place as foreman—a position I still hold today. My son went to the Paterson public schools and graduated from high school. He went to college and finished with honors two years ago. At present, he holds a good position at a large banking concern in New York City and is definitely on his way up.

My ideas are those of a true American. I believe in democracy and peace. I have no sympathy for dictatorship or any isms. I am very happy and grateful to be an American citizen. My boy is the same way. No politics for him yet, he says. I have no time for that, and that is the same with the rest of our large family. We Hollanders are a peace-loving, democratic people as a whole. We have not as yet buried any of our immediate family. We still all stick around pretty well. During my lifetime, I only attended a couple of funerals of people I used to know. As a rule, I stay away from them. I don't like death and funerals. I guess it is all the same—a brief church service, a family gathering, and then the mourning period for a year, I guess. Well, I hope I don't have to attend any funerals for a long time to come. To me it looks pretty good. As far as I know, we all are in perfect health. May the Lord save us for a few more years.

I am in good health myself, and, outside of the regular children's diseases, I don't remember being seriously sick in all my past life—a cold or a sore throat or a headache, but nothing worse. In my early youth, all our amusement was at school with the other boys, and later on at home and in our several church activities. Nowadays, we go to the movies and other social entertainment of the several Holland societies.

Arthur Vermeire

My Own Store in America

My interviewee is a little, snappy old gentleman, who wears glasses. His hair is gray-white. He is very active and helps around the property when he feels like it. He is a very friendly person.

My father was born in the city of Nijmegen, province of Gelderland, Holland, in the year 1840, the son of a confectioner, that is, a maker of all sorts of sweets, candies, and chocolates. My mother was born in the same town in 1842, the daughter of a building contractor. My father had a long-established business and was a very prominent citizen. I have one brother and two sisters. We all received a good education. My sisters were sent to a boarding school a few miles away, and my brother studied five more years after he graduated from grammar school. He tried his hand at different jobs, but could not get to like any. Finally, he quit trying and decided to be a candy maker too. I was already working at home with my father for a few years, so from then on it was a family affair. With the additional help, we increased production and decided to enter the wholesale business. It went very slow in the beginning, but my father had a good reputation, and the number of customers increased from day to day. Within a couple of years, we built up a wonderful trade, and we hired a helper to deliver the merchandise to our many patrons.

After a while, my brother married a young lady he went to school with. They came to live with us, and now we had one more in the family. My father and mother were lovely people. They brought us up the best way they knew how. They were very religious too and, naturally, very strict. Every Sunday the whole family went to church in the morning and again after supper to evening services. Then we mingled with the other members of the congregation for a little entertainment, and then home early and to bed.

This was just about the general way our people lived in the city, a hardworking humdrum life with very little or no public entertainment, a dreary life compared with today's here in the United States. Well, every once in a while we heard of this family or that family emigrating to America. A couple of them we knew very well—real friends of ours—had gone that spring to get rich in America.

At that time, things did not stand too good between my brother and me. He was a couple of years my junior. I was easygoing. I let him have his way most of the time, until he started to take advantage of me and regarded me as his inferior. He, his wife, and little boy lived with us ever since his marriage. I guess he acquired bossy ideas and wanted to tell me what to do. Well, I was still a single man and allowed him more rope than I should have, him being my younger brother. But he got more and more bossy and conceited, and one day we had it out. I told him then what I wanted to tell him long before, and, of course, from then on we were at odds, much to our parents' displeasure. I decided to leave home and country as soon as there was an opportunity to join the next emigrant party. The captain in Rotterdam advised me that he was leaving for New York in two weeks and would make room for me, too. I made all arrangements and said goodbye to my family, much to their grief, and away I went.

I was then thirty-one years old and full of confidence in the future. We had a terrible voyage across the ocean. I thought we would never get there. The weather was stormy, windy, and rain aplenty. We have very few days when it was nice enough to come up on deck. To my estimation the ship went too slow—sometimes it seemed we were not moving at all. But, finally, after eighty-six days, someone shouted "Land!" and the next day we landed in New York. From there, I took a train to Passaic, where I met my old-time friends. They had left Holland five years before and were making good. I boarded with these good people for two years.

One week after my arrival, I took a job in a Passaic woolen mill. I did not like it so very much, but I was getting good pay of twelve dollars per week. I started an account in the bank with the money I had brought with me, and I was able to save a little every week. I was thrifty, and I had my eyes on the future. We had a Holland church in our neighborhood. We lived just about the same life as in the old country. During the week, we all made ourselves comfortable after the evening meal, read the newspaper, or played checkers, and talked with the other members of the family—one boy and two daughters. The oldest was twenty-four years old and was destined to become my wife later. It all seemed very natural that, after being with them over two years, she answered yes to my question.

I liked my newly acquired family very much. I was treated like one of the family from the beginning, and I, of course, always appreciated their friendship toward me. We decided to do the proper thing, and we got married two months later. I took off a couple of days for a honeymoon at home. We had a very happy life together. I especially was happy to have a home, although I always did feel at home there. We lived a quiet, everyday life, until one evening some Paterson friends of my father-in-law dropped in for a visit. He worked in a big Paterson mill, and he knew me too and the work I was doing. Before he left for home that night, he told me his foreman told him a couple of days ago they were going to hire a few good, experienced workers at a salary that was three dollars more than mine. I was tempted, and I told him, if he would talk to his boss about me, I would take the job and move to Paterson. So he promised.

I talked things over with my wife that night. We decided I would take the job and move there with an eye on the future. I knew there was a big Holland colony there, and I wanted to go in the confectionery business because I never liked the mill work. By the end of the week, I received a card in the mail asking me to come and see the foreman next morning. I went down and met him. He was a very fine and friendly Irishman. After a little talk about my experience, he told me I could start the next Monday. I went home with the good news. My in-laws did not like to see us move away from Passaic, but they agreed it was all for the best. I went to work at my new job the following Monday, and, on the next Saturday, I found a note in my pay envelope stating my work was of the best. It made me feel good to know my labor was appreciated. After I got my bearings in Paterson, my wife and I made a few flying visits to Paterson on Sunday afternoons and found a nice, clean, three-room attic flat on the Hill, now Prospect Park. We went shopping a couple evenings for furniture, and we were soon installed on our very own. My wife was a little lonesome at first, but she took the trolley home at least once a week and sometimes twice. Everyone was satisfied. When my little boy was born a year later, that was the peak of our happiness. He was a sturdy, healthy youngster of nine pounds. My mother-in-law and my old landlady attended my wife. She was afraid of doctors, but we did not need one. They understood everything. They had plenty of experience in their day. Two years later came the little girl, also a picture of health, with the same attendants.

Then, a few weeks later, a Holland contractor finished building a nice house, containing a spacious store with twin windows and four rooms in the rear and a very roomy and dry cellar finished in cement. We went over to take a look around and found it just what I was looking for. At last, I was going to realize my ambition—my own store in America. I soon had everything arranged with the owner, and, before I knew it, I was making my own first stock of merchandise in my own candy kitchen, down the cellar. I did not make much at first. I was very careful. The first customers soon found out I was making the right kind of goodies, and my business grew with leaps and bounds. Everything went along smoothly for years. The children grew up, went to school, and graduated. After graduation, my boy wanted to stay home and help in the business. It made us very happy. He was our only boy, and I had always hoped he would be my successor.

The children were very fond of us. They were obedient and grateful. We brought them up the way we were raised—in the fear of God. All our neighbors are of national Holland origin, and it is just like living at home in the old country here. We bother very little with politics; we have no time for that. We love peace and contentment. We do not want dictators or the like. Most of us Hollanders belong to a burial fund, some sort of insurance to bury our dead. In that event, we have a simple funeral service at home and a family reunion. The nearest relatives wear mourning for a full year. We appoint our own ministers and support our church adequately. We have different kinds of societies for religion and for entertainment. Being a home-loving people, we have most of our pleasure home. Our meals are plain, but very substantial. Therefore, we are a healthy people and seldom need a doctor.

My wishes and hopes are fulfilled. My daughter is a happy mother and housewife with a good breadwinner for a husband, and my son, as my successor, is not dependent on anybody. He worked hard with me and now owns a good business. He is happily married and has a nice family of six children, four sons and two daughters. I am now sixty-seven years old and retired. We live with my son, and I could not be happier. We have a lot of fun with the grandchildren and get along fine. We are a happy family.

Shoemaking Runs in Our Blood

My interviewee is of slight build and medium height. He is fifty-seven years old and very active. He has very little gray hair and is of an amiable disposition.

My parents were both born in Haarlem, North Holland; my father in 1850, and my mother in 1852. They married in 1878. For generations, my father's ancestors have been in the boot and shoe business, from the time when a person who needed a pair of boots or shoes had to come to the shoemaker and have his shoes made to measure, until the present time of mass production. Almost everyone in the city knew my father. There were very few shoemakers in those days. He made shoes for old and young, rich and poor. He specialized in shoes for crippled people. Therefore, he kept very busy at all times, and his four helpers never had to worry about slack times; there was no such thing.

The displays were also different in those days. We just had a small, very neatly arranged store. I had one display window with a few of my father's masterpieces for men and women. He had his regular customers, who traded with him for years—that same trade his ancestors had built up before him. Shoemaking runs in our family blood. We never knew anything else or saw anything but shoes in the making. Nobody else but my father took a customer's foot measurements. He did not trust anybody but himself for that very particular job. After that shoe was finished, it was sure to fit. Good shoes were very expensive; ten to fifteen gulden was a very common price for a good pair.

Well, we had a good-size family, a brother and five sisters. When we grew old enough, we all finished our education in Haarlem. Three of my sisters took jobs in the city in large business offices. One took care of our own business's bookkeeping. The youngest one was my mother's helper and her best friend; they are inseparable. My older brother got a job with a large coffee and tea importer and was doing real well when I last saw him.

My parents, especially my father, were very stern, but good. We loved them very much. We all went to church on Sunday, and nobody was allowed to do a thing. My mother even did all the cooking on Saturday. The only pleasure we had was in our own home. It was not until I came to the United States that I enjoyed a little freedom.

I had always been around the shop, watching and helping at one thing or another. When I asked my father to teach me all about the shoe business, he was very happy because my older brother was never interested in it. After I finished school at age sixteen, my father personally taught me all the fine points of the trade, and I could build a shoe as good as the best in the shop. My dad was very proud of my ability, and he told me how someday he wanted me to continue the tradition of the family. Well, I had other ideas about that.

I had an uncle—a brother of my mother, a few years younger than herself—who worked for a large and very fancy bakery in town and who was always talking about America. He was married, had two children, and had quite some money saved up. Whenever he was with me, he would tell me about all the opportunity in the New World, how some of his former friends were doing so well there, and how some of them had invited him to come on across and become somebody.

My father told me how wrong he was, how people had to start all over again in a strange land, and how well off I was at home with the rest of my family; but still I was always glad to see Uncle Ed and to hear him talk about that great country across the sea. I became more interested in the proposition; and before long, America became the dream of my life.

I went to Uncle Ed's house every time I had a chance, and you know the trend of our conversation. I told him one day how I decided to give up everything at home to go to America with him, if he would take me, and how I would extend my father's reputation as a shoemaker to America. He told me they too had made up their minds. At first, my aunt was not very keen about leaving parents and brothers and sisters behind; but, at last, her husband's enthusiasm got the best of her too; and, if I could get my father's consent, they would take me along.

A few days later, when my uncle came over with his wife, we talked everything over for a long while. My father was convinced nothing could shake my determination. I told him how, sooner or later, I would go anyhow. So they finally capitulated and handed me over, so to speak, to Uncle Ed.

After the decision, the last letter was written to America for advice. The work in the shop went on, but the days seemed so long, waiting for that last message with all the last instructions. Finally, more than three months later, the news came. Everything was in readiness over there, and it did not take long to make reservations in Rotterdam. A big sailing vessel was leaving in two weeks with a total of about fifty more Hollanders, crossing the ocean to New York.

Then, the happy day came, when we all took leave of our parents and relatives. We were all very sad at the parting hour, but we promised to be back in a few years with enough American dollars to live a life of comfort ever after. That is known to be the general goal for everybody who leaves for America, but it does not always turn out that way. I found that out.

On the way across, we encountered some real bad weather. We spend many anxious hours below deck, during heavy rainstorms on the gale-swept ocean. Many of us who had never sailed on the ocean became very sick, and we had a real miserable time almost all the way across. Especially the families with children had a very bad time. At last, after sixty-two long days, early one morning we saw land and America for the first time. Everybody, sick and well, was on deck to look at the vague and still far-off outline of the American shoreline, and we all remained there until we almost reached the harbor.

After arriving at the dock, the ship was fastened, and we all went on land with light hearts and full of hope. A large welcoming party was on hand. Each of us had some relative waiting for him. Some had been there over a week, sleeping in their wagons overnight; but it was all over now, and everybody went his way to his final destination, some near and others very far. I was born in 1884, so I was twenty-three years old when I reached these shores in 1907. My Uncle Ed's friend was there too, waiting for us, and was he glad to see us. He assured us we did not have a worry in the world, and, after a few days of complete rest, he would show us the town.

We lived at that time where the Prospect Park section of Paterson is today. One day, on a Saturday, our friend took us for a walk downtown. It was not far. When we came home again late that afternoon, I was much impressed with our new home—the city and its beautiful stores. We decided to take another trip downtown the next Monday by ourselves. Our friend had to go to work.

On that Sunday morning, we all went to the Holland church, not far from where we lived, and again to evening services. The *dominee* was on hand to welcome the new members from the mother country.[14] Everybody asked a lot of questions about the old country. They all wanted to know the present conditions there and were generally very much interested in their old homeland. But, as a rule, nobody wanted to return there again to live unless they could go back and live a life of ease. The next day, Monday, we walked downtown again, alone this time. We made ourselves familiar with the principal streets and got home that evening good and tired. Afterwards, we decided to walk downtown every day. As we walked on upper Main Street one afternoon on our way home, Uncle Ed and I noticed a sign on a bakery window: "Baker Wanted." We knew right away what that meant, so Uncle Ed took a chance and went in. The proprietor was working in the rear when his wife entered the store. He could not talk English, so he asked his question in Dutch, and to his amazement the lady understood. She said they came from Bremen, Germany, and she could understand Dutch quite well. The baker invited him in where he was working. He asked him a few questions. My Uncle Ed told his story, and he was hired on his first job in America. He turned out to be a first-class man. At the end of the first week, he was paid first-class wages of twelve dollars. My uncle was delighted and grateful to Mr. Otto, who kept him on the job for almost ten years.

After a few weeks, my aunt found a nice, clean five-room house, which she rented right away at eight dollars a month. They went shopping the next Saturday afternoon and bought just the necessary furniture. They were soon installed in their own home.

I wanted to open a shoe store of my own, but I thought it wise to work awhile for someone else and learn the language first. All my new-found friends in the church congregation were on the lookout for a job, and a few days later I was told to go to a shop for an interview and a test.

I could not speak English, so the friend who had recommended me came along with me as interpreter. My prospective boss liked my appearance right away and took me in the rear to show me the place. He did not want to give me a test, he said, "just come in tomorrow, and we will see." I came to work the next morning, was handed a measure chart for a new pair of shoes, and told to go at it. It took me a little while to get used to a few tools that were different than the ones I was used to work with. But then there was nothing to it, and I made a pair of shoes I myself was proud of. The boss looked them over and looked at me. He patted me on the back and said simply, "You'll do." He showed me his appreciation when he paid me the highest wages that Saturday—eighteen dollars. I was very much surprised myself, but happy to have a good job. In those days, jobs could be depended on. When a man knew his trade, it was like a life job. After working about three months, a new customer came in. He was a cripple and asked to see the boss. I called him and told him that the caller was deformed. He was going to send the man away because he never made shoes for deformed feet. I told him that was our speciality in Holland. After assuring him of my ability in that kind of work, I took the man's measurements and made him the best and cheapest shoes he said he ever wore. He came from another town and told me he was charged a much higher price for his made-to-order shoes, and they did not have a comfortable fit at that. Well, here was a new customer, and from then on I made all that man's shoes.

Twice a month, I wrote a long letter to my family, and everybody congratulated me on my success here. I was really happy. Sometimes after supper, I went to visit one friend or another. On Sunday, we had a good time after evening service. There was always something going on in the church hall. There, I met the girl who was to become my wife. She was the youngest of nine children, also born in Holland, and came over with her parents several years before. Her father was a mason and a builder. She was twenty-three years old, a picture of health, and had a smile like I had never seen before. We became good friends and seemed attracted to each other. When I asked her for a date, she invited me to come to her house some night first to ask Mother. Personally, she said, she was more than willing.

I came over one night. While I knew her parents, I was never before introduced to them. We got acquainted that evening, and I was permitted to go out with her the next Sunday afternoon. I was alone here and got pretty lonesome once in a while. She knew it, too. When I asked her for her hand, she was very glad to say yes. She knew I was a good worker with a steady job. Besides, her whole family had become very fond of me. Three months later, we got married and went to live in our own quarters, with new furniture and everything necessary for housekeeping. I took a week off to stay home and enjoy it. Believe me, I was a happy man after being without a home of my own for so long.

I worked for my boss five years. I received a raise in pay and could stay there as long as I wanted, but I planned to own my own business. I was well-known by my own people by now; so one day, I had an opportunity to rent a very convenient store with the rooms in back, right on Main Street. I decided this was it.

My employer was very sorry to see me go, but he wished me all the luck in the world in my new undertaking. In another week, I started in business and was very successful from the beginning. After a while, with the advent of the factory-made shoes, the demand for custom-made shoes dropped considerably because they were more expensive than the others. After a few years, I stopped making shoes altogether and devoted my entire time to selling factory-made goods.

We had three children, one son and two girls. The girls are the oldest, all of them born the natural way, delivered by the family doctor, with my mother-in-law taking care of my wife. They are all healthy children to this day. They all went to public school in due time and graduated. The girls married and are good housewives and mothers now, and my son is in the store with me. I come and go when I feel like it, and he is really in charge of the business. He is also married and lives in the back of the store. My wife and I live with one of my daughters and are all very happy. My children are all married with mates of their own nationality, so there is no intermarriage. That does away with much trouble. With the same beliefs and customs, it is like living in the old country, only life is much fuller. We can buy anything we like, and, in comparison, live like kings. We have plenty of pleasure when our children come to visit us. Our grandchildren come and want to play with Grandpa, and Grandma spoils them, believe me. There is no happiness like it.

Oh, when we die, let's not talk about that. The last minute is soon enough. When the time comes, we will go the way of all others—the Holland way of our fathers. With politics I never bothered; no time for it. As to dictators, not for me. No one man should be allowed to lay down the law to the masses. We love peace and democracy and are happy and content in our own family circle.

Arthur Vermeire
March 6, 1940

A Mistake to Go to Another Country

My friend is of more than medium build, around fifty-six years old, and in the best of spirits. He doesn't have a gray hair in his head and would rather talk than eat. He is a very friendly person.

I am fifty-six years old. I was born in 1884, in a little hamlet on the Dutch-Belgium frontier called De Valk. I was named Albert. I'm the oldest of five children. I have two brothers, Cyriel and Emiel, and two sisters, Martha and Alice. My grandmother helped to bring me into this world, as she did with the others. The doctor lived in the village about eight kilometers away and was not even considered at any child-birth in our house. We lived in a two-room brick-house on the side of the highway that was used at the same time as a dike. There was a kitchen with a tile floor; a big white-top table; five chairs and a bench; a clothes closet; a woodbin by the old Dutch stove; an aclove deep in the corner, where my parents slept; and a fairly large attic, where all the others slept in three separate beds on straw mattresses. We had no furniture except a couple of large trunks, where our clothes were kept. It was very simple, but clean. We reached our quarters under the roof by means of a homemade ladder that was pulled away in the daytime. In back of the kitchen, my father built some kind of an addition, where everything was kept that we did not need in the house—pots and pans and kettles and farming tools of all kinds. Beyond that was a stall for the two goats, a pig pen, and a coop for the rabbits and one for our few chickens.

My father worked in the big sugar mill a few miles away since he was fourteen. He had a dependable, steady job. I don't remember how much salary he earned, but my mother could always buy us whatever we needed most. That was not much. Shoes we only wore to go to church. We all wore wooden clogs in the winter, which kept our feet real warm and cost but little. In the summer, we children did not wear any shoes at all. We even went to school barefooted. A pair of overalls and a shirt of blue denim constituted our daily clothing, and a cheap dress for the girls. Each of us had three of these outfits, so there always was one clean and ready.

Our meals consisted of homemade rye bread, spread with home-rendered lard, and coffee for breakfast; the same again at noon; and for supper every night, boiled potatoes, mashed with cabbage, white turnips, carrots, or onions, with a small piece of smoked meat of some kind. Every fall, my father butchered our biggest pig, mostly around three hundred and fifty pounds, that furnished the family with all our meat. It was salted and cured. My mother made headcheese and real delicious sausages, which she hung up to dry under the attic roof.

Sunday was the big day. My father killed a chicken or a nice fat rabbit, and we had that for dinner at noon with potatoes, vegetables, and white bread. Then, again around four o'clock in the afternoon, my mother made good strong coffee and homemade raisin bread, baked the day before. You see, the food was very simple, but nourishing. That is why we all grew up healthy and strong.

On Sunday, the whole family went to church, to the seven o'clock mass, rain or shine. We never missed. When we got back home, everybody changed clothes, and the Sunday duds were pack back in the trunk. The girls played around the house, and my brothers and I went fishing in the creek. Fish were plentiful. Most all of the time, we caught a nice mess of eels or panfish, which my mother fired for dinner.

Sometimes I think back to those happy-go-lucky days of the simple life and carefree existence. We helped our parents, of course, but we knew what to do every day. Each of us was to perform some duty, according to age. When the work was done, we played with some neighborhood children, who lived about a quarter of a mile away on each side of us, until sundown, when everyone was called in the house and the door locked. You know, we did not have any streetlights out there, and at night it was pitch dark. None of the children would venture out for fear of meeting Crockemitaine, who was supposed to be an evil witch who rode around the countryside with a black wagon and invisible horses to pick up children who went out after dark.

In the summertime we were allowed to stay up until after dark, but in wintertime we all went up the ladder not later than seven o'clock. The next morning, we went one at a time to the back shed to the old pump to wash up. What a time my mother used to have with us. The water was ice cold, and the shed was cold. Sometimes, we forgot to wash our necks, and Mother went back with us to show us how to do it right. We could not go to school with dirty necks. After Father went to work on his bicycle, we had our breakfast and hot coffee, and off to school. We all took lunch along in a little box and ate it there. It took almost one hour to walk to school, so we could not come home at noon.

We had one and a half hour for lunch, a big playground for the kids to play. When it was cold outside, we all played in the recreation room under the school building. Anyhow, we had lots of fun in our school days. We all started our education at four; some before, some a little later. Some who lived in the village could go to school as soon as they could help themselves without the aid of their mother, and they were taken care of by a woman teacher. All the other grades had men teachers, who used a long stick to good advantage when behavior was bad. When a boy's or a girl's conduct was repeated, then the teacher would send a message to him or his father explaining the situation. Most everytime the next morning, the result was marked in the conduct of the errant pupil. Too bad we could not finish grammar school. We all had to quit around the age of ten or as soon as we were able to read and write.

In the spring of the year, we went to work for the rich farms in the district—some dairy, some cattle, and some grain or general crop farms. The boys took the cows to the pasture and watched them all day and were paid about ten gulden for the summer season, or twenty-five gulden the year round. They got paid at the end of the year. Sometimes, the boy was lucky to strike a good-hearted farmwife who fed the help good. Others were sometimes the stingy kind, who ate good themselves but considered their help only just a little better than their cattle. Those poor kids were required to do almost a man's work.

Long after their marriage, mothers would not see their daughters. However, when her mother was stricken very sick, my mother just could not stay away. She went to see and care for her every day. Well, she found out they were very happy together. After her mother got well again, her parents invited us all over on a Sunday after church, and all was forgiven. You see, they belonged to the Reformed Church, and my father was a Catholic. My mother, too, was converted to the Catholic religion and brought us all up in the same faith. That difference of religion was really the main reason of my in-laws' objections. You know, in Holland the population is 95 percent Protestant, or what is called Reformed, and only 5 percent Catholic, mostly in Zeeland and Brabant in the south of Holland.

Well, when I was ten years old, I went to work on my grandfather's farm. My duty was to take the herd to the pasture in the morning, bring them back again at night, and to watch over them so they did not wander too far. I took my lunch with me—a good-size jug of coffee—

and I was set for the day. Sometimes I fell asleep for a short time. It was a very dull job. Nothing to do but lay around.

One morning, before going out, I found my uncle's old pipe in the barn. Right there, I decided to take it along. I went to the kitchen and took a handful of Uncle Isidoor's tobacco, and off I went. That morning, I took my first smoke, and the last for quite a while. I was puffing on my pipe, and it was not long before I felt a terrible commotion in my stomach. I sat with my back against a tree. I don't remember how long, but I know I brought my lunch and coffee back with me. I could not eat supper that night. After my Aunt Pelagie found the pipe in my pocket, she knew. The next morning, when I came to the table for breakfast—I felt OK again—my uncle put his pipe in front of me, but did not say a word, and smiled. So I told them I was all through with smoking for a spell.

My mother's family grew very fond of me, and I loved all of them. My grandmother was always doing something special for me when nobody was looking, and my grandpa took me along whenever he could. On Sunday morning, he always brought me home to my family and called for me with the buggy at night.

In the next five years, my aunts Pelagie, Marie, and Gusta got married. All three took farmers' sons as husbands. My brother Emiel worked on his Aunt Marie's farm, and he was very happy there. We visited each other every chance we got. My Aunt Gusta's husband was persuaded to stay with us on our farm because my grandfather was getting on in years, and Uncle Isidoor had made up his mind to go to America. He was young and healthy and a good farmer. He decided to try his luck there.

He was really my best pal, and I was very sad when I heard he was going away. I always slept with him, and I was asking him about America every night before I fell asleep. So he promised me, if I was a good boy, he would call for me in a few years if I was still willing. I told him I would be ready anytime, no matter what happened. When he left, I cried all that day. We all went along to the railroad station to see him off and say a last farewell. I was last to clasp his hand and to wish him good luck. For the next few weeks, I missed my uncle terribly and cried myself to sleep, but I soon remembered what he told me about having patience. So I consoled myself and went to work as usual, but with a solid idea of going to America someday not far off.

By now, I was doing general work—milking the cows, churning milk, and making butter. I went to market with our dairy products on Friday, and soon I became acquainted with every face of the business. After my uncle left, I went home every Sunday to my family, and I sat and talked to Father and Mother about him. I waited for news from him about his new life in his new country. So, when a few days later the postman walked through the big gate with a letter he was waving, we knew news had come.

My grandfather received the letter, went into the kitchen, got his glasses, and sat down by the table, his eyes moist. He read it in silence, smiled when he finished, and then read it over again aloud for all of us to hear. My uncle wrote how he had intended to buy a farm at first and then had taken a job at a small dairy farm, whose owner had died quite suddenly and left a widow with two daughters. He had met the family a week after he arrived from Holland, after mass on Sunday. Some friend had introduced the new arrival to them. When Uncle Isidoor learned of their misfortune, he went to visit them. After talking things over, it was decided he would take charge and see what could be done. The letter ended there with greetings for all of us and a suggestion to me that he might need me soon.

The next Sunday, the last of my sisters was to have her first Holy Communion and receive her confirmation. She was eleven years old. The bishop came back in the afternoon and confirmed the Holy Communion class of boys and girls. This was usually a family feast day. After weeks of special teachings, it was the last Catholic function before marriage. We all partook of a special, good meal of chicken with a homemade dessert of preserves, fruit, and pie. Everybody was happy. My father took me to the village that afternoon, where we met a lot of old friends. My father told me about Uncle Isidoor and his letter from America, and everybody was glad about the good news. That day, I drank my first glass of beer, and I liked it, too.

Filippine was just a small village, with a main street composed of the church in the center of a big square, where the weekly market was held on Friday. A block from there was a small Reformed church; a bakery; a butcher shop; several beer parlors—as a rule, a combination grocery-saloon; two hardware stores, where the farmers could buy farming tools, kitchen utensils, and all kinds of seeds; a big house where the doctor lived; the town hall; the big clothing store; and a short side street with the railroad station at the end and the hotel across the street from it. At the railroad station, you could find a few of the regular old townspeople almost every day of the year, who did not have anything else to do but to find out who arrived in town on the two daily trains and gossip the rest of the time.

Across the street, on the church side, was the big house where the undertaker lived. He was about the most prominent man in town. When someone died, he took full charge. The deceased was dressed up in her or his best togs and put in the best room of the house, which was made up like a chapel. The townspeople came to view the body and say a prayer. The last night before interment, an all-night vigil was held by friends or members of the family. The casket was closed in the morning. After a short religious service in the home, everybody walked behind the casket to the village cemetery just outside the town. The village priest performed another short ceremony, the casket was covered up, and everybody went home.

Oh, yes, my youngest sister, Alice, went to work for my Aunt Pelagie, to whom a second child—a boy—had been born. Her little girl was not yet two years old, and my sister was supposed to take care of her cousin and help her aunt with some light work in the kitchen. She, too, liked her job; and, when she came home on Sunday, we all talked about the happenings of the week. After supper, we all went back to our respective jobs. Martha was to stay at home and help my mother. Martha would not hear of leaving her. She was especially attached to Mother ever since babyhood; and she always was, for she never married.

My father was promoted to foreman in the factory. He cut down his livestock to just enough to provide for his now-small family. The same with his land. He cultivated just enough potatoes, wheat, and vegetables for our own needs. Mother could take it much easier with Martha doing the housework. She could sit down and sew and darn and do just the light work, besides the baking, which nobody could do like her. I was always glad to go home on Sunday morning for Mother's raisin bread alone. I could never forget the cake and pies she used to make for St. Nicholas Day, which we celebrated on December 6. It takes the place of Christmas in America. My sisters got a cheap doll and some new clothes, and us boys just got some new clothes, which we needed anyway. No toys for us. That was just a waste of money. My mother baked a pot full of cookies and made honey cake, and all were satisfied. That day, we went visiting our relations on both sides and were given small presents and more cookies and fruit from the many uncles and aunts. Those were the happy days.

Every year, we had two fairs in the village; one was in the spring and one in the fall. Then, a carnival came to the village square for a whole week with a merry-go-around, Ferris wheel, shooting galleries, small circus, strong men, etc. Everybody dressed up in their best clothes; the women and girls with their white lace bonnets and golden horns, wide skirts, and fancy corsage of homemade lace; the men with their high, soft black caps and fancy pipes, wide trousers, and long black topcoats. That week, there was dancing in every taproom in the village, with an accordion furnishing the music. A good time was had by all. On Friday, market day of that week, there also was a cattle show, and prizes were awarded to the winners. The last Sunday was family reunion. The one with the biggest room invited the whole family for dinner. On that occasion, the best in the house was displayed, like silverware, fancy dishes, and the like. We went to Mother's father's farm. Grandma sure knew how to give us a feast.

My Uncle Isidoor kept writing us regularly about his life and progress in New Jersey, U.S. of A. He was very happy to announce he was to be married to his boss's widow's oldest daughter, Emma, in the near future, and he wanted to know how I felt about coming over afterward. Everybody was surprised and happy about his good fortune. To become the owner, so to speak, of his own business in such a short time. His mother-in-law was not surprised. She saw in him, right from the beginning, that he was an able, sturdy, and hard worker—a man on whom she could depend after her misfortune.

We discussed the news that Sunday at home with my parents. Father told me that, if I set my mind on going to America to join my uncle, he would not stand in my way, and that I could keep and save my wages until I had sufficient money to pay for my crossing. From that day on, my heart was light and hopeful. Every week that went by was so much nearer to the fulfillment of a wonderful dream.

My mother's family was very pleased about my going, mostly for Uncle Isidoor's sake. He would not be alone there anymore. The day of my departure grew near. It was in the late fall. That week, I was busy packing my belongings—a few personal things besides my clothes. I was then nineteen years of age. The last week I stayed home. As the news spread among the neighbors, everyone came to wish me luck and say goodbye, many of them with the hope in their heart that someday they would be as lucky as I was to be able to come to the land of opportunity. I left Filippine on a Saturday morning on the early train to Rotterdam. Father took the day off, and Father, Mother, and my two brothers and two sisters all saw me off, some of them to join me later.

I arrived in Rotterdam around noon. A Holland-American guide took me to a large room in the enormous railroad station, where all other passengers to sail on the steamer were waiting. When we came back after dinner, our luggage was already taken care of, and we all marched to the ship in a body just a short distance away. All aboard amid the noise of steam cranes and grinding machinery. The loading was soon finished. Then a few last details, the blasts of the big steam whistle, and we shoved off. Soon after we sailed, supper was served. All passengers hurried up on deck after the meal to take a last glimpse of the homeland they were leaving, perhaps never to return. The crossing was uneventful. Very nice weather. It was stormy only a few days, during which time we stayed indoors.

There was quite a group of Hollanders. I made friends with quite a few of them, and we had plenty of fun. We played games on deck and took long walks. The days passed quickly. I got acquainted with two families who sat at my table during eating periods. They wanted to take me along to the state of Michigan to work on the farm. They would be glad to have me, but I told them I was heading for New Jersey to join my uncle on his dairy farm.

Eighteen days after leaving Rotterdam we arrived in New York. I shall never forget the sight—the ships in the harbor, the tall buildings, the noise, the great traffic on the Hudson River, the majestic Statue of Liberty inviting the many peoples of the earth to enter the gates of freedom and opportunity. So now I was in America. My dream came true.

Pretty soon the boat docked, and we third-class passengers were transferred to another ferry-like boat that took us to Castle Gardens. There interpreters took us into an immense hall with benches in the middle and around the walls. There we waited until our turn came for inspection by the immigration inspectors. I never saw such a scene in all my life—old people; young men and women with children from the different countries of Europe, loaded with bundles and grips; noise; dirty children, talking to others without understanding, crying and shouting—a veritable Babel. I was glad when our turn came.

From the inspection room, we again were put on a boat that took us to the Battery and into the wide world. My uncle had sent me a good-sized note with his name and address and the name of the station in Jersey City where I was to take the train to a little village outside of Paterson. When I arrived in Jersey City Station, the first thing I did was to send Uncle Isidoor a message telling him I was on my way on the last lap. When the train stopped at my destination late that afternoon, there he was waiting for me. With tears in our eyes, we fell in each other's arms. We loaded my trunk on the buggy, and away we went to my new life and home.

I was introduced to the family. His mother-in-law was a very friendly woman, and my new Aunt Kate received me as if she knew me all her life. The next few days, we talked and talked about the family at home, the state of their health, and every little thing that happened since he left. We went to bed late every night for a week. I busied myself around the place. Although he wanted me to rest a while, I was not used to being idle, and I started right in. Before he died, his father-in-law was selling his dairy products to a wholesale firm that picked everything up in the morning. After my uncle took over, he talked things over with his widow, and she agreed he would go out himself early every morning with the milk, butter, and eggs and start a retail business—more money, you know. So he started to go to Paterson with his clean, fresh products. Before long, he had a number of steady, everyday customers, who found it very convenient to find their fresh milk, butter, and eggs right at their back doors, even before they got up in the morning. Long before I came, he could not accept new customers because he could not do the work without help. A week later, Uncle Isidoor bought two new cows, and as his business increased, so did his stock. When he had twenty cows, we had our hands full, and he stopped increasing his herd. We had a flock of five hundred Plymouth Rocks.[15] My aunt took care of them. She loved that, especially collecting the eggs. Nobody else could do it. We all worked hard, but we were happy and contented.

On Sunday, I helped Uncle on his route so we both could go to church—he to his and I to mine. The others in the family went to the village nearby. It was the same every day of the year—work today, tomorrow, all the time. There was very little amusement but what we got out of our labor. We did not ask for other kinds of amusement. I, for one, did not care. I was used to it. We had plenty of fun evenings after supper. Our work was arranged so we had everything finished by supper time. After that, we read the daily paper; we played games, smoked, and talked together; and so the days passed. I loved my work because it was so much like home to me. It was practically the same as home. Uncle Isidoor was my teacher there, and I was teacher's pet. Here we worked together again, same as before. Besides, Aunt Kate, Nellie, and their mother treated me as one of their own.

In the summer, Uncle Isidoor and I went fishing many times together in good lakes and streams nearby. Sometimes, I went alone and was always happy to bring home a good string of fish. I cleaned it right away, and, as every one of us loved fried fish, we had it for breakfast in the morning. So it was during hunting season. My grandfather gave one of his shotguns for a present. Many a crisp morning I got up early, took my gun, hunted for a couple of hours in the nearby woods, and came home in time for breakfast with one or more rabbits or pheasant, which my aunt prepared for our supper. It was enjoyed by all.

Uncle's mother-in-law, whom I called Grandma, reminded me so much of my own mother. She did almost everything like her, especially her cooking. I loved the raisin bread she made, her pies and cookies, and those same delicious meat gravies, just like home. One big reason why I was so contented, I did not want to go out. Girls did not attract me, nor any other amusement. I put on my best clothes once a week to go to church. Outside of that, I did not need any Sunday clothes. My leisure hours were spent on the lakes and in the woods.

I was paid ten dollars per week and my board right from the start. I wrote a letter home every other week to keep my family informed of what was going on and sent a ten-dollar money order, which I never forgot, for the first two years. My parents wrote back to me that I should keep the money, that it was not necessary, and that they did not need it. But I insisted that they take it; I did not need much money. Clothes I did not buy often, and there was nothing else hardly to spend it on. So I saved it in the bank. I wore wooden shoes around the farm. They kept my feet warm and dry. We bought them from a man in Paterson who used to make them in Holland. It was just about three years after Uncle's marriage that a little baby boy was born to my Aunt Kate—eight pounds of noisy and kicking humanity, as healthy as could be. They had reserved the services of a good Holland midwife for the occasion, and between the two of them, they had a great time. Grandma took full possession of the baby and was crazy about it. It was the same with the other children that came around—six more, two boys and four girls. They all grew up with me, and, naturally, I was very much attached to them all. They called me Uncle Albert, and I played with them and took walks with them as soon as they could stand on their own legs. They came to me when in trouble and whenever they got hurt. I took them on my lap, and the pain was soon forgotten.

On Sundays, I took them for a ride in the country in the buggy. That gave their mother a couple hours of rest in the afternoon. I sure had a grand time with those kids. Later, when they started to go to school, on rainy days or bad weather I drove them to school and back home. I really spoiled every one of them. So, even today, don't ever say anything about Uncle Albert unless it's good.

In the meantime, Uncle's sister-in-law, Nellie, got married to a young man whose father had a big farm nearby. They had been going together for a couple of years. On their wedding day, we all went down to the groom's house, sat down to a swell dinner, and had a real good time. They received a bunch of beautiful presents from relatives and friends. I bought them each a comfortable easy chair, which they are still enjoying. They ask me once in a while why I don't get married so they can buy me a present, too. But I tell them I did not meet the right partner yet. They live with their parents and are very happy. Every Sunday evening, they come over for a while. Sometimes, they walk down during the week and stay a while. We all like her husband. He is a fine man. I don't have to tell you; he is a Hollander, too. That is one thing about our people—they will not intermarry as long as there is a Hollander left.

I became an American citizen within the next few years. When the United States declared war on Germany, I enlisted in the army. I was put in the commissary department in Camp Dix. Not long after, they put me in charge of the food stores, but I wanted to go overseas. I asked for a transfer, but I was told to wait. I stayed at camp for three years. One day, my superior asked me if I would like to take horses over to France. I accepted with enthusiasm. I was away from the farm, and I missed everybody terribly, but this was a change. This was different, and I welcomed a change. I made six round trips to Le Havre, when the armistice was signed and the war ended. I stayed on a couple of days to help celebrate. Everybody was crazy—French and English and Americans. All suffering was forgotten again.

My first thought was for home in Holland. I was in France now and not so far from home—just a couple of miles across the Belgium frontier. I thought I would ask for a furlough. Yes or no, I would take a chance anyway. So I went to see my superior officer, to whom I explained the situation. He said he could hardly refuse my request at a time like this, so he granted me thirty days' leave. The next thing was to find out how to get there. So I started out. I caught a supply train to the Belgium frontier at Roubaix. The next day, a half-dozen trucks started for Ghent in Belgium, and I got a ride—one of the roughest in my life. In Ghent, I bought an old bicycle from a Belgium soldier and pedaled home. I was not used to it anymore, so I was dead tired when I got there. I had a little trouble getting across the Belgium frontier into Holland, but a lot of people recognized me after I told them who I was. And my American uniform helped me, too. So over I went, and in fifteen minutes I was hugging and kissing my own mother and father. Oh boy, did I surprise everybody, and was everybody happy! My mother's parents were now enjoying a peaceful old age and could not keep their eyes off me. Then, to my father's family. Everybody was so happy. It took me a week to get around. In that thirty days, I never went to bed before one o'clock in the morning. We talked of everything, of all the things that happened in the past. The only one home with my parents was my sister Martha. She was still single and took care of Father and Mother. Father retired from the mill and received a pension. My brothers and other sisters all married and had growing families. I had a number of new relatives, whom I now saw for the first time in my life.

I will never forget that furlough. Those thirty days went like the wind, and believe me, it was a sad parting from all your loved ones.

Ever since the day I left them for the second time, I knew it was a mistake for anyone to go to another country and leave parents and loved ones behind. I almost gave in to the temptation to stay home again.

I said goodbye to all, three days before the end of my leave. Things were getting organized already. Trains were running, but not very often. The first day, I got as far as the French frontier. All during that day, I got off and on several trains and never saw a conductor. It did not cost me a penny to go home, outside of my food. The nicest part of my journey was made by American army trucks. The roads in the north of France were full of them. It was more than a month later that I took my ship back home, probably with the same horses I brought over before.

We landed in Newport News in January. It was terribly cold that day. We went to bed right after supper. Everybody was tired, but glad to be back. Time dragged from then on, waiting for my discharge. When it finally came, I hurried home as fast as I could. Before I went home to Holland, I wrote my uncle a postal card to let him know. When I got home, they were all anxious to know how everyone was getting along. I sat in the big chair that evening with a little girl on one knee and her little brother on the other, while I talked and talked until they fell asleep. For a whole week, we went to bed late; there was plenty to say. I did not start to work for another two weeks. I went to see all my friends and neighbors, who had invited me after my return. Then I was glad to go back to work. For a few days it was a little strange after the layoff, but it did not take me long before I was right back in form. During my absence, Uncle took on a young man from the neighborhood to help him in my place, and he was a very satisfactory worker. Between the two of us, the work was more divided and much easier. I had a little more time now, so I took advantage of it to whitewash the stables and the chicken coops, also to do a little repairing here and there, fixing up wagons and farm implements, and getting everything ready for the coming spring season.

The business was fine. Uncle was a good businessman, well liked wherever he went. He went around his route with an attractive and clean-looking wagon, pulled by two beautiful young and lively horses. The harnesses were cleaned and polished every day. He was proud of his whole outfit. Also, our farm was exemplarily clean at all times. In the summertime, a good many of our patrons paid us visits, mostly on Sundays, when they took rides in the country. They expressed their surprise at the tidiness all about the place and went away more than satisfied after their visit.

As life went on, all Uncle Isidoor's children received a good education. Roy, the oldest, liked the farm. After graduating from grammar school, he expressed his desire to stay home and help on the farm. His father was most happy for his decision, so he let him go along on his route. Very soon, he got to know every one of the customers. He was a very handsome and friendly kid and made a hit wherever he went. At the end of that summer, Uncle could take a day off once in a while. On a rainy day or in snowy weather, he stayed home and enjoyed the friendly, open log fire in the dining room and smoked his pipe in comfort. The other two boys, Jan and Peter, graduated from high school and got jobs in the city. Mary, the oldest, took a normal-school course and became a school teacher.[16] Katie studied for nursing and is now doing private work as a registered nurse. Nellie and Bertha are home and divide the housework, leaving Mother to do the supervising. The work, as a whole, is so evenly spread out that none of us works hard. We all have our tasks assigned to us, and we do them with a will.

We still have a lot of fun at home. We play games in the evening and talk about the war, the possibility of our mother country's involvement in the carnage, and the fate of all our relatives there. We most sincerely hope they can keep their neutrality intact. We very seldom talk about politics. We are a busy people with no time to bother with that. I, for one, am satisfied with the present order of affairs. I am a lover of peace; I hate arguments. That's the big reason why I am still a bachelor. But you never can tell. If I ever got lonesome—but I hardly think so with this happy crowd around.

Now the fifteenth of this month is the opening of the trout fishing season, and Roy is going to take off the first two days, and him and I are going out bright and early after the wily trout. So wish us luck because we will need quite a few for Tuesday's or Wednesday's breakfast. The pans are already greased. From now on, all my spare time will be taken up with my favorite sports. If you are a Walton disciple, you know how I feel.[17]

Jan got married a couple months ago, and I live with him. I have a nice big room and board there. I go up to the farm when I feel like. I got a little car to take me all over—at the farm, too. The horses are gone. Deliveries are made by truck with Roy at the helm. So, you see, I have nothing to worry about.

T he case histories of Jews in the New Jersey Ethnic Survey are a reminder that there were also deep divisions within ethnic groups, such as that between the German Jews and the Eastern European Jews. Even within the Eastern European Jews there were divisions between the Lithuanian Jews (known as Litvaks), the Galician Jews (called Galitsianers), the Rumanian Jews, the Hungarian Jews, the Ukrainian Jews, and the Byelorussian Jews. The level of identification was often even more local. First-generation Jews tend-

Jews

ed to associate with people from their own city or province, forming organizations known as *landsmanshafn* (hometown associations). Thus, within the overall group of Polish Jews, the Białystok Jews and the Łódźer Jews maintained their own identities. While some of these divisions continue today, they are not as widespread as they were before World War II.

The German Jews began arriving in the United States during the 1840s. Those who settled in Newark came primarily from Alsace-Lorraine, the western part of Germany, and Bohemia. They settled in the German Hill neighborhood, in the vicinity of Springfield and Belmont avenues, which became known as *Schmierkase* Country (a reference to the cottage cheese they ate). One German Jew, Louis Trier, came to Newark in 1844 and founded a small tannery. Others included a currier (a person who dresses and colors leather after it is tanned), a peddler, a cigarmaker, a basketmaker, a jeweler, a tailor, a trunk maker, and a grocer. There was even a German Jewish farmer—Isaac S. Cohen, who started his farm in 1847.[1]

By the early 1860s there were about two hundred German Jewish families in Newark. They became prominent in business, owning real estate, food stores, restaurants, theaters, and retail stores. In 1871 Leopold S. Plaut and his partner, Leopold Fox, founded L. S. Plaut and Company, which later became Kresge's Newark Department Store. Louis Bamberger, whose father came from Bavaria, Germany, and his brothers-in-law, Louis M. Frank and Felix Fuld, founded Bamberger's

Department Store in 1892. Bamberger became a major benefactor of Newark institutions, donating large amounts of money to help found the Newark Museum, the YMHA of Newark, the Beth Israel Hospital. In 1930 Bamberger and his sister gave five million dollars to Princeton University to establish the Institute for Advanced Study.[2]

In 1848 the German Jews in Newark founded Congregation B'nai Jeshurun (Sons of Righteous in Hebrew). It was described in 1939 as "the wealthiest Hebrew temple in New Jersey." In 1863 the congregation established a day school with instruction in German, English, and Hebrew. B'nai Jeshurun was originally an Orthodox congregation, but gradually from the 1860s through the 1890s it underwent a transformation to Reform Judaism, finally becoming affiliated with the Union of American Hebrew Congregations. The German day school was discontinued, and the congregation established in its place a Talmud Torah (a community Hebrew school).[3]

The history of the German Jews in Paterson followed a similar pattern. The German Jewish synagogue in that city was founded in 1847, and was also named Congregation B'nai Jeshurun. It, too, began as an Orthodox congregation and gradually moved toward Reform Judaism in the 1870s. In 1894 it moved to a new site on land donated by Nathan Barnert and was consequently renamed the Barnert Temple in his honor. As the profile of him in the New Jersey Ethnic survey indicates, Nathan Barnert was an important figure in Paterson's Jewish community. He was born in Posen, which today is the Polish city of Poznań, but in the nineteenth century it was part of Prussia. He went to California during the gold rush and then settled in Paterson, where he made his fortune. Barnert was elected mayor of Paterson three times, and, like Bamberger in Newark, he was the foremost Jewish benefactor in Paterson. Besides donating land to the Reformed Jewish congregation, he donated land and/or money for the establishment of the Miriam Barnert Hebrew Free School (named after his wife), the Barnert Memorial Hospital, and the Daughters of Miriam Home for orphans and the elderly.[4]

Beginning in the 1880s Jewish immigration to the United States shifted to Eastern Europe. Their emigration was caused in large part by a series of pogroms. Between 1881 and 1921 there were a series of such anti-Jewish riots in Russia. Unlike the German Jews, the Eastern European Jews spoke Yiddish (sometimes simply called Jewish), which is a dialect based on the medieval German dialect of the Rhine Valley, written with Hebrew script, and containing some Hebrew, Russian, Polish, Czech, Lithuanian, and Latvian words. Between 1877 and 1907 the Jewish population of Newark increased from thirty-five hundred to thirty thousand as a result of this Eastern European Jewish immigration.[5] They settled in the vicinity of Canal and Mulberry streets, and then began to spread out into the Third Ward, especially in the vicinity of Prince Street, which, like Hester Street on New York City's Lower East Side, became famous for its pushcart peddlers. The Polish Jews founded their own synagogues, such as Congregation B'nai Abraham established in 1855.[6]

In Paterson, as the New Jersey Ethnic Survey case histories show, the German Jews, the Russian Jews, and the Polish Jews had their own neighborhoods and institutions. The German Jews owned many of the stores on Main Street and lived on the affluent East Side. The Russian Jews were peddlers, either junk peddlers or custom peddlers who sold dry goods, such as clothing and linens. The Russian Jewish peddlers lived along the Passaic River, where they had their own synagogue, or *shul*, which was called the "Junkman's shul." The Polish Jews came after 1900, primarily from the Polish textile centers of Łódź and Białystok and settled on and around River Street in Paterson. One Jewish woman said (in a fragmentary case history not included in this collection) that "in Łódź, when one spoke of America, they referred to Paterson." These local identities among Polish Jews were expressed in their many landsmanshafn, including the Bialystoker Society, the Lodzer Sick and Benevolent Society, the Independent Lodzer Young Men, the Ozorkower Society, and the Pabianitzer Society.[7] According to Irving Howe, these landsmanshafn were "probably the most spontaneous in character of all their [the immigrant Jews'] institutions, and the closest in voice and spirit to the masses."[8]

The Polish Jewish textile workers in Paterson brought with them a socialist tradition that contributed to the labor movement in that city. The Workman's Circle (Arbeiter Ring), which was a Jewish socialist fraternal organization founded in the United States in 1900 to provide mutual aid and health and death benefits to its members, had numerous branches in Paterson, including a women's branch. In 1904, in response to increases in the price of bread, the Workman's Circle established the Purity Cooperative Bakery. A Workman's Circle children's school was opened in 1921 in Paterson, providing a secular Jewish education. Also active in Paterson was the International Workers Order (IWO), which was established in 1930 by dissident Communist factions within the Workman's Circle who decided to have their own fraternal order. In 1954, the IWO was broken up by the federal government as a subversive organization. One especially interesting organization was the Freiheit Gesang Ferein, or Paterson Jewish Folk Chorus as it was later called, which was founded in 1915. This chorus sang labor protest songs in Yiddish and, later, in both Yiddish and English. Many of its singers were also members of the IWO.[9]

The New Jersey Ethnic Survey also contains one particularly interesting case history that pertains to neither Newark nor Paterson. It is the life story of a Ukrainian Jew from Odessa who settled in one of the Jewish agricultural colonies in southern New Jersey. These colonies, founded in the 1880s and 1890s, included the towns of Alliance, Rosenhayn, Carmel, Norma, Brotmanville, Mizpah, Six Points, Estellville, Hebron, Garton Road, and Woodbine. They were funded by German charitable societies, such as the Baron de Hirsch Fund, as a more wholesome alternative to the city ghettoes in which Eastern European Jews were settling. Active in this movement was American-Jewish intellectual Michael Heilprin (1823–1888), who was born in Poland, lived in Hungary, where he was active in the revolution of 1848, and came to the United States in 1856. The agricultural colonies died out because they had problems convincing the younger generation to remain in farming.[10] One historian argues that the Jewish agricultural colonies appealed to German Jewish philanthropists as a way to Americanize the Eastern European Jews.[11]

Lived More Than a Thousand Years

This woman was very good-looking. She is tall and strong. She seems able to fend for herself and make the best of opportunities. She must have been remarkably attractive at one time, because she can still make a man spin. She speaks in a rather nasal tone and hurriedly. She sang a few Jewish folk tunes at my request and has a rather pleasant voice. She seems to be capable and resolute and has a tendency, I believe, towards strongheadedness. I think she must have her way and will not compromise. She is hospitable and kind. She had a huge portrait of herself that some artist friend had done in New York some eight years before. She is very proud of it and made sure I saw. She dresses well, if not a bit stodgily. Her attire smacks a bit of the oldish European mode, with high frilled collars attached to her dress. She has a fine throat, and her dress if poorly adapted to her physical qualities. She reads many newspapers, which clutter up her room. I noted this and also the interesting fact that she must write. I saw a typewriter in her room with many sheets of typed material strewn about. The woman she lives with sat in on the interview. When the respondent had to leave for a moment, the other woman told me she was a very nice person, with whom you can get along.

I am close to forty years old, and I have lived more than a thousand years during my life. When I was a little girl, I knew what it was to suffer. During the war, we lived like dogs, running from one cellar to another —first to get away from the Cossacks and then the Polacks. My father and mother were both killed by soldiers who didn't like Jews. I was young, but I will never forget these things. My brother had to go and fight for the Tsar. My younger brother we got out of the country, and he came to America. He lives in Detroit now. My older brother, the one who was in the army, lives in Newark. My father was a blacksmith and made a pretty good living before the war came. All the farmers came to him with their horses. I went to school and learned to speak a very good Russian. I never knew how to speak Jewish until I came to America years later. I had a good voice when I was a child, and I used to sing for the family. My older brother had a very good voice, too, and we used to sing together. My father liked to hear my sing. He was very good to us. He was not an Orthodox Jew. My mother was very religious and taught me how to light candles and say prayers on Friday night.[12] I always thought it was foolish. After he died, I never did it anyway.

I had a young cousin who was in the Tsar's army. He was killed during the beginning of the war, and my aunt—his mother—almost went crazy. She didn't live very long after this. Most of the young men of our village were killed off at the beginning of the war. They used to take almost children to fight. In our village, one of the young men cut off his trigger finger and tried to make it look like an accident. Other men had done this before, and the Russian officers knew all about it. They gave him a trial for about fifteen minutes, and they took him outside of town and shot him. We had to carry him back and bury him, or he would have laid there until he got rotten. After the first year, nobody wanted to go to the front. Nobody saw any reason to fight. My village was alright the first few years. There was no fighting near us, and we found enough to eat. Near the end of the third year, the German army began to march into our land, and then the real fighting began. Our village saw armies marching through all the time, and all of them were hungry and took our last piece of bread. The German soldiers paid for what they took. They were good to us and didn't bother the women. The Polish soldiers used to steal from the Jews, and the women suffered from them. If you didn't want to give them something to eat, they would shoot you like a dog. There was no law when they came into a village. The Russian soldiers were not so bad at first; but later, when they began to lose, they were disgusted, and they didn't care what they did.

After the war, I went with my older brother to Poland, and we lived there for about nine months. From there, we went to Germany, and there I met my husband. He was from Rumania. We became good friends and went to America together. We lived at first in New York, where I married him. We were very good friends. In New York, we had a lot of friends after a while. We went to parties and to the theater with them. We only used to enjoy together. We lived in New York a few years, and then my husband got a job in Newark, and we moved here in the Clinton Hill section in a nice apartment. We fixed up the house, and we lived a good life together.

I am not a person who makes a fuss over people. My friends think I am a cold person. I am not, but I don't like to make too much noise and fuss. I like people, and I like to sit in a group and sing the old songs from Europe. I learned to speak Jewish when I began to sing with a Jewish choir in New York. I belong to a choir now in Newark. My husband and I are separated now. We have been this way for two years now. I live here with my friends. I am used to it now, but at first I was almost crazy. You can get used to anything after a while. Even if you are not too much in love with a person, when you have lived together for fifteen years you get used to one another. I have no children. I do not care too much for children, and I never wanted any. My friends can have the children if they want to; I have no patience for them. I like to be free to go when I want to. I see my husband once in a while, but there is nothing there now. I worked for a while in a dry goods store, and the people were very nice to me. I am working now in a garment factory on Elizabeth Avenue for an Italian boss. The girls like me. Once I didn't get along very good with the women. Now, I guess I am getting older, and they like me more. What do you think? I am nice? I am glad to know it. It is no good when a woman gets old and the other women begin to like her. The girls in the shop come to me and talk about everything. It is slow season now, and I'm looking for something in New York. If I can find it, I will move to New York. I do not like Newark too much now. I haven't friends in New York now, but I will find them. I like to sing, and I will belong to the choir in New York when I go there. I would not get married again, but I would like to have a friend. I like to tell the truth to people, and some people don't like this. They think I am too much like a man. I say what I feel. I am not ashamed.

Irving Zuckerman

To Know What Education Means

A Jewish-Ukrainian female, about twenty-four or twenty-five

I was born in Odessa on the Black Sea. When I was just a little girl, the most exciting experience I remember was my schooling. You see, we had to study behind closed curtains and in a basement of our district rabbi's home. One day, the police came, chased all of us kids out, and took our teacher away. Later, we learned he was sent to Siberia for ten years. Imagine. Just for teaching us, he was exiled for ten years.

Naturally, when my parents came to the United States they appreciated the free school system. I graduated high school here long ago. And my elder brother is a college graduate who took to law. He is now a fine lawyer. Believe me, if Americans had to pay the price for education like the Russian or Ukrainian Jews did in the old times, they would know what education means.

Another exciting experience I had as a little girl in Russia (Ukraine) was when my father decided to move the family into a small town called Alexandrovsk, where Jews were not supposed to live in those days. We had to move across the border of the province at night and through swamp land. My mother nearly died from pneumonia, when we got to Alexandrovsk. I was very ill, too, from dampness and cold in the night. But we got through the lines, undetected by government officers; and, believe me, I have never forgotten that night of hell and freezing. It was late in the fall.

That is all I can tell you that may be of interest. Remember, education of the Jews in Old Russia was practically a criminal offense. One had to get it on a steal, and many Jewish teachers paid dearly for their part. If education meant anything, it meant suffering and persecution in Old Russia. If Bolsheviks lifted that one point off the Jewish population, the revolution was worthwhile. But I have an idea the persecution of the Jews to some extent is still going on in Soviet Russia.

A. Basil Wheeler

Lived from Hand to Mouth

This interviewee seemed keen about the idea of offering me his biographical sketch. Although he appeared to be a man who is ordinarily suave and self-assured, when I approached him with the idea of the interview, he expressed an interest that bordered at times on the verge of plain conceit. He was tall and somewhat Semitic in his features. He was sallow enough to be mistaken for an Arab, had he but worn the customary turban. He spoke slowly and enunciated each syllable. As he spoke, he drummed his desk with his forefinger, with which he is no doubt concerned because, as the others, it was well manicured and boasted a large ring with a birthstone. That to me seemed a bit ostentatious. He interjected every other remark with asides, which the more fastidious among us might have considered pornographic. At times, he became so obsessed with what he wanted to say that he stopped talking for the moment and seemed completely entranced. It seemed that he was a bit affected when he recalled his early suffering. All in all, however, he was courteous and considerate throughout the interview. His office was large and very neat. The furniture was not cheap and was well selected. However, he seemed out of place behind his large mahogany desk.

I was born in Russia thirty-six years ago and came to this country at the age of seven. In Russia, I remember not having enough to eat. We were a family of eight. I remember living in a house with no floor. We were jammed into two rooms. We slept above an old country stove to keep warm. I remember my mother taking all of us in great haste outside of the village in which we lived. She anticipated a pogrom the following day. Pogroms were frequent in our village.

My father left for the United States when I was two. When I was three, my three older sisters also left for the United States. Later, we followed and landed in New York in 1911. We moved to the East Side, where the entire family, including my father, were reunited. We lived in a four-room railroad flat. The younger children slept on the floor. The older children doubled up in the available beds, which cluttered up the two bedrooms. The toilet was in the yard, and there was no hot water.

My sisters worked fifteen hours a day in a dress shop. They had to supply their own machines. When the season slacked in one shop, they had to cart their machines in a pushcart to another shop. During the busy season, for about four months out of the year, there was ample food in the house. During slow season, which was the balance of the year, we lived from hand to mouth. We were evicted from two places for nonpayment of rent. I remember some very bitterly fought needle-trade strikes, in which my sisters were involved.

My three older sisters sacrificed opportunities to be married at an early age in order that their younger brothers should have an opportunity to receive an education, of which they were deprived. Father was an Orthodox Jew. We were sent to religious schools. This education was stopped, as far as I was concerned, at the age of twelve, when I went to work in order to help support the family. I continued to go to school during the evenings. I went through high school and for a short time attended college.

I did not know there was such a thing as pajamas until I was sixteen. Did not sleep in a bed until I was sixteen. Until that time, I slept on the floor or on a bed composed of chairs and the extension boards from our dining-room table. One of my older sisters once treated my mother to some fancy vegetables by bringing home a bunch of celery. Never having seen celery before, Mother thought they were flowers and put them in a vase in the center of the table. My first job was as a printer's devil.[13] After that, I was a shipping clerk, an errand boy, and a salesman. I trouped with a dramatic group. I was also a longshoreman, a plumber, a roofer, and an auto mechanic. At the age of sixteen, following one of the strikes in which my family was involved, one of my sisters, who had become a Socialist, enrolled me in the Rand School of Social Science. Here I took some courses under Scott Nearing and Nellie Seeds Nearing.[14] From this developed my conscious interest in the problems of the working people. We never had money for the movies. In the summertime, if we went to Coney Island once, it was a real treat. As for my conscious interest and active work in the labor movement, that started at the age of twenty-two. I was out in Seattle, Washington, at this time, and I became involved in a strike purely out of interest in helping the people who were out. It only amounted to being on the picket line. I was not employed in the shop. I returned to New York in 1924, and I was involved in the unemployment demonstrations of 1930, 1931, and 1932. I participated in street meetings on the waterfront at this time, too. I helped organize the longshoremen, and I spent several years organizing youth clubs. I also spent a short time doing club work for a Jewish settlement house. I did some statistical work at one time for a Jewish education institution in New York.

I have been married for thirteen years, and I have two children. One is ten and a half; the other is seventeen months old. The reason for the gap in ages is purely economic. During the intervening period there was never sufficient money for the support of more children. My wife has worked the greater portion of our married life. I have been a professional organizer in the labor movement for the major portion of the period since 1931.

Irving Zuckerman

America Is a Man's World, Too

This woman was very short and almost as large around as she was tall. Her features, however, were quite lovely. She has eyes that constantly express affection and sympathy. You might say that they were the eyes of one who has truly suffered. She has a powerful jaw line and a particularly broad forehead. She appears to be a woman who might have once possessed a great will and determination. Now, because of her illness no doubt, her throat is flaccid, and her skin has a tendency to droop. She speaks very quietly, and it is difficult at times to hear her. She does not speak at all times articulately, which conveyed to me not a speech difficulty, but a nervous condition. She wandered occasionally in her speech before the interview. During the interview, however, she made a great and intensive effort to stick to the point. It was a slow and painful process, but she succeeded admirably. She was very neat and well-dressed. Her home was very clean and tidy. She was polite and offered me tea. As she spoke, she occasionally looked toward the top of the room. I think she may have been attempting to suppress a tear. She was sad and sometimes bitter. I don't recall that she smiled once. A few times she may have been somewhat wistful, when she recalled her early days in her father's house—the time she smoked a cigarette, one of many she had made for her father. At one time, this woman must have been thoroughly charming.

I am forty-nine years old; I was born in a small town in the Ukraine. I had three sisters and one brother. My father was a businessman; he sold wine and whiskey. We were very rich, and I went to a very good tutor. Almost fifty men worked for my father. My father was a very educated man, and he wasn't a fanatic. He dressed like the men in the city. Many people came to visit us and to talk to my father. I used to make cigarettes for my father with a small machine. It was the same as the machines you can buy in Newark today. It used to roll the cigarette. Once I tried to smoke one of them, and I got very sick. My mother wanted to kill me. My father was not religious, and I never went to Hebrew school. I studied with private teachers, and I spoke very good Russian.

When I was sixteen, I went around with a young man; I think I was in love with him. I didn't know then what this meant. If I did, I think I would have stayed in Russia. He was very smart. He was a writer. I don't mean that his writing was printed. He used to write poetry. We read together from Pushkin.[15] I would sing to him. Today, I sing in a Jewish choir here in Newark. I am a contralto today. In Russia, when I was a young girl, I was a very good soprano.

When I was eighteen, I went to a dental school in Kiev. My older sister went too, but she didn't like it and stayed only a few months. I stayed for two years, studying mechanical work. I learned to make teeth and plates. Not many girls were lucky enough to learn such a trade in Russia. The tools cost a fortune, and my father spent a lot of money to educate me. In school, I had a very good friend; we lived together. She was not as rich as me, and I helped her to buy many tools. Her family lived near Kiev, and we visited there many times. I met her brother, who was very quiet. I went out with him many times. Most of the time, I paid for both of us. I stayed in Kiev for a year after I finished school. I looked for a job, but I couldn't find one. My friend and her brother wanted to go to America. I read about America, and I decided to go, too. We went together. My mother cried, but she let me go. I think my father's heart was broken, but he bought me a complete set of dental tools and hoped I would find work in America. He asked me if I loved my friend's brother. I told him no. He said that I should not think about marriage until I learned to take care of myself. My friend was a very good mechanic. Her brother was a paperhanger and a house painter.

When we got to America, my friend met a businessman, and they got married. They went to Milwaukee, where her husband had a delicatessen business. They had one daughter together, but she died very young. I was all alone, and I married her brother. I cannot say I was too much in love; but we were both lonely, and we thought it would be better to live together. We went to Cleveland, and here my daughter was born. I almost died in childbirth; I was very sick for months. I could not nurse my baby, and she was not a very healthy child. When she was not even a year old, she got a chill; and since then she has had very bad eczema on her arms and neck. She gets her attacks during the summer, when her skin gets very dry. We went to every doctor, but it cannot be cured. She suffers.

My husband was sick all the time, too. He is a very nervous man and was complaining all the time of having snakes in his stomach. We went to the Mayo brothers, and it cost us over two thousand dollars to cure him.[16] He was operated on a few times. The doctors said it was more nervousness than anything else. They operated on his appendix and then his gall bladder. The second operation was needless, but he complained so much that they operated only to satisfy him. I don't think they touched anything. Afterwards, he said he felt better. Doctor Mayo told me that if he ever complained again, I should take a whip and beat him until he stopped. I laughed at this, but I wonder sometimes if the doctor was not serious. Later, my husband got lockjaw and wanted to jump out of a window. He said all the time that he was going to do this, and my life was very bitter. My husband wasn't stingy, but even when he earned good money—sometimes seventy dollars a week as a paperhanger—he did not like to buy things for the child. She never had toys like other children. I used to make her playthings out of rags. My husband said it was a waste of money to buy such things; it would spoil the child. On his own brother he spent over five hundred, when his brother came to live with us from Russia. He is a very strange man.

My daughter was my whole life. I used to read to her in Russian. She did not understand me, but she always wanted to hear me read. I had good books from the old country. Here are some. (*Note: She had works in Russian—excellent volumes by Tolstoy, Dostoevsky, Pushkin, Turgenev, and others.*)[17] My daughter recited and sang like a big person.

We lived in Cleveland until she was nine. Then, we moved to Twelfth Street, Newark. My sister lived here with her husband and two sons. They were very good boys. They worked after school to help their father, who was a peddler. I went to night school in Newark for a year, and I learned to write English a little and read. I tried to find a job in my trade, but they would not take a woman. America is a man's world, too. I did some work for my neighbors. I make good teeth. We bought a machine. I cost eighty-five dollars. I never made enough to pay for it. My daughter went to the South Seventeenth Street School. The principal loved her. His name is Murnaghan. When she graduated, he kissed her and said she was going to be a wonderful woman. Her teacher cried when she left. She went to the *mitlshul* of the Workman's Circle.[18] Her teacher here, Mr. Simon, thought she was a very good student. She can speak and write Yiddish as well as I can. She acted in a Jewish play, when she graduated from the mitlshul.

We moved to Irvington, and my daughter had to transfer from West Side High School to Irvington High. She did not like it here, but she got along with the other students. They were mainly Christian. They invited her to parties once in a while, but not too much. When she graduated, she sang in the operetta. She has a wonderful voice. After she graduated, she worked in a five-and-ten for a few months, and then she worked in Bamberger's for about a half year. She did not like to be a salesgirl, and she cried more than once. She met a girl who was a model for photographers and painters, who made a lot of money for a young woman. Before I knew what had happened, my daughter was a model, too. At first she modeled without my knowing about it. Then, one day, the father of the other girl came to my house in great anger and said to me that my daughter was leading his daughter from a good path—that my daughter had made his daughter into a model. I almost fainted, when he showed me pictures of both of them naked. He told me that he followed them and found them both on High Street at a photographer's club, modeling for a man, naked. I chased him from my house. I was heartbroken. I begged my daughter to stop modeling, but she didn't want to stop. She said it was decent. I had a nervous breakdown for almost a year. Even now I'm not so well. She works for the WPA now. She gives us few dollars a week. How much can she give with such a job? She is a clerk on the library project. I am sick most of the time. When she became a model, I was in bed for over two months. I never was so sick in my life. Maybe if my husband was a stronger man, he could have stopped her. She has a very strong mind, and she is a very stubborn girl. That was four years ago. Now, I am afraid to stay in the house alone. My hands are weak, and I can't do housework like I used to. I make a few teeth once in a while, but I think this is a man's world; and even they are bitter, too. My husband works day and night for a boss painter in Morristown. When he gets home at night, he is so tired sometimes he doesn't eat, but reads a few minutes and goes right to sleep. I pity him. My daughter goes with a young man. He's a salesman for a cosmetics company. He doesn't make much, and they can't get married; I wish they could. My daughter isn't getting younger. I sing in a chorus and I belong to the Workman's Circle. I used to be secretary of my branch, but now I can't go to meetings as much as I used to. My husband belongs to the IWO. He is insured by them. But he never goes to meetings. He is not a sociable man; he doesn't like to be with people. Once in a while, we go to a friend's house. He likes to play cards. This is our only pleasure. What more can I tell you?

Note: I asked her about her political outlooks. She said she had no interest one way or the other. She said that she would rather I didn't mention it.

Irving Zuckerman

Never Turned Down a Dare

This young girl aroused my sympathy as nothing else ever has. She has the loveliest face I could ever hope to see. It is placed on a body that has been cruelly deformed around the back by a treacherous accident in her youth. As she walks towards you, you cannot see the hump. Her body in front is shapely and pleasant. Her face is lovely, and she smiles at you in a very shy and awkward sort of way. It is only when you have seen her back that you begin to understand the smile. She is always self-conscious, even with those she knows quite well, she told me off the record. She made me promise that I would not inject any sympathy for her into my interview. She spoke well and reflected upon her life clearly and rationally. She is not given to eccentricities or uneven temper. She is calm and sometimes a bit defiant. She can be hypercritical in a most caustic way. She likes people in a general way. I took her to lunch before the interview, and she insisted on paying for both of us. She likes to feel that she can do things for people. I think she likes to feel that people may perhaps lean on her for certain things.

I was born in Newark on Eleventh Street, August 23, 1917. They tell me I was a very spoiled child; I always wanted my own way. I was very devoted to my father. I remember his taking me to the West Side Park, where he rolled me in the grass and played with me. I never wanted to go out with the family. I always wanted to stay home, and I used to insist that the family stay home, too, even on Sunday night—the night they all liked to go out together.

My father used to tell me stories of his childhood. He used to tell me about his youth, his experiences when he worked in the forests of Lithuania. My grandfather, who was in the lumber business, owned a lot of territory. My father worked for him. He used to tell wonderful stories of the forest. They were beautiful stories, and I never got tired of them.

I was never particularly fond of school—not in the early grades anyway. I resented being imprisoned, more or less. I was always a little afraid of the teachers—afraid of not being in step with the rest of the kids. I think that ever since I was a little kid I've had a terrific inferiority complex—never sure of myself. I changed schools often. I was pretty good in my lessons. I was tops as far as athletics were concerned. I loved gym. I was pretty much of a tomboy.

I never turned down a dare, which was the beginning of the end for me. I went roller skating down a very steep hill one day and ran into a Mack truck. I never took another dare. I was never able to again—not one that had to do with athletics. I injured my back. After that I stopped taking gym. Everything I was most interested in—sports, athletics, playing with the kids—I had to give up. I went to all kinds of doctors. I ended up wearing a cast for six years. I was in the hospital six months. I went through terrific agony, pain, and torture—and operations. I started high school, but I always felt that the kids were sneering at me, because I looked bulky because of the huge cast. Finally, I discarded the cast, and that business was all over as far as my ailment was concerned. But it left its scars. Then, came the depression. We lost our home in Irvington, which was very, very dear to me. My brother couldn't find a job in Newark, and he was very desperate, so much so that we were worried about him. Finally, he was offered a job in Texas; and when he was only nineteen, he left the house, leaving both my mother and myself heartbroken and close to a breakdown. We were always a very close-knit family, and this was practically the first major break in our unity. He remained in Texas a year. He worked in Dallas and came home by plane, sick and half-starved. We had to send him the money for passage.

When he left us, I was the only child in the house. At a very early age, I realized my responsibilities—always worrying where we were going to get our next meal from. My father became seriously ill—a nervous breakdown. There was no money in the house, and we went on relief. The relief check was very inadequate; it never provided half enough to offer food my father needed. We were pretty bitter during this period. I realized all this, and I tried to comfort them as much as possible. I had a girl friend, whose mother was very good to me. After school, she would invite me to her house for supper. She would talk to me and comfort me. We got to be great friends. I realized, too, that if I had supper there, it would save on food at home. I used to go there sometimes as much as three times a week.

Then, I graduated high school. My brother and I were very intimate and friendly. It was a very special kind of friendship we two had. I can't describe it. I don't know what it was, but it was swell. We never took each other for granted like most brothers and sisters. We always managed to retain interest in one another until he went away to Texas. We used to have swell fun together. He went to engineering school for a while. I used to do little things for him to help him out. After he came from Texas, I resented him very much. Through all this period of trial and tribulation, my mother and father and myself had become very closely knit. I felt that my brother was an intruder, but I got over it.

When I graduated high school, I got a job in Bambergers. I worked in the office for about four months. I didn't like my job a bit. I was very unhappy, and I injured my finger. I wasn't able to do the work as well as I could before I injured my finger. There was one girl who was my boss. She picked on me no end, and I used to go crazy. I was in a constant state of upheavel. I was fired at the end of the Christmas season, and I was delighted.

Then, I got on WPA in the Department of Agriculture. I liked my work, and I got along well with the people there. It was quite pleasant. My emotional life on WPA—and it may sound funny—became the transitional period in my life. I was laid off the agricultural project after eight months because of general reduction in forces. I waged a hectic struggle for eight weeks and finally got on the recreation project. But I didn't like working with children, and I got transferred to the city hall. Through these experiences in working with people, I've gotten to learn how to get along with various types of individuals. I met one girl in the city hall whom I disliked intensely. She was very gay and seemingly empty-headed. I can't have based my dislike on any particular reason; I had no grounds for it. She never did anything to me.

Then, we were transferred to the police department. Some of the cops were pretty nice; others weren't. Most of them were wolves where the girls were concerned. They pinched us when Sergeant X wasn't looking. X got a pinch in now and then, too, when the others weren't looking. They threw parties for us every once in a while. Christmas we planned a party, but we girls weren't paid. We were all blue and disappointed. About eight o'clock, we saw a big tray being carried in full of sandwiches. Sergeant X had bought them for us. We had a swell time. There were candy and drinks along with the sandwiches. When we were transferred to the police department, this girl and myself became very close friends. We're still friends. I'm as close to her as I could be to anyone. She turned out to be anything but flighty and empty-headed. It was all very pleasant—the happiest job I ever had. After we would come back from supper, we either sang or discussed current events. Sometimes, the cops would join us. I worked there for a year and a half.

Then, I was transferred to the planning project. I worked for the consultant director. He and I used to have very serious discussions on everything. I was quite interested in the social aspect of the work we were planning. He was the type of many who would advise young people because he thought it was for their benefit. Instead of encouraging me in my work, he would sit for hours and tell me what was wrong with it. The result was he broke down every bit of self-confidence that I had built up. When I first knew him, I had a lot of respect for him because of the education that he had and his prestige. When I have a lot of respect for people, I usually put them on a pedestal. Only he let me down tremendously. I was very upset over the possibility of leaving my job over the eighteen-month ruling.[19] I was discussing this with him one day, and he told me that I really had nothing to fear—after all, I had a home, a mother and father. We could always go on relief. After that, every idea I had about him was shattered. He had years and years of training in social science. He worked for the Chicago Commons. I had credited him with more intelligence than such a remark. After that, I refused to have any sort of discussion with him, and I did my work. I typed briefs that came through, and that was all. The last day I worked there, as a final gesture, he invited me and the other people who were being laid off to the Newark Athletic Club for luncheon. After luncheon, we were all saying goodbye to him. He shook my hand and his last words were, "X, be good to yourself!" That was all. My brother had married. We have drifted apart and have nothing in common. His unhappy marriage has made me somewhat cynical about marriage as a whole. It has taught me how to get along with men.

Irving Zuckerman

Always Lived in Dreams

This man was wizened and small. He couldn't have weighed a hundred pounds, yet he was equipped with tremendous energy and optimism. He was very genial and extremely friendly. He seemed to be trying very hard to josh me. At times he became profoundly serious, and he carried it well. He was poorly dressed, but neatly. He does not eat well. That is quite apparent. He takes himself and his relationship with life very earnestly. He does what he does in a thorough and competent way. He is one you feel you could rely on in a pinch. He looks as though he would be pretty tough in a scrap. He is sympathetic and possesses a psychological acumen that is really astonishing. He can measure a man in a flicker. He is a very sound judge of things and people.

I was born in Newark in 1898. The Third Ward at that time was a Jewish and Polish neighborhood. We lived in three rooms—a family of four. The toilet was downstairs somewhere. Everybody in the house used one toilet. My father worked at Public Service. He received fifteen dollars every two weeks. Later, my father, after a few years of working at Public Service, took ill, and I was compelled at the age of ten to go out and sell papers to support the family. I went to school as far as the eighth grade. That's about all as far as my youth is concerned.

The Third Ward had no playgrounds, and we used to play ball in the streets. Because of the poverty in the neighborhoods, most of the boys had to earn their living in any which way they could find. This toughened them up to the extent that some even went to the extreme of stealing and robbing. Fights on the streets were nothing unusual. Neighborhood gangs were being formed all the time, and got together and waged fights over anything at all—just for the fun of it. The homes in the ward were poorly built. Most of them were wooden frames with little or no fire escapes.

Some of the boys I played with are today leading citizens of the city. Judge S—— is one of them. The gang used to go out and steal bicycles and took tires off cars. We used to rob corn on Lyons Avenue, which was all farm area at that time. We used to hire a pushcart for ten cents and then sell it. Some of the boys were sent to reformatories. Some of these became hardened criminals to this day. Some of the boys were the best you could meet for a friend; but if you crossed them or did them dirt, they'd just as well cut you from ear to ear as look at you. They had a very hard sense of justice. They had a strong social sense, all of them. I was the smallest one of all, and many a time I was pushed through a drug store transom to "lift" alcohol, which we sold to make whiskey with. A few of the boys got the electric chair, but none of them were really criminals at heart. It was the poverty. When they got older, they became more friendly to one another in the neighborhood. They became like a big family. The playgrounds came when we were fully grown up. There was no relief at this time, and we were always dressed like bums and starved half the time. The parents never made enough to clothe and feed a family. We went hungry more than once with nothing at all to eat. Prince Street has always been a dirty street with pushcarts from Springfield Avenue to West Kinney Street.

I went to learn my trade at the age of sixteen. I was an apprentice for about four years. Later on, I began to work in various industries throughout the city of Newark. I advocated unions all the time and soon landed on the blacklist. Today, I still live in the ward and help out my father sometimes. He can't do much. He's a glazier and is very sick most of the time. I'm unemployed right now. I have to be on relief most of the time because I can't get a job in my craft. I guess I'm too stale to take a shot at it anyway. Yes, once I used to be a very skilled worker—a good machinist, if I say so myself. My father is a very Orthodox Jew. He's always having controversies with me over something. Not so much lately. He's too sick. We thought he was going to pass out only a few weeks ago. My mother is a very sympathetic soul who understands a problem much better than my father, who is very strict and cold.

Today, the housing conditions in the ward are not much better than they were when I was a young kid. Since I can remember, the homes haven't been fit to live in, and some of them, which were condemned when I was a kid, are still there today with people living in them. Nothing much has changed, except that on Spruce Street you have more liquor joints than ever before, and there has been in all this time a huge influx of people from the South. I guess today the population is 50 percent Negro. The same places that rented for twelve dollars a month once, cost twenty dollars and more a month now. These places aren't fit to live in anyway, but what can the people do? This housing project is pretty slow for the needs.

The trouble with me is I was never practical enough. I've always lived in dreams, seeing things which only today are beginning to come around. I worked on the ships and went to Europe from 1920 to 1922. I liked this life very much. I have gone through some of the most interesting parts of Europe—France, England, Germany, Sweden, Denmark, Norway. But in my travels in the United States, I've found it to be more beautiful than any other spot you could name. I've lived through Yellowstone Park. I've seen most of the state of Pennsylvania. I've also been through the Blue Ridge Mountains and the Allegheny Mountains. I've loved the scenery, like something I've never seen. I worked up in the Blue Ridge Mountains for a time, building munitions dumps during 1917. I've worked for Butterworth and Judson chemical works. I've seen men turn from white to yellow and pink from chemicals. I've seen men become tubercular, right before my eyes. I was a bathrubber too at one time and made some real dough at this, mainly because of the tips. It's shot now. Right now, I'd like to tell you more, but I can't think of it. Maybe some other time.

Irving Zuckerman

We Were Actually Desperate

This woman was portly and rather obtuse. She seemed to possess not even the slightest degree of sensitivity. She called to my mind people I have known who are concerned with nothing but their palates and their stomachs. People of this kind usually have one guiding principle, and that is themselves, absolutely nothing outside of themselves, and only that which serves to gorge themselves. She spoke hastily and seemed very anxious to impress me. I was very uncomfortable in her presence because I could feel a strong wave of concupiscence emanating from her. I was glad we were not alone. She seemed a veritable man-eater. She told me I could come again to get some more information from her. I have no doubt that her conception of life is at times very vulgar and contemptible. She was dressed in a housedress that could have used a washing. Her hair was unkempt, and I was completely revolted by the condition of her skin and teeth. She spoke English with an effort to be fancy.

I was born in the slums of New York. Due to an accident, my brother was killed in the slums, and we moved to a farm. Most of my childhood was spent on the farm—the usual farm routine. I was the oldest child of the family, and I had to help my mother and father with the farm work and the housework. I did most of the manual labor. There was always a mortgage to pay. My mother used to say the notes drove her crazy. We had a fire, and the barn burned down with the cattle. We were supposed to build a new barn with the insurance, but the mortgage company wouldn't give us a release. They wanted the insurance money to go towards the mortgage, and we were left out in the open. We had some stock left, and we didn't know where to house it. So we had to put them in an open shed during the whole winter. We suffered four years like that. We sold the place, and my father got a job in the Ford Motor Company. At that time it was in Kearny.

My father was very strict. In order to escape my strict homelife, I married. I married a man much older than myself, but he had a very good income at that time. Things went along alright for seven years. Then he got sick. We bought a little farm because he had to retire from work. We bought the farm for his health because the doctor said he had to rest and have plenty of fresh air. When he felt better, so that he could work, he couldn't get any work. He became very discouraged and got worse, and I had my hands full after that. I had my last two children, during this time. Things were very bad for us. They had a reverend out there in the country who took over the relief, and he'd tell the people he was giving them relief out of mercy. He refused us relief. At that time, you had to work for relief. My husband was willing to work for relief, but he couldn't do any very hard, physical labor. He was an accountant, but they wouldn't give him what he was fit to do. In the meantime, I had my last baby. Things were very bad. The baby almost passed away on us; we never had enough milk or food for it. My husband was very ill by now, and they refused him the proper food, which the doctor ordered. We were actually desperate.

Well, things got so bad that he got terribly sick, and he died. And I was left with four children—the baby barely seven months old, the oldest about twelve. The place was under foreclosure. I placed my children in a home—all except the baby— and I went to work. I had to take the baby to a nursery every day. The management of the home was so bad the children were very unhappy there. Thinking that I could make things better for them, I decided to take them home. The state board promised to give me as much as necessary to take care of them. After I took them home, they did what they wanted about everything. Nothing that they had promised did they give me. I was desperate and didn't know what to do. My baby was so sick from malnutrition that I had to send him to a preventorium in Farmingdale. He almost had the active tubercular germ. After he came home, the neighborhood to which we had moved was rotten and dirty. The children didn't have any room to play. I had to go to work, and I made them stay in the house. We lived on the third floor, and there wasn't much light in the house. I was forced to send the two young ones back to the home, so that I could work without worrying what they were doing when I was away. I have two in the home right now. My oldest girl can't get a job, and she worries me. She makes all kinds of remarks about doing anything for a little money. Life must be terrible for a young girl who can't find a job. We're on relief, and I get state board for one girl. I could tell you lots more, but that's all right now.

Irving Zuckerman

Tried Everywhere, but No Dice!

This was a very young woman. She was blond and extremely attractive. Her eyes were pale blue, and her figure has been well preserved for one who has undergone her kind of life. She was interesting and had much vitality. She appeared to have a strong desire for life and experience. Her attitude towards her child was that of a friend. Her child, a sweet little girl of five, addressed her by her first name. The atmosphere in the house was cheerful and intimate. The furniture was good, if a bit old and outmoded. The house was neat and well-ordered. Her relationship with her husband, despite their poverty of former days and the difficulties they are encountering today, seemed stable and of mutual comfort. All in all, I shared a feeling with them of utmost trust and confidence in themselves and in the future. Such a feeling may have been due to the feeling of warmth and sentiment that pervaded this home.

I was born in the heart of the Third Ward. I don't recall much about my early years, except that most of my activities were confined to playing with my sister and brother. My mother didn't like us to play with the other children. She thought that they were too rough and that they might spoil us. I think, however, that despite my mother's caution, I turned out to be quite a tomboy.

After my father had saved money from first sweeping floors in factories and then learning a trade, he decided to give in to my mother's lifelong wish of living where there were trees and flowers. They looked for a home in the suburbs, and they saved money. First my father swept floors, and then he operated a pleating machine in a cleaning and dyeing plant. With lots of skimping and doing without, they were able to save a little money. My mother had had a tendency towards tuberculosis in her youth, and two years spent in the Third Ward didn't help her condition any. They found a lot of land in Maplewood, which was then mostly woodland, and laid plans for building a little home. We children attended the school system of Maplewood, and the contrast was very marked. It was very difficult for us to adjust ourselves to playmates whose fathers were big executives in corporations, after having lived in a poverty-stricken area.

Life continued more or less quietly until I was in the fourth year of high school. Then, a new machine came out in the factory in which my father worked, which made it possible for any child to do his work. A young girl was hired at twelve dollars for a job at which he had formerly been paid seventy-five dollars. From then on, our economic conditions became difficult. The difficulty of paying taxes on our home forced the mortgage company to take away the house in which we lived. This was very hard on my mother because for ten years she had carefully and lovingly cultivated lovely plants and flowers surrounding the house. When we were children, we indulged in a sentimental pastime of buying my mother a plant every year at Mother's Day. She had planted these around one side of the house, apart from all the other flowers. When notice came for us to move, she asked the agents if she could please dig up the plants, which her children had given her over a period of ten years. They said no. It's part of the property as long as it's in the ground. And so my parents moved to an old deserted house on a dead-end street, which had formerly been the offices of a lumber-shipping company, where they live now.

My mother writes poetry in Jewish. She's been published in some of the Jewish dailies. She always nurtured a desire for the children to be artists of one type or another. Early in my teens, I attended the old Fawcett Art School in Newark, while at the same time keeping up my studies in school. A month before my graduation from high school, the stock-market crash forced me to go out and look for a job. I had already completed a course in fine arts and hoped to get work in that line. When I finally did get a job, after a six-month search, it was in a sewing factory at Eighty-eight West Market Street. I worked here several months making children's cotton dresses. My average salary was six dollars a week. I was laid off there and got a job at Del Pack on Central Avenue, Newark. My job consisted of making the flies on men's cotton pajamas at two cents a dozen. I worked here one week and received $4.92 a week.

Feeling that a change was necessary in my life, I got married. But the only change in my life, because of some very tough luck, was that I went to work in another factory. Two months after I was married, I discovered that I was pregnant. Because we had no money and lived in one little furnished room, I continued working in the factory. A month and a half before the baby was born, the boss told me that I could no longer do the work required of me. I went to the social service for help on my confinement. The hospital where I gave birth had a shortage of doctors and nurses, and my baby was delivered under the supervision of an intern. Not being able to afford her upbringing and not being able to go to work immediately, I was forced on the relief rolls. My mother offered to have me live with her in the five-room apartment that my sister, my brother, my father, my sister's child, and my mother shared. The three of us—my child, my husband and myself—moved in with them, making a total of eight. There was, naturally, a lot of crowding, and we weren't very happy.

Fortunately, I soon got a WPA job on the recreation project, and we were able to move. This job, plus the few pennies my husband made driving a cab, permitted us some comfort with the child. I worked there for two years and was then laid off under the eighteen-month clause. I have now been forced back on relief, but I hope to soon be back on the project. I've tried everywhere for private employment, but no dice! My countless searches for work have been in vain. My work on the project was interesting and creative. I was very much interested in it and should naturally like to continue it, if possible.

Irving Zuckerman

Pilfered Junk to Make a Few Pennies

I found this man to be very sober and quite absorbed in the serious-ness of his profession. He is a refreshing contrast to the "ambulance-chaser" type of legal mind that has cropped up in the past decade. His work is his passionate advocation, and his clientele are human beings with human qualities who are to be served and not mulcted. I enjoyed his company immensely. He is not sparkling or buoyant; but in his presence, I think one is inclined to feel a certain air of steadiness and confidence that is all so rare in our present milieu. He wears strong glasses, which indicates that he continues to burn the midnight oil in the earnest pursuit of his practice. He is about five foot six and of stocky build. He has pleasant features and an ingratiating smile. He likes to appear bucolic in his demeanor, but I'm afraid it doesn't work as he would like it to. He has a healthy outlook and disposition. This is a most startling virtue in a community and world which is so full of cynical barristers.

I was born in Newark thirty-four years ago. My parents were born in Austria. I lived in the Third Ward. It was a tough neighborhood; and, as kids, we pilfered junk to make a few pennies. A few of my friends were once arrested for stealing material from a wagon, with the owner unfor-tunately in seeing distance. We used to play in the lots with iron junk piled around, jumping from one pile to the other. Looking back at it now, I begin to realize how dangerous it all was.

Once, in matching our strength—I must have been about thirteen at the time—by throwing cobblestones, one of our boys struck another in the head with one of the stones. I'll never forget that incident. We were all arrested and held at headquarters for investigation, pending the boy's recovery. Of course, our families were all upset—very panicky.

They must have thought we were going to be electrocuted or something. Fortunately, however, the boy showed signs of recovery after a week, and we were reprimanded by the judge for not being more careful.

We had a boys' club—the McClellan Boys' Club of the Third Ward, founded by Thomas B. McClellan, principal of the Montgomery Street School. It was a boys' club to better the conditions in the ward, and it served a very good purpose until it was disbanded. There's a move afoot right now to revive the club.

I remember distinctly the first call that came out announcing the armistice. It was the false armistice of 1918.[20] I couldn't realize the full significance, but my mother and father did. I understand now. My brother was scheduled to leave for France the following month. There was much joy, and then the word came through that it had been a false report. This was no real armistice. I can imagine the despair of my parents. I remember, too, when the real armistice came through. The whole neighborhood seemed to be gathered into the streets. I'll never forget that time. It's in my memory right now. Broome Street was jammed with masses of crazy-eyed people.

Let me tell you something about Broome Street. You might find it pretty tough to believe. Broome Street at one time was a residential section and very clean, too. In the early twenties, there were trees and foliage on Broome and none of the dilapidated shacks and homes you see now. The Broome Street I speak of stretched from Spruce to Avon Avenue. I used to go with my mother to a moving-picture house that charged five cents. This movie was on Spruce near Barclay. I think there's a fish market in its place now. It was a very novel sight to see the early comedics. There was also another movie house on Prince Street near Spruce. There was one movie on Belmont Avenue that I remember particularly. You could see the program in the closed house, and then, for the same admission, you could go next door to an adjoining lot where they showed open-air movies. The pictures that I recall seeing and that give me real pleasure were *The Iron Claw; The Perils of Pauline*, with Pearl White; and *Neil of the Navy*. I remember John Bunny.[21] He was a great comic. I also remember Slim Summerville, when he played with Fatty Arbuckle.[22] "Slippery Slim" they called him then. Another movie was on Belmont and Court, where the bank is now. This is the movie we always sneaked into. The picture that is so vivid in my mind to this very day is called *The Forbidden City*. More than once, I've had a yen to write to Hollywood and ask them to revive this movie. Funny, isn't it? But I sometimes dream about this movie.

Ringing doorbells seems to have been one of our major hobbies.

Every evening almost, we used to gather in the residential section of the ward—that part of Spruce above High Street, an area in which there lived mainly the professional people, such as doctors, dentists, and lawyers—and we rang their bells till thunder came. We often pushed the bell down and held it there with a pin. When the person would come to the door, we would laugh like hell and then run off. Another pastime was pilfering from the stands on Prince Street, which was just beginning to become the dirty hovel it is today. I remember when there were no junk carts in this part of the ward. We would pilfer bananas and potatoes, and we were never caught. We would always manage to steal potatoes, and we would go to a lot on Broome Street and hold them over a fire until they were good and crisp. I almost wish I could do this again today. I've never had potatoes like those we used to roast on Broome Street over that fire in the lot. Around Halloween, especially, we used to masquerade as various characters popular during that time. I used to like to dress up like Charlie Chaplin. I could imitate him pretty well. The fellows used to get a kick out of it, and it didn't do me any harm with the girls, either. We used to have neighborhood amateur shows, and I once enacted a role of Lon Chaney. At the age of twelve, I joined the Boy Scouts—something I had been avidly looking forward to for years. We used to meet at the neighborhood house at Seventeenth Avenue and Boyd Street. It's still there, with Miss Miller still in charge. We had some swell times with our troop. We used to go on overnight hikes to Eagle Rock and Singac.[23]

I graduated from Montgomery Street School at the age of thirteen, and then entered Central High School. High school for me was very difficult, at least the first two years. I took part in the debating team and what was then known as the Liberal Club. Today, it is probably called the Problems of Democracy Club, or something of the sort. Football was the main sport of interest to me. The enthusiasm was great. Such outstanding players as Billy Helkig, Charlie Giskey, Ernie Cuppard, Barney Kopling, Joe Krieger—all under the coaching of Charlie Schneider, who turned out some pretty swell teams in his time. In 1922, they copped the state championship.

In 1923, I graduated and entered law school. Law school was, of course, an entirely new phase. During the day I worked in a lawyer's office, and in the afternoon I attended classes. We had as one of the professors Charles Masson—who since has passed away—who left some contributions, not only to the city, but also the state. He was an authority on bankruptcy law. He contributed much to the development of Newark Law School. Another professor was former judge William King, who instructed us in federal law and procedure. He did a good job with us, too. In 1927, I graduated law school, and I continued my clerk-ship until 1930. When I finished my clerkship, I decided to take a postgraduate course; and I studied for a year post graduate at Miami University and received my degree LLB in 1932. I got the right to prac-tice law in Florida and New Jersey. In 1933, I returned to Newark and was admitted to the New Jersey bar.

Since then, in my practice in the city I have specialized particularly in certain phases of law known as the federal protective branch, dealing mainly with helping out of small storekeepers who find it impossible to continue business and who can avail themselves of the National Bankruptcy Act. I also specialized in deportation and accidents pertain-ing to federal projects of one type or another. I'm practicing right now in the city of Newark. As I said, I specialize in federal work. I deal mainly in that branch of administrative law which has become popular in the last six years—the functioning of the courts, the National Labor acts, Old Age Pension, Social Security, National Labor Board, etc.[24] They have established a new kind of law practice in which I am deeply interested. This work occupies most of my time. I find it valuable and important because it brings me into close touch with the social and economic aspects of my clientele. We are able to develop a very close relationship, which is not of the usual lawyer-client type.

Irving Zuckerman

The Lore and Meaning of My Life

A young Jewish man; second generation; parents born in Rumania
   I interviewed this fellow at the Retail Workers Union at 34 Park Place. I couldn't get his address, unfortunately. I'm trying to do so through the secretary, with whom I am somewhat friendly. He was a rather tall young man and powerfully built. He spoke in a slow, drawl-ing tone and never seemed to rush about anything. He was polite, but he seemed to affect a disinterested attitude, which I resented, and which I think others are inclined to resent. He was a bit condescend-ing at times and seemed to drift from the interview and then come back to it, as I waited patiently for him to do so. You might say that his personality was antagonistic. He said I would be able to see him again if necessary. I was inclined to suspect that he was more than pleased with this opportunity to talk about himself.

Some of my first impressions of my early youth would offer wide contrast to the present conditions which exist in my place of birth. I was born on South Nineteenth Street, Newark, about twenty-eight years ago. This section at the time was divided from Irvington, New Jersey, and Grove Street, which was the boundary line, by a huge lot about five hundred yards across, stretching from Nineteenth Street to Grove Street and facing my house—in fact, right across the street from it. This lot held for me some of the keenest and most thrilling experiences of my early life. It was here that we used to dig trenches and hurl at one another our heavy artillery of snowballs, concealing within them sharp pebbles and sometimes formidable stones. It was here, too, that the circus, for some three years consecutively during my youth, pitched its camp to the enraptured interest of myself and my young friends. It was also into this lot that my young friend, Herbert, fell from the second story of his home and miraculously escaped with only a broken leg. Yes, it was this lot that held the lore and meaning of my early life, and it was to this lot that most of my early life was dedicated.

In school, I was constantly on edge, passionately anxious to get out and rush to the lot and play with the boys. When away for a few days to visit relatives in New York, I was sulky and brooding; I wanted to be home playing on the lot. Yes, the lot held in its grasp the full import of my early years. We had through it easy access to Grove Street and all the magic of apple orchards and vast chicken farms that then existed in the comparatively farm-like area that was then Irvington. I remember, however, the awful dread I had of being there at night.

Once, I remember distinctly, I had to go to a farm across the lot for my mom to get some eggs, which were urgently needed for the completion of a cake. It was twilight, and I knew that by the time I was ready to go back, it would already have been pitch dark in the lot. I was morbidly afraid, and I tried in every way to get out of the assignment, but to no avail. I had to go, and go I did. On the way over, I was calm and defiant. I went to the farmhouse, which was supervised by a gray-haired woman, whom I vividly recall to this day. She was usually quite stern, but on this night of all nights she kept me for a while and asked me a lot of questions about myself and whether I liked school, etc. I wanted to break away, but I couldn't. Finally, she let me escape, and I started across that vast tract for home. I want you to understand that it was during this time precisely that stories of Jack the Ripper were all the vogue. It was because of the story of this fiend that kindly parents used to keep their kiddies indoors after nightfall; and it was this story, with its butchery implications, that pounded in my brain as I began to cross the lot. Baby, was I scared! I'll never forget. I think I must have matured during that walk. Every gust of wind was Jack snorting in my face and preparing for his brutal attack on my entrails. Every shape, familiar as my own face to me during the day, on this night assumed all the wickedness and frightfulness of "the Ripper." I remember that when I got to the last fifty yards or so, I clutched those eggs to my chest and spurted with fury for my home. I must have broken a few records, if not a few eggs, in that last dash. My mother was alarmed when she saw me. My face must have been a fright. I shall never forget that night.

I remember pretty clearly, too, when my mother first took me to school. I wailed and howled and scratched at the pretty teacher's face; but I think after my first experience with kindergarten, I became quite acclimated and settled down to a serious and consequential school-life experience, which I would not surrender for all the wealth of Araby. It may have been that the sweet cakes and fancy embroidery that my mother made for some of my teachers may have assisted me in my early days in the old, brown building that first received me as a scholar of five-and-a-half ripe years. In school, I was one of the more popular people. I was class president in my last year and read the Bible at each assembly. I remember how I used to affect great pomposity when I read the Lord's Prayer. I think I impressed more than a few of my more impressionable classmates, too. In high school, I fared rather well. I made my letter in track—ran the half-mile. I never shattered any marks, but I was a pretty dependable man in a pinch—when a few points were needed.

Oh, yes, I omitted this, but it may be of some interest. I've never been able to sing a note, you know. I must be tone deaf or something, but I remember that I always got a doubtful seventy in voice throughout my school life, probably because they never knew, where voice was concerned, whether I was neuter of otherwise. They played safe by not having me sing and giving me seventy. This never was a problem, however, because I could always move my mouth and simulate singing when surrounded by hundreds of caroling throats of my more beneficent schoolmates; and I would get away with it. But came the time of my thirteenth year, and I was to be confirmed.[25] This necessitated my singing certain prayers by myself upon my confirmation in the synagogue. This was absolutely necessary under the Orthodox laws. I was desperate. My family along with me were fearful of imminent disgrace if I once opened my yap before their friends and relatives. It was a crucial situation, and something had to be done. Omit the prayers? Impossible! Well, sir, my rabbi sweated blood and thunder to train my ear, but he failed. He taught me to chant in a rather high-pitched way, and in this manner I got away with it, but belatedly. My Yiddish speech, however, of gratitude to my parents and the community more than overbalanced the ill effect of my singing, or should I say "chanting," voice. I put into that speech all the sincerity and fire of my vigorous youth. When I saw my mother and my aunts bawling there in the audience, I knew I had clicked. I shall never forget, either, the fabulous banquet my people feted me with. It was an ornate affair. Wine and liquors flowed, and I, before it was over, fell soundly asleep. It had been too much for me. I remember that for this affair an older cousin of mine had smeared my head with pomade—a process I had always marvelled at and now experienced for the first time. It made me feel grown up.

In high school, I majored in literature in preparation for a college prep course. My average for the four years was fair. I stood among the first third of the graduating class. I was assistant editor of the senior book, and this gave me a lot of prestige in the class. Under every photograph in the graduation yearbook, it was customary to include a quotation from some classic poem, intended to characterize or aptly describe the student above it. I was virtually flooded with special requests. For the first time I was accosted with genuine vanity in its most naked form. Lord, what requests I got from some of the ladies!

After high school, I got a job through that older cousin of mine, who by now was a buyer of menswear in a pretty-well-established department store in the Bronx. I worked here at a men's tie counter for three years. I also did the odd jobs about the place. Never work for a relative, my friend! After this, I got some work around the local department stores here in Newark. I worked in Chicago for a while, too. I didn't like it much there, and I scurried home in a hurry. Five years out of high school, I completed some credits by attending colleges at night. I attended some college in New York, which it would be discreet for me not to name for many reasons. I graduated from another school in Brooklyn as an alleged resident of Brooklyn, where I have relatives. I hope my name is not going to be used in connection with this interview, because it would be embarrassing and damaging for this to be widely known. I have a B.A. degree, which represents for me a certain degree of learning with no practicability whatsoever. There isn't much I can do with it at the present.

Perhaps, however, in the future—don't you think?—I'd like to teach. I always wanted to do this. It appeals to me. I think I'm something of an idealist in regard to teaching—molding human minds for the good of the community, or something. Sincerely, however, I think that teachers are the men and women I've admired most in life—if not for their immediate work, which suffered in the main from limitations imposed upon them by the school system, than for their amazing potentialities for training and scholarship. I must admit, I have been sometimes awed by the magnificent eruditeness of some of these people. It has seemed phenomenal to me that men and women could amass such learning in the short sphere of life that many of them physically represented. It is perhaps the most commendable commentary upon our present setup— that it has offered educational facilities for those who might be intelligent enough to exploit them. I like to read, but I find little time or concentrative effort to do as much as I would like. Occasionally, for exercise, I go to Weequahic Park on Sundays and ride a bike.

I'm not overly concerned with political currents of the day. To my mind, they all have a particularized and personal axe to grind; and this depends upon a particular bias. I work in one of the stores in Newark today as a shoe salesman; and I happen, by coincidence, to belong to a union. I have no opinions on unionism. It may have its purpose, and it may not. It is purely optional, as the case may happen to be. There isn't much more I can say, I guess. I might say that I do look with a certain amount of dread upon the present conflagration in Europe, but purely from a personal point of view. I wouldn't like to be involved. This life isn't a particularly sweet one, but it's the best I've known, and I'd like to know it a bit further.

Irving Zuckerman

Never Avoided a Fight

Mr. X's father came to this country from Austria in 1891. He left behind a wife and baby son. He had been a cattle dealer; but, as the needs of his immediate family were increasing, and he continued contributing to his father's needs, he thought that by coming to the United States, he would improve his economic condition. Upon arriving here, he went to live with and work for his cousin, who taught him the baking business. Here he stayed for six months. Then he moved away and established his own business. Mr. X's father had only a Hebrew-school education, and so he was never able to read or write anything but Yiddish.

In a short while, Mr. X's father sent for his wife and baby son. Upon their arrival, a home was set up, and they lived very happily. This family soon had nine more blessed events. Mr. X was the third in the brood. He was built round. Ten years later his mother had twins. From the time this family settled here, they lived continuously on the same street. They had the bakery here, and all the children had to help in delivering and soliciting customers. The living conditions, economic as well as physical, called for a hardy individual, and X was, beyond doubt, very hardy.

X went to school up to the eighth grade. The prevailing economic conditions forced his parents to take him out of school and use him in the bakery, as were his older brother and sister. The first five children were withdrawn at the eighth grade, while the later five were all high school graduates, the two youngest girls becoming grammar-school teachers. Mr. X was confirmed at thirteen, as were his brothers, as is the custom with Orthodox Jews. During the time, X worked to help his parents. At the same time, his reputation as a fighter grew. He tried to avoid getting into arguments, but he never avoided a fight. At fifteen, X ran away from home. He fled to Connecticut, where he falsified his age and enlisted in the United States Navy. When his parents learned of his whereabouts, they got him out. His father gave him a good whipping, and tried to control him, but it was all to no avail. His great job in life seemed to be fighting. He traveled around with a group of fellows, of which he became leader because of his ability; and his fighting ability brought him respect of the people, not of his faith.

Soon, the United States joined with the other nations to make the world safe for democracy. Immediately, he signed up. His parents had tried to discourage him, but it was of no use. In a short while, his elder brother joined the National Guard. X was sent to France. He was here for eighteen months, and he partook in several major engagements. Two weeks before the armistice was signed, his family received an official letter from Washington, stating that X was lost in action. A few days later, another letter from the War Department stated that X was found in a field hospital and was well-nigh recovered. This was indeed a joyful day in X's family home. In a short while, X returned home, where the entire neighborhood turned out to welcome him back. After being honorably discharged, X went back to work for his father.

In about six months, he won an appointment to the local police department. At this time, he was about twenty-three years old. In this position, X won many plaudits, being cited for bravery and good work. X kept this position for about three years, and then he quit. He claimed that he wasn't making enough money. These were the boom days of 1926.

His first business venture was to rent a garage. His uncle bought a half block and built a new garage. X undertook to manage this place. He paid $550 per month. Business boomed. He sold this place and opened another garage, just as large but in a better location—the theater district. Here he was very successful. He inaugurated the first U-Drive-It in town. In this he prospered for a while, and so he sold his garage and devoted his entire time to the U-Drive-It business. Sorry to relate, the bubble bursted, and he lost his business and investments. He did nothing for about six months. Then he opened another garage in Newark. Here he was fairly successful. So he attempted to branch out, and he opened another place in East Orange. These places went along fairly well, but X didn't see any future in this. When Roosevelt repealed the Eighteenth Amendment, he entered the liquor business in Newark. He has had several different locations and many partners. He claims that all the locations were good, but his partners ruined the business. Today, he has no partners and is making a good living.

As with many other veterans, X never married. Many times, professional matchmakers, his sisters, and his mother attempted to marry him off to fine, Orthodox Jewish girls. It was no use. He merely said that he wasn't interested. He never cared for the opposite sex, and so he never bothered much with them. X is not very religious. He observes the duty of the kosher laws, but not the holidays. Upon the recent death of his mother, he did not recite the *Kaddish*, but he did observe the week of Shiva.[26] He does not belong to any synagogue. He has bought cemetery plots from the Newark War Veterans, Jewish Post. X never bothers much in politics. He is a Republican, but he voted for Roosevelt. He feels that every Jew should vote for Roosevelt because of his liberality and outspokenness toward anti-Semitism.

His physical description is about five feet, nine inches tall, but very fat, weighing about 250 pounds. He has never been sick, but at present he has trouble with his kidneys. The only operation he has ever had is the one in France in the field hospital. Here, his nose was fixed. It had been smashed as a result of a bomb explosion while in action. He received partial war-disability insurance from the government until about 1926. He has a faint trace of shell shock and suffers some ill effects from mustard gas. Sometimes, he finds it very hard to breathe. He has no amusements nor recreation. He hopes to make enough to secure himself in his old age. He is very fastidious in his dress, and he buys a new car every year. His clothes are very expensive. He tells me each suit costs him one hundred to one hundred and fifteen dollars, tailor-made in New York. He keeps his car like new, wiped each day, washed each week, and polished every month. Thus, one can see his only pleasure is personal and material cleanliness. Because he has no wife or children, he spends his money on his nephews and nieces. He takes great joy in their company, and especially likes them to ask his advice. In this way, he feels that he belongs to the wonderful institution of the family.

Herman Bader

A Movie Review: *A Brivele der Mamen* (A Letter to Mother)

Produced by the Sphinx Film Company, Warsaw, Poland, featuring Lucy and Misha Gehrman, at the Little Theater in Newark.

As I entered the Little Theater I was somewhat startled. It was the first time I recall in my many visits to the "Little" that it was so completely occupied. I even experienced some difficulty in finding a seat. Finally, after a perfunctory search, I found one next to a portly, well-dressed gent. Once seated, I looked about me and became interested for a few moments in a swift observation of the people about me. I was surprised to note that not a few among them were comparatively young Jews, possibly, like myself, second generation. At the moment, I ascribed this to the fetching qualities of the title.

The film itself has its locale in the White Russia of prewar days. It presents no insight into the ghetto, as might have been expected from past films of the same type.[27] It deals primarily with Jewish life in a small agricultural village close to the Polish border. The Jew, it is clearly manifested at the very outset of the film, is not a farmer; his lot is that of the small town businessman, occupied with the retail sale of goods, housewares, and the artisan manufacture of clothing. In fact, not the least enjoyable segment of the film for me was the characterization of the village tailor. Here is a fellow, full of life and vitality, fully imbued with a higher sense for his menial lot—a lot which he, in his inimitable and idyllic way, makes into a resplendent pattern of life—a pattern richly hued with the qualities of his soul, as he constantly says, and the haunting music of the Hasidim.[28] Throughout the film, our tailor hums softly and occasionally breaks out a bit more boisterously with the beloved Jewish melody, born of a long line of European tailors, "Azoy neyt a Shnayder," (This is the Way a Tailor Sews). It may have been the intention of the direction for this tailor to lend a purely comic note to the whole affair—and he often does—but it seems to me that this characterization, compact with its rich background and significance of purpose, penetrates much deeper into a larger, moral sense. It seems to me that this tailor offers a key to what is sometimes termed "the Jewish riddle." In short, here is a man of poverty; here is a man afflicted materially from every side; here is a man who cannot call his home his own; and yet he sings, he dances, he brings the utmost of cheery optimism to those about him, and in his work he expresses joy and confidence. Perplexed, historians have referred to the Jew as a constant challenge to their formal concepts of historical logic. How, they have questioned, has this people been able to survive in the face of a cruel and relentless historical fate? See the tailor of this small Jewish town and perhaps you may have a key to this riddle. The tailor is a community phenomenon, incredible at times but at all times indispensable to the milieu in which he has found himself. Need it be said that he is beloved by all? Even his wife, a somewhat buxom Dame Quickly in her own right, though she nags and berates him, cannot help but gather him to her ample bosom after he has quixotically offset her wrath with a lilting tune.[29] The audience loved our tailor and chuckled knowingly and affectionately at his generous escapades. One factor that perhaps impressed me above all others was the utter craftmanship of this man and his passionate desire to perform a laudable task

Another character who earns his share of abundant treatment is the village *chazan*.[30] Here is a man revered by the community because to them he is not only voice and music, but he is their poet, chanting their folklore. As the cantor sang, many of the men in the audience and some of the women hummed and sang softly along with him.

The story is a simple one. It concerns itself, in the main, with one of the many families living in this remote village of White Russia. No one would doubt for a moment the memorable qualities of this Jewish family group. It has for a father a man of delicate features and physique, who finds greater joy in the spontaneous composition of tunes than in any attachment to the menial requirements of life. His wife, devoutly in love with him, nurtures this tendency and is the sole support of the family. Thus, the disrespect of the children and the village folk generally is incurred, and the father is off to America. Here he consummates his lyrical career in complete failure. He is not fit for the rigorous life before him; the streets of America are not paved with gold. He becomes a park bum and later a pushcart peddler in the East Side. Despite his penury, however, he manages to accumulate enough money to send for his young son—a boy who is considered to be a musical prodigy as an excellent singer. When the boy embarks for America, his mother weepingly admonishes him to write to his mother—*A Brivele der Mamen*. At this point in the film, I heard a violent outburst of weeping at my side and discovered to my amazement that it was the portly gentleman. There was weeping all around me—men as well as women. Was this due to excessive sentimentality on the part of those who wept? Or did it strike a familiar chord in their own European past? I do not know. I only know that many handkerchiefs were in evidence at this point and throughout the film, until the reconciliation between mother and son.

The film emphasizes the role of the HIAS—an organization that rendered some very meritorious service after the war in bringing together families that had been scattered as a result of the turmoil and confusion.[31]

During the film, I overheard many remarks commenting upon the respective acting ability of the cast. These remarks were made in the most casual way, as though they in no way interfered with the concentration of others upon the film itself; and yet nobody seemed to mind. It was accepted as a matter of fact—as the natural thing to do—and everybody indulged in it.

In its depiction of refugee flights during combat between the Russian and German armies, the film no doubt served very sharply to invoke for the audience a somewhat similar fate to that of the Jew in Europe today. More than one remark I overheard attested to this. One that I recall particularly was uttered in Yiddish: "We poor Jews. When will we get a chance to be at peace and rest?"

The younger people in the audience seemed to react to the film with as much enthusiasm as their elders. Strangely enough, I detected more young women than men. If it had done nothing else, I think *A Brivele der Mamen* proved beyond any doubt that there is a considerable audience in Newark for whom a Jewish film is yet a keen source of entertainment.

Irving Zuckerman

The Little Theater

I have this day interviewed Mr. Franklin, manager of the Little Theater, 562 Broad Street, Newark, New Jersey.

The Little Theater, so named because it is a small place on one of the world's busiest streets, has a seating capacity of three hundred. This year it has shown to New Jersey's Jewry three Jewish movie-talkies: *Tevya, Moisha-Oisher,* and *Motel, the Operator.*

Tevya, made by famous Russian Jewish artists, was filmed in Moscow and in St. Petersburg, Russia. It depicts early Jewish religion, customs, habits, and costumes. It also has a love scene. It was shown for one week, and 80 percent of its patrons were old folks of the first and second generation, 10 percent of the second and third generation, and 5 percent youngsters. The manager also reports that from his personal observations that 3 percent to 5 percent of the old folks generally enjoy the picture so much that they see it twice.

Moishe-Oisher and *Motel, the Operator,* were made by American Jewish stars, and they deal with the themes of love, romance, comedy, and music. Seventy-five percent of the patrons were younger people, mostly from the third and fourth generations, 10 percent first generation, and 15 percent second generation.

Each picture is shown for a week, and the theater is always filled to capacity at each performance. The Little Theater management has a contract calling for the exclusive rights to be the first to run Jewish pictures in the state of New Jersey.

Fischman

Prince Street, Newark

Seven blocks long, Prince Street extends from Waverly Avenue to South Orange Avenue in Newark, cutting through the city's Third Ward—a neighborhood not without reputation in the annals of the police. By day, the thoroughfare is a noisy center of cheap trade, operated almost exclusively by Hebrews; by night, after its business has been locked away, it is a thoroughly Negro community.

I

Prince Street sells cheap, out of pushcarts, out of open barrels, along the sidewalk, and across seamy counters. Lentils, dried peas and lima beans, mountain nuts, coffee, tea, and peanuts are sold out of bins. You can fill your pockets with loose tobacco, pungent and moist, scooped out of a glass container to your order; you can buy a suit of clothes, new or secondhand, from a curbstone peddler. You can purchase headache tablets, suspenders, a hammock, or a statue of Popeye the Sailerman, or Joe Louis, "the Brown Bomber."

Bananas, talcum powder, herrings, sunflower seeds, and pickled apples vie with Japanese toys, silk petticoats, balbriggan underwear, and lamp wicks for attention.[32] Prince street sells cheap; it will sell even more cheaply if you haggle. It invites you to buy, to bargain, to take advantage of its cheapness in Yiddish, German, Ukrainian, Polish, and Russian. It also speaks English. And, if that is not enough, it argues its prices and values with a frenzy of elbow, hand, and eye.

Pushcarts nudge against the curb, lean over and thrust their merchandise at the passerby. Every weary building has a storefront, and before each one racks of goods crowd against the knees of the shoppers.

No space is allowed to go unused—even the cellar entries. Smells of dried fish, peanuts, and vegetables creep up from basement storerooms, whose entrances are banked by sacks and briny barrels.

Across one entryway, secondhand shoes dangle forlornly by their laces from a wire. The store in this building is a Jewish bakery where are displayed *mandlbroyt, kuchen* of every variety, and the round, doughnut-like hard rolls called *bagels;* here too is a tray of the soft *zeml*—a plushy roll in whose center coyly nestles an odorous slice of onion. On Friday, the shop will sell *challah*—the sweet white bread of the Hebrew Sabbath.[33]

Before the bake shop, there is room for two pushcarts. Beside one of them a shriveled little man, his stringy overcoat turned up about his ears, shouts endlessly, "All kinds toys, chip," and shifts from foot to foot like a chilly bird. At the other pushcart, a foghorn-voiced woman in an imitation leopard-skin coat, wearing cracked white shoes, shouts the virtues of the radishes, cucumbers, and lumpy carrots she sells.

Over the stores there are rooms. Trade goes on there too, though the faces upstairs are Negroid. Prince Street sells cheap, upstairs as well as down; but for this commerce, there is no display, no clamor. A few years ago Prince Street upstairs clustered its gaunt wares among the racks of dried figs and neckties and grabbed at its prospect's elbow avidly. It was as vocal, though not as loud, as the Prince Street of the pushcarts; it whispered to passing men, both black and white. Nowadays, the gaunt merchandise hides upstairs, while its salesmen, smiling and winking, pick up customers among the crowds.

Prince Street sells cheap—its merchandise fills the needs of every appetite, at bargain prices. And often it gives more than the buyer bargains for.

II

The beginnings of Prince Street, over fifty years ago, were similar to that of any popular shopping district of the day. Its stores served the immigrant workers of the neighborhood, particularly the Germans, employees in the nearby breweries. As the city's industrial expansion brought the factories' smokestacks closer to their doorsteps, the more prosperous of the workers moved into the suburban districts—Vailsburg, Irvington, Bloomfield, and the Oranges. Those who remained and those who refilled the vacated dwellings in the now less-desirable community demanded cheapness above all else from their shopkeepers. The merchants who had grown used to catering to a more prosperous patronage could not satisfy this new type of customer. They sold out one by one to others, who operated on principles of clever merchandising rather than through personal appeal and neighborliness. The majority of the new shopkeepers were Jewish.

Only the most shrewd and canny could survive the fierce merchandising competition that began during that period. Price wars raged. Merchants accosted possible customers on the street and dragged them into their stores to astound them with stupendous bargains. The fame of the street as a place where much could be bought for little spread through the city. Trade increased. Shops were partitioned to provide space for as many businesses as possible. In the frenzy to use all available room for business, the shopkeepers moved their families out of their dwellings behind the stores, turned the flats into enlarged shops or storerooms, and took up residence on the sidestreets. The more prosperous set up homes in the suburbs.

Property values boomed. The second exodus from Prince Street was underway. The original dwellers had left because the street was made unattractive by factory smoke; the merchants' families moved because the street had been made valuable by the clamor of trade. Finally, families in the flats above the stores were driven out when landlords demanded exorbitant rents. But those Prince Street property owners who had gloatingly envisioned their upper floors profitably rented to sweatshop clothing stores and jerry-built furniture emporiums were disappointed. The unpredictable public refused to patronize the upstairs enterprises, and they were soon abandoned. The upper floors, above the teeming trade, stood vacant for many years. Finally, hopelessly deteriorated, they were rented to the poorest slumdwellers at a fraction of their original rates.

But street-level space became increasingly valuable. The pushcart appeared, and after many a wrangle, in which fists as well as curses flew, the shopkeepers were able to demand and receive a fee from the peddler whose two-wheeled business darkened their door. In the tumultuous days near the turn of the century, peddlers paid as high as one hundred dollars a month to the merchant whose shop they stood before. The rate nowadays is from two dollars to ten dollars. Though the practice is wholly without legal justification, neither party has ever abrogated this long-established rule of the street.

By 1900, all of the many and various businesses on the street were operated by Hebrews. Through a species of race solidarity—as evinced by price and trade agreements from which the few non-Jewish merchants were studiously excluded—and because the Semites were willing to work long and killing hours for quick turnovers, the Jews won the battle of Prince Street. The neighborhood that had once housed a polyglot community of Germans, Poles, Italians, Irish, and Russians had become a ghetto. Thus it remained for over twenty years.

III

Through subsequent years the number of kosher delicatessens, meat markets, and dairy stores increased. Jewish bakeries, Jewish bookstores, and stores selling the paraphernalia of Judaism crowded between stores whose produce had a more secular appeal. On the three blocks at the southern extreme of Prince Street, known as the "upper section," synagogues were built, or were enlarged from little sheds in backyards to impressive brick edifices. Wispy old men, at whose ears dangled the *payess*—locks of the faithful—and bent old women, who wore the *sheytl* wig over their stringy hair, pushed their way along the narrow pavements.[34] A Hebrew school was erected, and Jewish boys attended it, after their school hours were over, preparing for the great occasion of their bar mitzvah, when they should be thirteen and become men in the eyes of the Lord, God of Israel.

Perhaps the height of Jewish influence was reached when the gilt-lobbied Metropolitan Theater on Montgomery Street, just off Prince, opened its doors, mirroring in a highly-colored fashion the drama and romance of Jewish life.

On Saturday night, Hebrews from all over Jersey came to Prince Street to shop. Customers stood three deep before the counters of the kosher butchers. Kosher restaurants and tea shops did a tremendous business; and in the throng, thrifty housewives haggled and bargained loudly with the peddlers. The second invasion of Prince Street was even then in preparation; its armies crowded at both ends of the throughfare and massed upon the side streets. Slowly they moved together. The Negroes swept into Prince Street.

IV

The migration of colored people to the industrial centers of the North during the world war period, when unskilled labor was much in demand, brought many to Newark. A majority of them settled in the Third Ward, where a Negro community had long been established. As the whites, enabled by wartime salaries to live in less-congested communities, moved away from the neighborhood, the Negroes took over more and more territory.

But labor became plentiful after the war. Wages dropped. Negroes were discharged from their well-paid jobs as the flood of returning white workers filled the labor market. With the war emergency gone, industrial production decreased. The Negroes, their incomes lowered, sought cheaper dwellings. The vacant, moldy rooms over the Prince Street shops were near their old homes, and the Jewish shopkeepers, themselves hit by the bad times, rented to them.

The Negro invasion of Prince Street was slow, but steady. Today, virtually all the upper floors of the houses on Prince Street are occupied by Negroes, though some few of the least-prosperous Jews have moved back from their foreclosed homes to the old neighborhood. In some cases, both races share the same houses.

Race prejudice between Negro and Jew on Prince Street rarely breaks out into the open. It expresses itself with mild baiting between the two; the Jews jeer the Negroes in Yiddish, and often the colored man's retort is couched in the same language. There have even been a few Negro converts to Judaism, and the Negro women are just as expert as their Hebrew sisters in haggling with the merchants. Although, from the cultural and historic standpoint, the two races are very far apart, they have poverty in common. They fight for the same bargains and go to the same relief stations. Their children play in the same schoolyards and attend the same classes.

The Negro businessmen, on the whole, have been unable to compete successfully with the Jews on Prince Street. There are a few Negro enterprises, but these are of the service variety, catering solely to Negro trade. Barbershops, poolrooms, and taverns compose the majority of them, although Prince Street has two shoemaking shops and a tailoring shop run by Negroes. There are at last a half-dozen Negro laundries, supplanting the businesses of yet another race—the Chinese. These are called "peace laundries" and are financed and sometimes owned outright by the Father Divine organization.[35] Their price lists are headed with the slogans of their sect: "Father Divine is God" and "Peace—It is wonderful." A laundry near South Orange Avenue, opposite the mosque-like Russian synagogue, has a large wooden sign which states that the laundress was stricken in body and soul and "Father Divine restored me to wholeness."

A significant expression of the evergrowing influence of the Negro on Prince Street life can be found in the stalls of the shops. Yams, okra, soy beans, and sugar cane are prominently displayed. The live-chicken markets are as faithfully patronized by the Negroes as by the Jews. The assistant of the *shochet,* who wears a folded paper bag on his head in imitation of the Jewish functionary's *yarmulke,* is invariably a Negro.[36]

With apron as bloody and knife just as keen, he plucks and cleans the fowl after the Hebrew has murmured his ritual over it and slit its throat. Flashy trinkets, curious medicines, and brightly colored cloths and garments appeal to Negroes from a pushcart opposite a display of Jewish religious candelabra and books. One shop, selling *tefillin* and *tallessim* and other Hebrew ritualistic accessories, prominently displays what is glaringly advertised as a "Jewish Lucky Piece"—a small *mezuzah* made up as a watch fob.[37] Since no Jew religious enough to ascribe mystic power to this talisman would desecrate it by carrying it on his person, the trinket is obviously displayed to appeal to the crapshooting element.

V

The poverty of Prince Streeters, particularly of those Negroes who live in the section near Springfield Avenue, is extreme. The houses there are in the last stages of decay, and some have neither gas nor electricity. Toilets are shared by several flats, and there are no bathtubs. The owners, paid a minimum of rent, neglect even the smallest repairs.

Slowly, organization of exploiting forces has closed in upon both whites and blacks. The pushcart peddlers, for example, have been reduced to economic slavery. The depression so weakened them financially that they cannot now afford to own their vehicles or buy their merchandise. Most of the pushcarts and their stock are owned by a corporation that collects the day's receipts from the peddler and rebates him a percentage of the profits.

The prostitution of the Negro women is also organized. Harlotry began in the depths of the depression when these women were faced with starvation. Police interference drove it undercover, but the women sought and used the services of panderers. Banded together, these procurers control this by-no-means negligible Prince Street commerce, which is patronized by whites and Chinese as well as Negroes.

Another systemized racket that operates on Prince Street is child slavery. The crowded tenements house many "baby farms"—establishments where children of Negro parents in domestic service are boarded. Often, when the mother or father is unwilling or unable to continue paying the child's board, the youngster's adoption by South Jersey farmers is arranged. That legitimate adoptions occur is unarguable, but too often arrangements have been made by which the children have become veritable slaves. A fee, collected from the adopters, is split by the boarding mistress and the racketeers.

Organizations, ostensibly benevolent or fraternal, mulct members out of exorbitant insurance premiums and assess them heavily for shoddy, gaudy uniforms. Operators of the number and racing rackets collect a daily toll, and pseudo-religious, spiritualistic, and a variety of other charlatan organizations cheat the credulous. In the well-patronized taverns and poolrooms, marijuana cigarettes, referred to as "reefers" or "dusters," are openly sold; more harmful drugs are also in circulation. Nostrums for venereal infection, miracle salves, ointments, and remedies for all the evils that befall the flesh and mind are to be had on street corners.

Rudolph E. Kornmann

German Jews Interviewed

In the spring and summer of 1939, in an ethnic survey of nationalities in Newark, first-, second-, and third-generation German Jews were interviewed. Although this group of Jews was small as compared to other Jewish groups, the questionnaires which were used disclosed three distinct types: the German Jew who have been here ten to twenty years and who have, at the most, a high school education; the German Jews who have been here the same length of time, but who have had some college education; the German Jews who have been in the United States for forty to fifty years. The attitudes of these people toward American life and toward other nationalities are presented in separate sections on the following pages. The account of an interview with a German Jewish rabbi is also included.

I

For the German Jews who have been here for ten to twenty years and who have not had the benefit of an education exceeding high school, it is difficult for them to realize that they settled in the United States long before the Jews of other nationalities and therefore were enabled to secure greater economic advantages. In the case of the respondents in this group, they came here only because relatives who were in business urged them to come. These relatives found places for them in the family business of various types.

It is revealing to note that such respondents tend to think that all Jews in America are in the same economic position as themselves, namely, in some business, earning enough money to live comfortably.

This mistaken tenent is the basis for such a remark as this: "After all, we (the Jews) make a fairly good living here in America. We work hard, and we get along. So I don't see why we shouldn't just keep on that way, without any fuss." Any attempt, however, to obtain some clearcut formula from such respondents regarding behavior of Jews in general in America elicits but vague generalities: "Jews should set a good example" and "They should live right and do right" are typical statements of advice on behavior.

Aside from the questionnaire, personal conversations brought to light various beliefs concerning the role of the Jew in America that are of interest in establishing the social attitudes of this first type of German Jew. It is the belief of such respondents that Jews in America must be especially careful not to offend anyone, especially in regards to their violating certain carefully established standards of so-called Americanism fostered among the upper-middle classes. In this category of standards may be included any and all types of prolabor and progressive activity. Because the respondents are mainly small businessmen, they view prolabor and progressive activities with fear and trembling. They feel that the non-Jews who control industry and commerce indiscriminately label all Jews as social agitators who exert an unsettling influence on the status quo. In their anxiety to disprove that Jews are a factor in the labor and the progressive movements, they tend to be more reactionary politically and economically than their own economic status would ordinarily warrant.

Many in this group seem to have been influenced by Nazi propaganda to the extent of sincerely believing Jews to be inferior to some other races, such as the British and the Scandinavian. This is shown by the fact that, when interviewed, the respondents favored allowing British and Scandinavian immigrants into the country, but believed Jewish immigration should be restricted. Also, this type of German Jew would marry only Jews of German descent, a choice which indicates that marriage with other types of Jews could be placed on the same level as with other ethnic groups. If given a choice to be considered "Jewish" or "German," the German category will be picked without hesitation.

At the same time, their ethnic attitudes have been so conditioned by Nazi propaganda that they wish to curb Jewish immigration. This contradiction, as with all other contradictions that may be found in this type of German Jew, lies in the fact that such persons have not been Americanized as yet in the best sense of the word. Many of their actions are those of Jews residing in a less democratic country, rather than those of Americans of the Jewish faith.

Politically, the respondents shy away from all activity. Far from taking any sort of aggressive stand against antidemocratic movements, the tendency is to hide, so to speak, from any kind of participation in collective citizenship. Whatever urge may exist to struggle against un-American forces is sublimated by attendence at a Reform temple (usually B'nai Jeshurun) and helping relatives in Germany to come to the United States. Here again is an odd contrast. This type of respondent spends a good deal of effort bringing relatives from Germany.

II

The second type of German Jew, like the first type, has been in the United States for ten to twenty years. Both have the same appearance. The only difference between them is that this second type has had a longer exposure to American education and has a viewpoint more nearly akin with the true American. He has had at least a couple of years in an American college. Like the first type, he has gone to school while working for a relative.

This second type of Jew considers himself to be an American, rather than a German Jew, although the difference there is still not so great. In many ways, his social activities parallel those of the first type, such as membership in a temple, etc. He is also active in organizations such as the German-Jewish Club. This was formed to provide social activities for recent German-Jewish arrivals. In business, he may hold a minor executive position.

Politically, he is opposed to all "totalitarian" states, which include Germany, Italy, Russia, and Hungary. He is opposed to both Fascist and Socialist forms of government. Although he may be devoid of the Jewish inferiority complex of the first type, at the same time he is caught in the grip of conflicting forces and impulses. For this reason, he belongs to progressive organizations such as the German-American League for Culture, which he considers to be a political organization in the sense that it is anti-Hitler. This shows that he is more aggressive and more active than the first type of respondent and that he is still strongly controlled by influences which may be considered remote from American habits and ways of thinking.

He thinks unions are a good thing, if properly controlled. He is willing to fight antidemocratic forces, but he is unwilling to come out into the open about it. If necessary, he fights them on the political front. In short, he does what he can in his own personal, limited way, but still as a German Jew first and an American second. If he saw such a statement, he would deny it vehemently. Therefore, in the essential respect of conduct, the first and second types of German Jew are alike in that they act primarily as German Jews, rather than as Americans of the Jewish faith.

III

The German Jew who came to the United States forty or fifty years ago has prospered economically because of thrift, industry, and the greater opportunities offered earlier arrivals. Although much more integrated as a type, and less torn, as it were, between two worlds of attitudes and behavior, he is more nearly akin to the first type of German Jew we have surveyed. His psychology is clearer and simpler. He represents the simplicity of the person who is consistently himself. The recent happenings in his native Germany have come rather late in his life and to his mind are temporary.

He is a member of several clubs—businessmen's clubs—and his economic and political reactions are the same as any other businessman. The German situation is apparently a separate order of business in his mind. It does not permeate everything he does, as in the case of the first and second types, who have been closer to the Germany of the recent years.

The children of this third type and their children will, we think, provide interesting contrasts with their parents. It is likely, however, that they are "100 percent Americans" who feel that whatever is happening in Germany is not much of their concern, save that their parents talk about it too much.

This third type of respondent has an antipathy toward unions—"They set class against class." He is typical of businessmen with moderate-sized businesses. They are more opposed to unionism than the big businessmen. The latter see it as an unescapable element in American economic life, and they accept it as gracefully as they can.

This type of respondent felt himself to be a German first, then a Jew. It can be safely said that the advent of Nazism in Germany hit the German Jews in America especially hard, because it made it almost impossible for them to identify themselves with a country that they considered their native land. Germany had been the fatherland to them, the same as it was to non-Jewish Germans, and Hitler's seizure of power left them stranded, high and dry. In compensation, they have built up in their mind's eye an imaginary picture of the "true Germany" that was in which no blemish can be found.

One would think that before Nazism, Germany was a promised

land. While that may have been true, comparatively speaking, still there is no validity in the unreal picture conjured by German Jews in America who feel the necessity for a "homeland," even if it be purely imaginary in composition. This third type of respondent is, of course, a German who first grew accustomed through the years to look back upon his boyhood years in Germany with a nostalgia sharpened by distance and the passage of time.

The advent of Hitler still further increased the nostalgia because now return to childhood scenes was no longer possible in view of the sweeping changes in Germany under Nazism. So, the respondent attends his Jewish temple with its German-Jewish rabbi (born in Americus, Georgia, and ignorant of Yiddish, as are most German Jews), delivering a solemn sermon in English about the blessings of American life as contrasted with the horrors of life in Germany. This is his escape from reality because he does nothing beyond listening to the sermons; action is far from his mind. He will attend to his business; God will attend to Hitler.

IV

One of the German Jews interviewed was a rabbi. When the rabbi was asked his place of birth he replied, "I was the first rabbi in America whose both parents were born in the United States." He made the statement as pridefully as a Mayflower descendent citing his ancestry. His mother's mother was born in Poland, otherwise his grandparents were born in Germany. His mother and father were born in Americus, Georgia, where he also was born.

When the interview was made, he willingly discussed a variety of topics. He talked on Zionism, anthropology, the local elections, trade unionism, Judaism, social activities, Americanism, Harry Bridges, and the Hobbs bill.[38] He himself brought up each topic. He had positive opinions, which he emphasized were "American." He boasted that his Jewish faith did not influence his opinions. He hoped that many other Jews were like him. He declared that Jews must not think like Jews; they must think like "Americans."

He stressed that Jews in America should be Americans, pure and simple; and that religion should enter their lives in the same way as it does non-Jewish Americans. Judaism must not be an all-embracing way of life, separate and apart, as in the case with Orthodox Jews, but simply a part of one as an American.

The rabbi is an anti-Zionist. He is opposed to Jewish nationalism in

Palestine. First, he feels that the Jew as an American owed allegiance to one flag—the American flag—and the sight of Jews hailing the Jewish national flag is a symbol of divided and foolish loyalty. Secondly, he feels that the Jewish dream of a Jewish nation provides the British government with a catspaw for its hot chestnuts in the East. Although the idea of a Jewish national homeland may provide pleasant thoughts to millions of Jews scattered throughout the world, he feels that such justification for Palestine means giving aid and comfort to Zionism.

The rabbi is extremely active organizationally. As the head of the richest temple in New Jersey, he is in demand for speeches and ceremonies. Occasionally, he delivers an address over a national radio hookup. He is on the boards of such diverse organizations as the Salvation Army and Newark University.³⁹ His attitude toward education is flexible. The rabbi understandably took the question, "How much schooling is necessary for a good job?" to mean, "How much schooling is necessary to succeed (in a business way)?" The rabbi's influence in the community is extensive, but he is careful to use it for such causes that are as divorced as possible from politics or economics.

He talked enthusiastically about a series of articles that were written by an anthropologist in a magazine of national circulation. The articles concluded that the intermarriage of Jews with gentile Americans would raise the level of the American people generally. The author of the articles based his conclusions on the theory that the Jews had become a selective race because of persecution, and, therefore, the level of their intelligence and adeptness had increased. The rabbi felt that anti-Semitic overtones may have been embodied in the articles extolling the cleverness of the Jews. On the other hand, he thought the articles compensated the overtones by being an education against persecution. In the ethnic attitudes section of the questions, he displayed complete tolerance, except on the marriage question. There he was careful to point out that he was thinking of the religious angle only. The articles really flattered his inner sense of superiority.

The local political situation was discussed. The rabbi felt that quite a mess was yet to be stirred up. He seemed completely innocent, however, of the fact that one block from his temple is located the headquarters of a national numbers racket, scheduled for federal investigation.

He seemed particularly disturbed over the case of Harry Bridges, the California labor leader. He is convinced that Mr. Bridges is a Communist and, as such, has no right to lead 300,000 workmen, who during a strike were inspired by him to cause bloodshed and millions of dollars of loss in business. It was pointed out that perhaps it did not make much difference in the final analysis whether Mr. Bridges or some native labor man led the workmen, but the rabbi seemed convinced that Mr. Bridge's removal was the key to the labor situation on the West Coast. He felt that no noncitizen should have the right to lead any organization or business of any kind—that is, be in any position where he could influence Americans. Foreign directors of American corporations, he felt, were not in leading positions and were therefore exempt. The rabbi has no objection to men like Harry Bridges being humble workmen—rank-and-file members of unions; but he feels that a law restricting any rise in leadership on the part of such persons is necessary. He also dwelt on the fact that apparently second-generation Russian Jews seemed more inclined to be active in the labor field than most other segments of the population. In such cases, he felt that religion was the only answer. It is not surprising that the Hobbs bill, which provides for the imprisonment of aliens unwanted by their native lands, meets with his approval.

Despite the rabbi's concern with Americanism first, there is an undercurrent of uncertainty struggling upward. The rabbi agrees that American democracy must not merely be defended, but an aggressive attitude in its behalf must be adopted. At the same time, he is powerfully affected by the widely-current distaste of even thinking about the future. So far as he is concerned, there is no tomorrow, only today.

Fatalism plays a great part in this attitude, despite the many expressions of confidence in Americanism, which has by now become more a fetish than a word. "This is the greatest country in the world," says the rabbi. We agree. But the rabbi doesn't feel quite comfortable about it. There's a man like Harry Bridges. There's the CIO. There are the young, second-generation Russian Jews, unconnected with the synagogue or temple, unconnected with Judaism. There are the dozens of conflicting tides sweeping the country—progress, reaction, unionism, industrialism, capital, labor, classes, religions, the chaos of Europe pouring through loudspeakers in every parlor.

The rabbi is first and foremost an American; furthermore, he is an American conditioned by the economic condition of his congregation. His attitudes are their attitudes. Their views, economically and politically, are his views. He points with pride to the members of his congregation who started in life with little or no education and became wealthy.

Sometimes, he seems more remote from the struggle for economic security than his congregation, much less so than the average individual. He feels that there is too much economic strife. However, he does agree there is room for adjustment in this rich country of ours, but he does not know how the adjustment can be made. After all, the rabbi does not pretend to be an economist or a businessman; he is concerned with the problems of the spirit, which he feels are the most important in life. While he delivers his solemn sermons on tolerance and the story of Queen Esther, the rabbi is not concerned with economic matters, and neither is his congregation. They attend the temple to escape such matters. But in his study the rabbi thinks of all these things and arrives at the conclusion that "Americanism" is the answer to them all. After all, isn't he an American first—he who happens to be of Jewish faith.

Ernest W. Pentz

"Paterson's Most Useful Citizen"

Nathan Barnert pointed with great pride to the fact that he was born on the holiest day in the Jewish calendar—Yom Kippur, the Day of Atonement— September 20, 1838, in Posen, in the kingdom of Prussia. He was as devoted to his people and to his people's God as he was when he came to these shores with his parents, Meyer and Ida (Newfelt) Barnert, in 1849, from his native home in Prussia. Nathan Barnert obtained his education in Posen and in New York City. It was a hard struggle in the beginning for this young immigrant. When he was not in his father's tailoring shop on Forsythe Street, New York, he was devoting his time to home study and in the Talmud Torah on Henry Street.

It did not take Nathan long to decide that his father's shop held little opportunity for him. At that time, the country was gripped with gold fever, and thousands were hurrying to the newly discovered fields of wealth in California. The boy became determined to cast his lot with the swelling crowd of fortune hunters. At that time, financing of a trip to the California gold fields was monumental. Nathan thought of many schemes to raise passage money. The electric light was unheard of then, and gas was a luxury that only a few could enjoy. So he decided to sell candles, with soaps as a sideline. It was a hard struggle from the beginning. Each day, he counted his small profits, and his enthusiasm increased with his slowly growing funds. After a few months, Nathan confided his plans to his parents one evening. They told him it was a fruitless effort, but he could not see it. So one morning, accompanied by another lad his own age, he went to Vanderbilt's steamshop agency on Warren and West streets, New York, and counted out $130 in small change for his passage to Nicaragua, and off he went.

A few hours later, the boys found out the money did not include meals on the ship. For a couple of days, they did not eat; but then, when Nature asserted herself, something had to be done to satisfy the cravings of hunger. The next morning, they entered the boiler room, where the coal passers worked under the direction of a big, kind-hearted man in uniform.[40] Pointing to the shovels, he said, "Cap, I am strong, and I can do what that big fellow is doing. Give me a chance, will you?" The officer was impressed with his boldness and engaged him along with his companion. For three days and nights, the boys worked hard, and then the announcement came that their destination was near at hand. After washing, they put on clean clothes, and they went to the purser's office, and each received thirty-six dollars for their labor.

After leaving the ship, Nathan overcame his sudden feeling of lonesomeness. He proceeded to Marysville, California, and then on to Sacramento. The mining camp was filled with stories of big strikes, and prosperity was everywhere. After figuring things out, Nathan went to San Francisco and bought a supply of candles and perfumed soaps. He made visits to the mining camps. He was at once very successful, and, in a short time, he had saved fourteen hundred dollars. Then he decided to take a little pleasure trip. One Sunday night, five of them went to the El Dorado—a prominent gambling house of that day. All sorts of gambling games were played—the Mexican game monte, the French game of roulette, and the American faro. Many handsomely gowned, pretty women were in evidence, all after the miners' gold. Young Barnert also took a chance, and, needless to say, he lost his hard-earned money and with it his gold watch, which he had treasured for years. He then raised his hand and took a pledge that he would never play cards again.

He went back to the mining camp, sold his depleted stock of candles, and determined to advance himself by becoming a merchant prince. He went back to San Francisco, where he learned that a man by the name of Dixon, who had once resided in Paterson, owned a big store. Nathan went to see Mr. Dixon and was fortunate to secure a position as office boy. He swept floors, did chores; and, through his engaging manners, he became well-acquainted with the Dixon family. He worked there for several months and then decided to go on his own. He thanked the Dixons for helping him and promised to return the favor whenever possible in the future. He purchased a mule and peddling outfit, returned to the mining camps, and, by close application, he amassed quite a lot of money. He sold his outfit and went into the express business for a brief spell. He visited the Hawaiian Islands, and then, hearing of the fortunes being made in the gold regions on the Fraser River, he took a trip to that territory.[41] He did not find what he sought, but he acquired a knowledge of the country that he always cherished as sweet memories.

Nathan then returned to New York and for two years engaged in the clothing business. Then, in 1858, he decided to go to Paterson, where he opened a tailoring shop in partnership with Marks Cohen on Main Street. Later he became associated with Solomon Mendelsohn, whose interest he later bought out. That was at 149 Main Street. Then came the Civil War. All business became stagnant, but Mr. Barnert was not idle. He secured large contracts to clothe the Union forces, and he was thus able to give employment to hundreds of persons who were on the verge of starvation. That was his first real service to his fellow men in his adopted city. When the war was over, business returned to normal again, expanding from year to year. He was always ready to invest in real estate and made a big success of it. Mr. Barnert continued in the mercantile line until 1878, when he retired to devote his attention to his real estate interests. He invested some of his capital in founding a new industry in Paterson—that of furnishing supplies to paper mills. He retired from that company in 1893.

On September 2, 1863, Mr. Barnert married Miriam Phillips, daughter of Henry L. and Jane (Chapman) Phillips, born in 1837 in Chelsea, England. She came to this country as a young girl and for some years lived in New York City. Mr. Barnert has often stated that he owed his success as much to her as to his own efforts, by virtue of her gentleness and her magnetic personality. She always helped the poor and the suffering and was beloved by all who knew her. She was also a dominant figure in the fraternal world. When she died in March 1901, men, women, and children mourned her. They had lost a dear friend. The Miriam Barnert Hospital, a building that occupies one of the finest blocks on Broadway and cost a quarter of a million dollars, was a gift from her husband.

The public life of Mr. Barnert was one of exemplary honesty and uprightness. He was a champion of justice and honest methods. His fellow citizens honored him, and he honored them by the faithful and conscientious discharge of official duties. Paterson at that time was a natural Republican city; the Republicans had control of public office. A sturdy Democrat, Mr. Barnert was delegated by the Board of Alderman in 1879 to investigate the city's finances. His work was so thorough that it finally landed a number of crooked officials in the New Jersey state prison. He became a power in Paterson politics and was finally persuaded to relinquish the comforts of private life for the toil of public office. He was elected alderman of the Sixth Ward in 1876, and he stood the test so well that he was returned to office for another term.

The citizens of Paterson were not yet satisfied and insisted that Mr. Barnert run for mayor. He accepted and was nominated as the Democratic candidate for that high position. After a bitter political struggle, Mr. Barnert was elected mayor of Paterson with a majority of 868 votes. That was on April 8, 1883. During his term in office, he served his people well, fighting for their rights and benefits and against loose methods and mismanagement, no matter whose toes were stepped on. He was not dependent on his office for his livelihood, and he made that very clear by donating his official salary to the hospitals and the city's poor to the surprise of the public and even his enemies—an example of political liberality very seldom encountered. He was, at all times, very alert, and he prosecuted and punished several high officials for malfeasance in office. Thereby, he won himself a legion of friends for his honest administration.

In the next election, through the influence of Mayor Barnert, the mayoralty nomination was given to Mr. C. Cadmus, who was then elected. But in 1888, the people of Paterson persuaded Mr. Barnert to reenter politics. He was unanimously nominated as his party's candidate and reelected mayor after a close and bitter fight. The citizens of Paterson were to be congratulated upon Nathan Barnert's election. It was a great victory for justice and against political crookedness and misrepresentation. The honest pursuit of his administration was a never-ending vigil. A city hall clique had to be watched all the time— and they knew it—resulting in a big savings to the Paterson taxpayers. At the end of his term, Nathan Barnert returned to private life and retired from politics, even though efforts were made to induce him to be a candidate for Congress. Mr. Barnert declined all offers of further political honors.

He was made a member of the committee of citizens who were in charge of the erection of a statue to Mr. Hobart.[42] On January 1, 1912, he was named by then mayor Andrew McBride to be a member of the Finance Commission, the governing body of Paterson. Mr. Barnert's selection was a most popular one and came unsolicited. He was grateful for his appointment because it gave him an opportunity still to serve the people of Paterson. At his home on Broadway, Mr. Barnert had a large number of gifts from friends and admirers. There are two manuscripts—both works of art—which are both interesting for the sentiments they expressed, gifts of the trustees of the Miriam Barnert Memorial Temple and the faculty and scholars of the Hebrew school.

The latter, a magnificent work of art, was presented to Mr. Barnert on the occasion of his birthday anniversary on October 13, 1913. On one parchment is inscribed the signature of scholars, showing in this way their appreciation for the many kind and generous acts of their benefactor. Had it not been for his love and generosity, there would not have been a Barnert Memorial Temple, Miriam Barnert Hebrew Free School, or Barnert Memorial Hospital as his noble and enduring monuments.

"By their deeds ye shall remember them."

Adjustment Difficulties

I was born in Lithuania, then called Russia. I started Hebrew school when I was four years old. The average length of the day's learning was ten to twelve hours, with no chance of any recreation during the day. When I was eight years old, the Jews were forced to attend a Russian school, in which both the school and the teacher were licensed by the government. The Jewish students were forced to attend the Russian school for at least three years, during which time they were taught arithmetic and reading. We lived a very poor life in the old country. Homes were heated by wood from the forest. The only means of light we had were oil lamps; and for water, we were forced to walk three blocks because there was only one water pump for every large area. Hospitals were very far apart, and doctors were few and far between. The Russian government had no interest in the health of the Jews. Conditions were very unsanitary. I recall when my youngest sister was born. It was a very sudden birth. There were no doctors or midwives called in. The only help we had were from the neighbors, who were always willing to help. They had gained their knowledge from previous births. There were a great many deaths at childbirth due to the unsanitary conditions. Many times there weren't any clean sheets, lights, or hot water. No instruments were used; baskets or drawers were used as cribs.

There was a great deal of farming in one territory, but the food, in general, was very poor. There was plenty of wheat and other grains. Our mothers did their own baking, and we ate a great deal of potatoes and apples. We had very little amusement in the old country. We used to take long walks on Sunday through the parks with our friends, and we would discuss letters and reports from our friends in the new, rich world—America. Then, towards the later part of the afternoon, we would walk toward the band concert and listen to the waltzes. If we ever took a girl out, it was usually to the beer gardens, where we drank beer and listened to the various entertainments and where we joined in with the other guests singing songs.

As we grew older, much of our time was spent in the synagogue, where a group of Jews led by a rabbi sat around the table the read the Torah.[43] We studied this very closely, going over it word by word. Many, many hours were spent on one page, and this continued day after day like a serial picture show. The rabbi explained every article to us very thoroughly, and thus we had a great knowledge of the Talmud.[44]

My father was a rabbi in the old country, and he taught me to chant the Jewish hymns because he wanted me to follow in his footsteps. My father had corresponded with some rabbis who had come to this country previously with promises of a golden opportunity here. We were informed that rabbis were earning as high as twenty dollars a week. With some help from friends in America, I decided to leave for America. I promised my wife that I would send for her just as soon as I could get myself located and earn a living. Therefore, I set sail for America, entering in the Lower East Side of New York City. I stayed with some friends who were rabbis. At once, I was told that if I wanted to be a rabbi in America, I would have to learn English, so that I could perform marriage ceremonies and other customs in American ways. I started at once in a night school. The teacher was a Jewess. We arranged that if I gave her some private lessons in Jewish and Hebrew, she would teach me English in return. She was a great help to me.

Two months later, I secured a position as rabbi in Elizabeth, New Jersey. This position was secured through some correspondence from my father in the old country with some rabbis in New Jersey. In Elizabeth, I went to night school, but there was some laughter over my way of expression and small beard that I had. I then secured a private teacher, and for four years, I took lessons from a young fellow who had graduated a high school. I lived in a furnished room for two years with some very religious people. During this time, I sent ten dollars a week to my wife in Russia. This was considered a lot of money. My wife was getting rich and soon saved enough money to come to America.

When she arrived in America, we had a little party in celebration of the event. For a joke, we placed a banana on a plate with a knife and fork and a salt-and-pepper shaker. She had never seen a banana before and did not know what it was. My wife took her knife and fork in hand and started to cut the banana like a piece of meat and then seasoned it with salt and pepper. This brought a great deal of laughter from all around. From then on, my wife was very careful before she ate any American foods.

In the evenings, we would sit home and receive visits from members and leaders of the synagogue where I was rabbi. We would return these visits, and this was our only means of entertainment. Many evenings I would spend at home, practicing our Jewish hymns to prepare for service on the High Holy Days. Many of the boys of other ethnic groups would shout at me as they passed the window. Then, the vandals would run away.

There were times when I passed the corner store where the boys hanged out, and loud remarks were passed about me being a Jew and having a beard. I did not mind this later on, because I was getting used to it. This was the only trouble I had with the other ethnic groups.

There was no trouble with other Jewish groups, because the Polish Jews lived with Polish Jews and the Łódźer Jews with the Łódźer Jews and Russians with the Russians. I was well respected by all Jews and received invitations by other Jewish groups to preach at their pulpits. I don't believe any Jews had any trouble with other Jewish groups, because they all had their separate synagogues, clubs, etc.

Two years later, I received a call to Paterson, where I made my new home. We had four nice rooms, and we paid twelve dollars a month in rent. The toilets were in the yard, and we used to bathe in the sink. This was a paradise compared with the conditions we had to live under in the old country. We had gas lights in every room.

Almost every member of my synagogue and most of those I met worked in the silk mills. Ninety percent of all the Jews who came to Paterson at this time came from the textile centers of Russia and Poland, such as Łódź, Białystok, and Warsaw. There was also a large number of peddlers, both junk and merchant, who were too ill to work in the mills.

There was a great need for additional synagogues in Paterson because of the mass immigration at this time. On the High Holy Days, large, private halls and auditoriums were rented, and cantors were paid twenty-five dollars for the three High Holy Days.[45] Cantors were also imported from New York, and chairs were rented from the funeral parlors. This was our emergency synagogue. Tickets for the High Holy Days were sold at three dollars, and about two hundred to three hundred tickets were sold for the holidays. Additional money was raised when men were needed to remove the Torah from the ark. The honor was sold for as high as ten dollars. Then, during the reading from the Torah, there were about eight blessings, and an auction was also held for this honor. These various activities almost made as much as one thousand dollars a year profit. When the time came to raise additional money for the shul, maps were drawn with a layout of all seats in the synagogue, and a committee would solicit new members, selling seats for permanent-life or periods of five or ten years for large sums of money. In this way, large sums of money were raised, and several synagogues were built. My income from the synagogue at this time was eight hundred dollars a year, but I earned additional money from the slaughtering of *kosher* fowl, which paid me three cents a head, and cattle, which paid me as high as one dollar.[46] Then, I performed wedding ceremonies and circumcisions. I also took care of ceremonies at funerals. For these, I received a donation of five or ten dollars, according to the wealth of the people. When the people were in need, there was no cost at all.

In the year of about 1910, I and several other Jewish leaders of Paterson got together and formed the United Brotherhood congregation, bringing all the synagogues and Jews in the city under one rabbi, who was head supervisor and judge. This brought a greater harmony among the Jews of Paterson.

My children received their Hebrew education from a rabbi who called at our house every day, spending forty-five minutes or an hour after public school. For this service, I paid him five dollars per month. Their higher Hebrew education was received by attending all services with me and gathering around the table with other Jews, learning the Torah. This is the same system taught me in the old country and is still being used in the Orthodox shul.

In the early part of the twentieth century, there was no trouble in obtaining kosher foods. The Jew realized this was a business by itself and entered it as a Jewish grocer or butcher. Many of the older members of my synagogue informed me that in the nineteenth century, the English butchers sold kosher meats, under the supervision of a rabbi.

From 1890 to 1910, there was an amusement park on top of the Passaic Falls and one out in Singac, where you could go with a five-cent ride on a horsecar. There were large picnic grounds; we would bring our lunches and enjoy the various rides. The cost of the rides were five cents; and for a very little cost, the families would have a grand time. There were a great number of Jews who attended these parks.

On Sunday evenings, we usually had a traveling rabbi stop at our synagogue, sing Hebrew and Jewish songs for us and also tell us clever stories. This entertainment was like a vaudeville tour, and it was arranged from New Jersey. There was usually a charge of fifteen cents for this—ten cents for the rabbi and five cents for the synagogue. It took me about five years to adjust economically, to learn to speak the

238   Jews

English language, the American way of wearing a beard, clothing myself to the American manner, etc. After this, I enjoyed American shows
and visited with a great number of Americans.

Since 1920, I have noticed from my synagogue and through friend-
ships that there are a great many Jews leaving the city of Paterson.
There are no more silk manufacturers left in Paterson, because of the
economic conditions, and no more Jewish workers. Many Jews have
followed the textile mills down South and to Pennsylvania, where labor
is cheaper. There were hundreds of heads of families who have become
owners of grocery and candy stores throughout the state with the little
money they had salvaged from the silk business.

Murray Koch

The Polish Jews Stuck Together

The interviewee was born in the city of Łódź, Poland, which was a very
large textile center. His parents were brought up in Łódź, and he
worked in the woolen mills. He left Poland to avoid the Russo-Japanese
War. He arrived in New York in 1897, after a ten-day sea voyage. He was
only twenty-three at the time. After a week in New York with relations, he came to Paterson and stayed with some friends, who had
come from Łódź several years before.

The food habits here were the same as in Łódź, with a greater variety
of fruits and vegetables here. They had meat once a day; before these
meat dinners, they had a piece of herring. On Friday nights, they started their meal with a glass of whiskey, noodle soup, chicken, and sometimes *gefilte* fish.[47] After forty-three years in America, the interviewee
still has the same Friday-night supper. On the other side, they baked
their own bread, known as *challah*, for the Sabbath.[48]

When he first came to Paterson, the interviewee stayed with friends
on Godwin Street, a very short block from River Street, which still is
the Jewish center of Paterson. This was in 1897. A year later, he was
married, and they took three rooms on River Street. It was a modern
apartment in those days, with gas in every room, running water in the
kitchen, and a toilet in the backyard, where they kept a candle for light.
For the next fourteen years, they moved several times to North Main
Street, Clinton Street, and then to Benson Street, which was on the
other side of the river. The Jewish section of Paterson was three or four

blocks on both sides of the river, running along the river for five blocks from what was then called Hamburg Avenue, which is now West Broadway, to Straight Street Bridge.

They had little difficulties with other ethnic groups. When they walked with friends through other parts of the cities, the corner loafers, who hung out at the corners, would make fun of them upon hearing them talk Jewish. The loafers would heckle them, making motions with their hands to their faces. Many times, small groups of these boys would come through the Jewish section and would poke fun at the elder Jews with beards.

The Polish Jews stuck together, especially the Łódźers. They had their own society; and, at their annual ball in the Hebrew Free School, they had a very enjoyable time, meeting with many of their former friends from Łódź. There were many visitors from New York, Passaic, and other cities, who came to meet with their old friends from Łódź, talk over old times, and see old faces. Many of them had received letters from home, and their friends were always interested in reading these letters. On most of these occasions, they would have a person who had recently come from Łódź go up on the platform and say a few words about conditions back home. Many of the people would ask questions about their friends and families in Łódź. This same good time was held at their annual picnic, which was held out in the parks during summertime.

There was little or no money that could be saved out of the earnings on the other side, and, in most cases, their friends and families in America bought tickets in New York and mailed them to Poland as passage to America. In this case, the interviewee's brothers, who had come to America several years previously, mailed home ten dollars a month, and in three years he managed to save enough money for passage. He arrived here with eighteen dollars in his pocket. He did not live beyond his means, and he always managed to save a few dollars a week, no matter how much he earned. He had saved three hundred dollars by the time of his marriage.

Most of the Jews—about 75 percent of them—earned their living by working in the silk mills. There were jobs for every member of the family in the mill. Most of the peddlers, both junk and custom, were Jews. A great many Jews were the owners of grocery and candy stores throughout the city. The clothing stores on Main and Market streets and on Broadway were owned by the German Jews, who lived in the East Side section of Paterson.

As mentioned above, the interviewee left Łódź in the year 1897 and arrived at Ellis Island after ten days at sea. His relatives from New York greeted him at the pier, and he stayed with them for a week because they were anxious to hear from their folks and friends in Łódź. Up until the time of leaving Łódź, he had corresponded with some friends and relations in Paterson. They had written him that he could secure work in silk mills because of his experience in the woolen mills of Łódź. After two weeks in Paterson, some friends took him to the mills where they worked to get some practical experience on silk looms.

In the old country, there were a great many synagogues in the basements of various homes. It was a daily, morning custom to go to synagogue and put *tefillin*[49] on his arm and forehead. In this country, it was done only on the Jewish holidays. In the old country, he always wore *tzitzit*, which he never wore in this country.[50] He at once discarded his foreign hat and was given an American-style hat by his friends. He was forced to work on Saturdays to hold his job.

He joined the Lodzer Society on coming to Paterson, which boasted about two hundred members at that time; today, it has over three thousand members. During the past thirty years, there have been many auxiliary organizations that have worked hand in hand with the Lodzer Society, the most important being the Lodzer Young Men and the Lodzer Relief. There were many other, smaller Jewish organizations in Paterson in the year 1900 that were named after towns in Poland and Russia; namely Bialystok Society, named after the city of Białystok; Ozorkow, after the city of Ozorkow; and others. All of these organizations have increased their memberships greatly with the mass immigration of Jews. There were many other types of organizations, like the Workman's Circle, that has its own new, modern building today on Carroll Street and Twelfth Avenue, and of which there are nine branches and a membership of three thousand. This organization started with thirty members in the latter part of the nineteenth century and met in a rented hall. There were many Jewish lodges, whose main ideas were to give the Jew a decent burial and provide the family of the departed with a small sum of money.

In America, Saturday was not a special day anymore, far different than in the old country. Here, they were forced to work in order to keep their jobs. Saturday noon was payday, which gave them a chance to do their shopping. On many Saturday afternoons, the men would go to the synagogue for a few hours before the evening service. In the study room, many men would sit around the table with the rabbi and follow the readings of the holy books, chapter by chapter like a serial picture. Many interesting and enjoyable hours were spent this way. Very few Jews did any reading to speak of outside of some New York Jewish newspapers. In these cases, one out of many would buy a paper, and after reading it, would pass it on to their friends.

The interviewee was very anxious to learn English, as were the other Jewish immigrants at this time. A great many went to night school; others had various schoolboys teach them at their homes. He went to evening classes at Central High School for six months to learn the English language. He always had a great deal of love and respect for this land of opportunity. He applied for his citizenship papers in the year 1912. In my interview, he boasted several times of being an American citizen, and he felt very proud of this. He explained to me how wonderful this country was in contrast to Europe, both economically and politically.

He has three children of his own, and he feels that the American children have not enough responsibility. All they think about is good times and clothes. They don't worry about where the money comes from or about saving money. He claims they spend money very foolishly. His daughter earns fourteen dollars a week, and she claims this is not enough to keep her in clothes. She has to buy stockings make of silk twice a week at one dollar a pair; in the old country, his sisters bought stockings for nineteen cents, and they lasted several weeks. Cosmetics were not used in the old country. When his daughter bought a coat last winter, she insisted on paying over one hundred dollars, which he believed is far out of proportion to what she earns. There have been no great difficulties with his children outside of difference of opinions. He claims he gave his parents far more respect than he received from his children.

He had no difficulties with his parents. For seven years prior to his parents' deaths, he and his brothers gave five dollars a week for their support. The children saw to it that their parents were never in need at anytime during their lives. It seems that in the case of his father and other elderly Jews, they turned to religion very strongly and spent a great deal of their time in the synagogue. Having been brought up in a textile center of Łódź, where there were a great many woolen mills, his parents and friends were weavers. At the age of seventeen, his father taught him this trade, and this was the only thing he knew. There was very little difference between silk and woolen weaving; so after being in Paterson two weeks, he entered the silk mill, where he was not paid for learning. After this, he answered jobs for experienced weavers and was out of work only a few days. He started off with eleven dollars a week, and his wages were steadily increased until 1929, when the mills went out of business. His average pay in Łódź was only seven to nine dollars per week.

In his thirty years as a weaver in Paterson, he worked under about twenty-five different bosses. He quit his job because of arguments with his boss or poor quality silk or lack of light. He never knew any other trade, so he just drifted along in silk. He never belonged to any business organization, nor was he active in any labor groups. Paterson always had changes in its labor unions, and whenever he received a job in a union shop, he paid his union dues. When he worked in a nonunion shop, the union was forgotten about. He believed in organized labor, but was never active. He never worked in any strike and always looked for a new job instead of picketing.

The only great changes in America were in religious customs and in dress. In Łódź, the lady of the house would do her shopping, her housework, and prepare all her food on Thursday evening and Friday morning. After lighting the candles on Friday evening, there would be no more work until Saturday at sunset. In Łódź, wood was brought in from the forests and burned off in the stove, and water was brought in from the pumps a distance away. Conditions at home were unsanitary, with very few doctors and hospitals a great distance away. In this country, they dropped a great many of their religious customs. Their homes were more modern in America, and their future seemed so different here. In the schools of Łódź, they were taught Polish, a little German, and picked up some knowledge of Russian. In the Hebrew school, they were taught Jewish and Hebrew. In this country, they only used the Jewish language.

He became a citizen after being in this country about fifteen years, but he never became interested in politics. He only voted when someone asked him to. In the past few political campaigns, both parties brought Jewish talent to Paterson and held a show to bring out the Jewish voters. There were various Jewish speakers, who came out between the Jewish acts, pleading with the Jews to come out and vote, always picking out a Jewish candidate as bait. This man claims that in the next presidential campaign, he and all the other Jewish voters are going to vote because of the European situation. Their love for our democratic form of government has become stronger than ever. They have the same ideas as our own president in his actions in dealing with the countries in the present war. When in this country only a short time, he attended night classes in high school for six months and then had a schoolboy give him lessons in reading in the evening. He claims he is a hundred-percent American now and needs no other improvements in his education.

Murray Koch

The Only Blacksmith in Paterson

The interviewee was born in the city of Warsaw, in Russian Poland, in the year 1862. Warsaw was a large, but very poor city, with very few improvements. Only the rich went to school here, and the Jews had very little education. He was one of six children, and he was brought up in a very poor home. This is his second stay in this country, the first being in 1884, at the age of twenty-two years. He remained in this country two years before returning in 1886 by way of Germany, England, and Montreal, Canada. He came to Paterson in 1916.

On his first trip to this country in 1884, he was unable to find steady work. He does not recall at any time during this two-year period that he earned five dollars a week. He had a very hard and poor life, and he went through a great deal of suffering. Some friends had given him an old mattress, and he begged permission to sleep in a cellar, without light and heat. During the winter, he was very cold with only two cotton blankets he had bought off a pushcart for one dollar and a half. His face was never washed more than twice a week. He ate all his meals in the various saloons of the Lower East Side of New York, where he bought a whiskey for five cents and walked back to the free lunch counter and had a "free lunch." After these meals, he would buy a five-cent beer to wash it down. He tried a different saloon every day to fool the owner. He never bought any clothes during these two years. He still recalls his home in the cellar at 130 Forsyth Street on the Lower East Side of New York.

After two years of this life, his relations back in Warsaw sent him a ticket to return home. He returned home the same month that President McKinley was shot. After two years in Warsaw, he wanted to roam again, but he had very little money. He saved a few dollars and went to Hamburg, Germany, where he secured a job in a coppersmith shop. He remained there for eight months and then went to Berlin, where he worked for one year in a boiler works. He then went to Liverpool, and a few months later to London. By this time he had saved enough money to come to America. He arrived in Montreal, Canada, in the year 1888, where he worked for one year in a boiler shop. He then left for Boston, where he remained for nine months. He then met a rich girl, whom he married, and they bought a farm in Ellenville, New York. He was a farmer for twelve years. During this time, he was told that Paterson was a very busy and booming city and that there was much money to be made there. He sold his farm and came to Paterson in 1916.

He has never eaten anything but kosher foods at home. He has a great many of his lunches in saloons, and he eats anything he can get there. He has always lived in the Jewish sections of Paterson, never more than five or six blocks from River Street. He has never had any difficulty with other ethnic groups. He is a very agreeable man, and he seems to get along with everyone. He seemed to get along with all the various types of Jews in Paterson, except the "Junk Man's" synagogue on Water Street. He has a bitter hatred for them. He claims he was a member there from 1916 to 1919. At this time, his daughter, who had been married six months, passed away. The synagogue was to give members and their families a free burial plot. In this case, they decided that the daughter did not belong to him any longer, but to the man she had married. He resigned from this synagogue and joined one on Godwin Street.

In his first two years in America, he never had at any time more than two dollars in his pocket. In his various jobs in Hamburg, Berlin, London, and Boston, he had always managed to save a few dollars. At the time he was married, he had saved two hundred dollars. His wife at the time of his marriage gave him enough money to buy the farm. After coming to Paterson, he opened a blacksmith and horseshoe repair shop and did quite well. Business has been bad in Paterson the past five years, but he has the help of his children at present. His main work comes from the Jewish junk peddlers from Water Street.

Most of the Jews who came to Paterson had made plans to come here. They had come from the textile centers of Poland and had some correspondence with men who had come previously. Most Jews came to Paterson directly, after a short visit in New York. When he lived in Warsaw, many of his friends had corresponded with friends here, but there was no great demand for blacksmiths here. This is the reason he did not come to Paterson until 1916.

This man still has most of the old Jewish traditions. He does not, and never did, work on a Saturday or minor Jewish holidays. He goes to synagogue twice a day and on every holiday. He claims that synagogue membership is steadily on the increase. He goes to synagogue every Saturday morning, and then goes home to a cold lunch that has been cooked on Friday morning because he does not permit cooking on Saturday. He reads and takes a nap in the afternoon. About three hours before sunset, he returns to the study room of the synagogue and sits around the table with the other Jews and the rabbi, reading the Holy Book. Once in a while, a member will donate a herring, already cut in slices, and a bottle of whiskey, and a challah bread. Challah is not to be cut on Saturdays, so each man breaks off a piece. They have a snack after finishing reading and before starting the evening service, which is at sunset.

He never read anything but a Jewish paper that his neighbor had bought and passed on to him after reading. Many of the Jews went to evening classes in the high school to learn English, but not him. Though he has been in America for fifty-six years, he cannot read or write English, and he speaks it very poorly. After his second visit to this country, he developed a great love for it. He claims this is God's country, and there is nothing like it on earth. He thinks the younger generation is OK. He has five children, and each helps him at home. He claims the children of today are just as good as those who came from the other side. He has no difficulties with his children; they all help at home. He has two sons who work in the Brooklyn Navy Yard, and they always help him on their day off. Both his parents had passed away before he was five years old. His children respect him and his wife very much.

Most of the Jewish people of Paterson were brought up in the textile mills. Most of this man's friends were the Jewish peddlers who brought their horses to be shoed and wagons to be fixed at his blacksmith shop. In this man's fifty-six years in America, he has always been a black-smith, except for the twelve years he was on a farm in Ellenville, New York. The girl he married had been brought up on a farm, and this was the reason he went on a farm after getting married. He never belonged to any labor organizations or other organizations except a synagogue.

He claims there have been no changes in his family life in America. He says he still gets his three drinks a day, as on the other side. He has always spoken Jewish at home, although his children talk to him in English. Many times, he and his wife talk Polish or Russian when they don't want the children to hear. He speaks Russian and Polish very well. Though not a citizen, he has no ill feeling towards local politicians. He believes they are doing a very good job. He is very much in favor of what our government is doing in European affairs and in the relief programs at home. It is hard to believe that our government is doing such a wonderful job on the WPA, Old Age Pension, etc.

He had very little education on the other side because of his parents' passing away when he was a child. He never had any American education or attended any immigrant classes in this country.

This man is today seventy-eight years of age and is the only living blacksmith in Paterson today. He is very active and is at work every day from morn till night. He is strong as a bull and is only about five feet, five inches tall. He has his original set of teeth. He has five grown children, the youngest being twenty-four years of age.

Murray Koch

Struggle for a Living

Mr. X came to Zolochev in Galicia, which was then part of Austria, when he was eighteen. He arrived in this country during the 1903 depression, and he lived with a married sister.

In the old country, Mr. X was the third child in a family of four; the two oldest were sisters, the youngest a brother. Mr. X's father was a big man who was always in fine physical condition. He was a general storekeeper, whose business was the hub of the surrounding farms and the other businesses that had located nearby.

Mr. X relates that his mother died when he was seven years old. He recalls how bad the weather was the day of the funeral. He says that the snow was so high that he was carried on the shoulders of a relation, and his younger brother was left at home at his father's request. He also states that while his father was big, his mother was just the opposite— small, but sturdy. His father remarried, and Mr. X says that his stepmother was one of the finest persons he had ever known. He says that she could not have treated him better if he had been her own son.

Of course, Mr. X's family were subjected to many political persecutions because they were Jews. Nevertheless, Mr. X's father was well liked and respected because he was able and was known to consistently punish any slight—political, religious, or business. He also was trusted and was not bothered by any of the neighboring people. As he was fair and just in his dealings outside the home, so were his actions inside. He demanded and expected each member of his immediate family to behave in a manner befitting a decent citizen.

Mr. X's older sister left for America, where her fiancé awaited her. They were married here and soon had a daughter. Meanwhile, in the old country, Mr. X grew up as an average old-country youth does—all work with very little play. He recalls an incident, which occurred when he was about fifteen. He was out playing "shimmey"—the game in which a person strikes a peg with a larger stick, both usually made from an old broomstick. Someone was batting, and he was out in the field catching. The batter hit the peg up into the air, and Mr. X ran to catch it as it fell. He missed, and it struck him in the eye. As a result, he had a black eye. Fearing his father's wrath, Mr. X ran away from home. He lived in the fields for a week, until his eye resumed its natural complexion.

It must be realized at this point that Mr. X was confirmed after having attended *cheder* for a number of years.[51] This event takes place usually at the age of thirteen for all Orthodox Jewish boys. But, as Mr. X's mother was dead, he was confirmed at the age of twelve, as is customary for all orphans.

As he was now nearing his seventeenth birthday, his father was afraid that he would be conscripted for Franz Josef's Austrian army.[52] Heeding his father's advice, Mr. X left for America, financed by his family's meager savings. He boarded the train about two miles from home to avoid embarrassing questions from the station agent. He then went through Lemberg, Kraców, Dresden, Vienna, Berlin, to Hamburg. In Hamburg, he boarded the ship for America, and presented his credentials and tickets to the official.

On the ship, he was shown to the third-class location. Mr. X says that the men were assigned to a dormitory and the women to another. He says the conditions were filthy as well as unsanitary. It was sixteen days, before the ship arrived in New York. After much red tape, Mr. X was greeted at the gangplank by his sister, brother-in-law, and a friend. He had six dollars in his pocket. He was taken to their home, where a hearty meal was enjoyed by all. After this meal, Mr. X went out for a walk. While walking, he was struck by a baseball in the back of the neck. He had to be treated by a doctor for possible injury, but soon he was allowed to return to his sister's home.

The next day, he went to board with his friend on Essex Street on New York's East Side, where he lived for four years. His first job was very hard to get. During the winter, he tried to get a job shoveling snow. Because it was during the depression and Mr. X looked so young, he was refused. He was told to go home, to let his father support him, and not to take away a job from a family man.

After a while, Mr. X got a job in a paper factory. He earned eight dollars a week, deducted his living expenses, and sent the balance to Europe. During this absence, a great fire destroyed his hometown, and his family's belongings were lost. He continued to work in the paper factory for six months. Meanwhile, he sought another job.

He found a new job in a lumberyard in Brooklyn. He worked here for about three months, and learned how to work on machines. While employed here, Mr. X made some contacts with the New York Central Railroad. In a short time, he was traveling all over New York and New Jersey as a special carpenter for the company. He worked for this outfit for two years.

Soon Mr. X got tired of this type of work, and he quit. He was unemployed for a few days, when he got a job in a grocery store. Here, Mr. X clerked and learned the business. His wages were four dollars per week plus keep. Mr. X kept this job for three years. He continued sending money to his family and living with his sister and brother-in-law.

Mr. X undertook a business venture on his own behalf. He bought a soda-fountain stand on a side street on the East Side of New York. He tells me that he had much trouble with the police and the politicians. His troubles ceased as soon as he got his citizenship papers and joined his precinct branch of Tammany Hall. He didn't bother with the workings of political parties. He merely was a good member. He went to all meetings and voted as he was "advised." Once, he didn't vote as he was advised, and, as a result, he had trouble with the Board of Health, Sanitation Branch, Police Department, and Fire Department for maintaining a fire hazard. This one example was enough to keep him in line. Mr. X remained here for two years.

His next business was a dairy store at Nineteenth Street and Ninth Avenue. Here Mr. X made a fair living. He continued to send money to his family in Europe. By now, his brother was a young man, who wished to come to America with his shovel to pick up some of the gold that was lying in the streets. Therefore, Mr. X sent for his brother. Soon, Mr. X's brother was here, outfitted and polished up in the American fashion of the pre–world war era. As Mr. X's brother couldn't get a job, he went to work for Mr. X. Mr. X saw that his brother was not adapted to this dairy, so he gave him some expense money and had him go out and look for a job. His brother got a job as a lugger in the wholesale butter-and-egg district on the East Side of New York. By chance, a new opportunity befell Mr. X. He was able to open a dairy store on Wadsworth Avenue, where a fine population of German people lived. Here, indeed, did Mr. X prosper. Still Mr. X continued to send money home and to pay for his board at his sister's home.

During these years, Mr. X went to various affairs and entertainments. He was considered a good dancer, but he did not strut on his dates. Soon, a friend of Mr. X took him to a small community about fifteen miles from New York, where Mr. X was introduced to a presentable young lady. Soon she became Mr. X's steady date. In about six months, Mr. X and his girlfriend were married. They continued to live in New York for two years. Then the X's moved to the hometown of Mrs. X. Here they opened a small dairy, because the United States was in a depression, and business in New York was bad. In this town, Mr. X endeavored to find employment, while his wife took care of the store. Now they had a son. Four months previous to the birth of his son, Mr.

X's sister died. It is the custom of Jewish people to name a baby after a dead relation. If the baby is of a different sex, the name is adapted to make it work.

Meantime, war was raging in Europe. Mr. X got a job in a lumberyard, and business picked up in the store. Soon Mrs. X's economic standard was raised. After a while, Mr. X gave up the store, but continued to work. But too soon the bubble burst, and Mr. X was without employment. Nevertheless, his economic base was soon restored because in a short time the United States entered the war on the side of the Allies. Immediately, he went to work in the army camps in South Jersey. He lived here and went home on weekends. During this period, Mr. X paid off many of his debts and put aside a few dollars for a rainy day

In the fall of 1917, Mr. X's wife gave birth to a daughter. This wiped out his savings. By working overtime, Mr. X was able to pay his bills without falling behind. Soon Mr. X's class was drafted. He was signed up and allowed to continue working, but he was told to report to his hometown draft office each weekend. This he continued to do during the beginning of 1918. Now he was told that he would no longer have to report, but he had to be prepared for any emergency. Although anxious about the political solution, Mr. X's family lived a happy social life because of financial stability. In November of that year, the armistice was signed, and Mr. X was given a honorable discharge.

The usual economic conditions prevailed after the war—depression. Mr. X lost his job, and he again tried to establish a dairy. This venture was fairly successful, but it was a hard job to make ends meet. The family lived over the store in a four-room flat for one year. During this time, Mr. X bought a small Model-T truck. He had to buy this because there was a strike of truck drivers, and trucking rates were exorbitant. In spring of the following year, Mr. X moved to a new location about five blocks away, where he prospered. He made a good living and entered the wholesale dairy business. Soon he had a thriving little trade.

One day, his landlord came to see him and saw the business. He raised Mr. X's rent five dollars. The third month, he raised to ten dollars. In six month's time, the rent was doubled. Mr. X attempted to have his landlord sign a lease at a reasonable amount of rent, but it was to no avail. The latter told Mr. X that if he did not like it, he knew what he could do. Before saying this, the landlord made sure that there were no stores in the vicinity.

Mr. X realized that this couldn't go on forever, so he looked around for a good location. Seeing none, he attempted to negotiate for a site, but to no avail. Therefore, he saw that he would have to buy a house in the vicinity if he wished to remain. So he contacted several property owners, but they asked high prices. Therefore, Mr. X went to a middleman to buy it for him. He saved himself three thousand dollars and moved into his own home. It was a four-family house, with a large store on the ground floor. Here Mr. X thrived and felt financially secure.

But all was not to go well. Mr. X's wholesale business went under, and he lost several hundred dollars, a large sum for a small businessman. In the meanwhile, Mr. X bought a new 1922 Dodge car, paying cash for it so as to save about eighty-five dollars in finance charges. Soon Mrs. X had another son, making it three children in the family. Meanwhile, the life of the family continued along its way. Then Mrs. X became sick. She was operated on, and had to get away for a rest. This incident set Mr. X back approximately five hundred dollars. While she was gone, Mr. X had a woman in the house to care for his family. Things moved along fairly well, but then the baby boy got the measles. Well, this was another hardship that Mr. X had to overcome, and he did so with a great deal of trouble. By this time, the family was reunited because Mrs. X returned.

As was the custom during this postwar period, the oldest son was taught the violin and the daughter the piano. Life ran along smoothly for his family for the next three years. Then there came a strike in a local mill, and many thousands of employees were out of work. Mr. X extended credit in his dairy, and did not press the tenants for not paying rent. Mr. X took out a second mortgage on his building, forced the people to move, and renovated his building. In the meanwhile, the strike was lost by the employees. Mr. X lost a great deal of money, and the people to whom he had extended credit now did not speak to him anymore.

After renovating the house, making it up to date in its entirety, Mr. X attempted to rent these flats. He was successful immediately. He received the rents, and the families moved in. Such good luck was not destined to last. The following month, two families moved, and third didn't pay any rent. The two flats were empty, and for six months the third tenant did not pay. Soon, Mr. X lost his property and had to move. He opened stores in various sections of the city, but they were not successful. Meanwhile, his children grew up and sought employment, but were only partially successful.

Today, Mr. X is located in a small store, struggling for a living. He leaves his wife and youngest son to mind the business, while he attempts to get some occasional jobs. Nevertheless, he is optimistic and believes that the future will take care of itself as long as he continues living carefully and righteously to the best of his ability. He votes very rarely in primary elections, and in the general election he votes for the man. He admits that he voted for Debs, the Socialist candidate for President.[53]

Herman Bader

To Have Her Own Family

The parents of Miss X were born and brought up in the same community. Their homes were near the Austro-Russian border. The town was Lvov. Her mother was the oldest child in a family of four. Her mother's mother died when her mother was a young girl. Because she was the oldest, a great deal of the work fell upon her mother. Nevertheless, she led a sheltered life, and she married at the age of eighteen. Her father was a distant relation of his wife. He was a very religious Jew—a scholar and a rabbi. He never shaved and had long hair along his sideburns, called *payess*.[54] He was wont to wander in the fields, lost in deep thought and meditation. He made a poor living, and, when he married, the young couple went to live with her mother's father. Of this marriage, three daughters and one son were born. The oldest of these is Miss X, born in 1908. She remembers nothing of her childhood, only that she was brought up in the usual manner of a daughter of an Orthodox Jewish home.

When Miss X was eight years old, the world war broke out. To this unhappy family's misfortune, their home province was a tramping ground for the opposing forces—Russian and Austrian. Their lives were in danger every moment. Many times, they hid in the cellar to escape death by stray bullets. The Austrian government decided to remove all people from this area, and so this family was moved. They were sent to Lemburg and from there to Warsaw—a city of war refugees. Many families became broken, parents separated or killed, and children lost. In this way, this nine-year-old girl became estranged from her family. When her family became aware of her disappearance, they thought she had been killed. She, on the other hand, feared the same about her family. When many of these refugee families were returned to their provinces, Miss X was left stranded in Warsaw. She was taken in by a kind family, for whom she worked for her keep, and these kind people treated her as one of their own children. Miss X continued to work for them for about eight years.

In 1918, when the war ended, and mail was able to pass freely from the United States and the Central Powers, Miss X wrote to an uncle and asked him to bring her to the United States. At no time did her uncle wish to do it, but, as perseverance will in time wear away the most stubborn refusals, in 1923 she was sent for. During this exchange of letters, she learned about the whereabouts and plight of her family. Her father had died the previous year, but she was in no condition then to aid her family.

Miss X was brought here in second-class passage. The trip took twelve days. She says that each day was happier than the preceding because she knew that she was that much closer to the promised land. She arrived in New York on a Tuesday in May. She was checked out at Ellis Island and immediately went to her uncle's home. That night, her aunt took her to the Turkish hot baths to clean her up from her long trip. The next day, her aunt and uncle took her out shopping and bought her a complete wardrobe.

After two weeks of inactivity, she got a job in a handkerchief factory. She earned ten dollars per week—the prevailing wage for beginners in this trade. She got this job through her aunt. She worked there for two years. By this time, economic conditions were such that everybody was making good wages. As she did not receive any advancement, she became dissatisfied with her work, and she quit this job. Fortunately, she did this around Christmas time. Immediately, she got a job in a downtown department store, where she received fifteen dollars a week to start. This season lasted three weeks, and then all the extra girls were laid off, including her. The following week, the proprietor called her back and gave her a steady job.

Miss X worked seven years at this job. She sold stockings and dresses, pots and pans, toys and school supplies, and all the odds and ends that are sold in a department store. She received several raises, until she earned twenty-three dollars per week.

During this time, she went to social affairs. She hoped to meet some eligible young man, but it was to no avail. Three years ago, she lost this job because of the depression. Immediately, she got a job in a corset shop, where she made out very well. With commissions and salary, she made twenty-five dollars per week. Here, she also got presents from various salesmen, who wished that she would push their particular merchandise and show her boss that the customers preferred certain brands of stock.

During this time, she still endeavored to fill her empty life—empty in the respect that she had no company of the opposite sex. Her boss was a bachelor, but he often said that he would never consider marrying a foreign-born person. Last year, he married a school teacher, who gave up her career and entered the business with her husband. The result was that Miss X again lost her job. This time, Miss X was unemployed for four months. Last April, she went to a New York employment agency and was able to get a job as a waitress for the summer at a hotel in Liberty, New York. She worked for three months, and, at the end of the season, she returned home with a little savings. After a while, Miss X and her mother used up this little reserve fund. She was unable to gain steady employment. This has continued to the present. She is now working part-time in a suit factory.

During this time, Miss X has had to live in a downtown section of town, where the rent is low. As you can readily see from the above information, at no time was Miss X fixed financially so as not to worry about her job. Since coming to this country, Miss X has moved only once. Miss X keeps the Orthodox Jewish faith. She attends the synagogue only during the High Holidays. Her physical condition is good. Her main defect is her height. She is only five feet tall. This eliminates her from many jobs. To be a coat or dress salesgirl, she must of necessity be at least five and a half feet tall. Because of her height and her lacking social recreation, she at times becomes moody, bitter, and cynical. Miss X has no particular amusements nor recreational activities. She would like very much to get married and have a family of her own. At present, she expressed deep sympathy for her two sisters and her brother and sister-in-law, who are still in Poland.

Herman Bader

Thanks God for America

Mrs. X was born in Minsk, Russia. Her father was a rabbi, and her mother was also from a scholarly family. Her family was never rich, but merely comfortably fixed. Her birth was normal; her mother was attended by a midwife. Her childhood was full of teachings regarding Orthodox Jewry and Russian culture—the little that there was.

Mrs. X came here when she was sixteen. She lived with an older sister in Brooklyn. Being that she was an experienced seamstress, she opened her own shop. She kept it for about seven years, and then she was married. She liked this type of work because she was her own boss. The income was very good, and she kept at it for about two years after her marriage. Then she went to Detroit, where she lived for five years. Her two older children—both girls—were born there. Mr. X was in the wholesale fruit business. At about this time, Mr. X began to fail in his health. The doctors urged him to move to a different climate.

Therefore, the family moved to California, where they stayed for three months. Next, the Xs moved to Jacksonville, Florida, where they lived for about one year on the little income from his wholesale business. The family then moved to Baltimore. They stayed there for two or three months because Mr. X was very sick. As soon as he got in a condition to travel, they returned to Brooklyn, where they lived for about one and one-half years. There the youngest child was born—a third daughter.

The family had a cousin in Paterson, who told them of a grocery store. So the Xs bought this store and moved to Paterson. They worked hard to make ends meet. After seven years, Mr. X died, but Mrs. X continued the business. Meanwhile, the girls grew up and continued their education. The two older girls graduated from high school, and the younger girl is a third-year student in East Side High. Mrs. X eventually sold her business. She is living today with her older daughter, who is now married. The second daughter is also married and has a baby daughter.

At all times, these two daughters have helped their mother in the store. At present, they still are helping her. Mrs. X continues to practice Orthodox Judaism. She goes to the synagogue only on the High Holidays. She likes everything about this country, especially its leniency towards the Jews. She thanks God for America after knowing conditions in prewar Russia. Mrs. X enjoys Jewish plays and radio programs. She is in fair health and makes a fine appearance. She is about fifty-two years old. Her hair is totally gray, and her hands show that she did much hard work in the past.

Herman Bader

The First Jew Killed in Action in France

Reuben Kaufman is known and remembered as the first Jewish Paterson boy who fought and died for his adopted country "over there." Reuben Kaufman was born in West Hartlepool, England, on July 10, 1897, and was brought to this country at an early age on June 28, 1904.

He was the son of Mr. and Mrs. Max Kaufman, who resided at Sixteen Cliff Street. He had five sisters and four brothers; his father operated a successful tailor shop. Reuben did not like the tailor business; the silk industry attracted him. He got a job in one of the large manufacturing plants and learned the business through actual experience. When still very young, he entered the manufacturing business—warping, entering, and silk twisting—and he was very successful at the time.[55] He was educated in the Paterson public schools, graduating from School No. 12, where he was an outstanding athlete, specializing in running. Shortly after graduating, he became an American citizen and proved to be of great credit to his adopted country.

Then, war was declared against Germany. At President Wilson's first call, Reuben was one of the first to enlist in the American army. He joined Company D, 114th Infantry, composed of members of the famous old Fifth Regiment. After the usual training period at Camp McClellan in Anniston, Alabama, his outfit was sent overseas and took part in the great offensives against Germany, which helped to turn the tide of the war. On October 12, 1918, his number was called, and he died fighting for his country—a hero. He was a volunteer company runner—an extremely dangerous assignment at that time. He was laid to rest at the famous Meuse Argonne Cemetery at Mon La Fana, Averne, France, October the 12th, 1918—the date that is sorrowfully written in the hearts of his family and in the hearts of many more who lost their kin in the great battles of that day. May his hero soul rest in peace.

On February 11, 1932, the Paterson Jewish War Veterans organized a post under the auspices of Jewish veterans and named it the Reuben Kaufman Post in honor of Reuben Kaufman, a Patersonian, the first Jew killed in action in France. The post is today a very prominent, patriotic Paterson organization, with an excellent band with Professor J. V. Dittamo as its director. They also have a very lively Ladies Auxiliary that keeps things humming for the post. The band was organized on January 11, 1933, under the leadership of Louis Glaser. On Armistice Day of each year, an elaborate service is held at the Barnert Memorial Temple to the memories of the departed Jewish service boys of Paterson.

The Kaufman family possesses the following testimonial scroll: "To Private Reuben Kaufman, Company D-114th Infantry, who was killed in battle, October 12, 1918. He bravely laid down his life for the cause of his country. His name will ever remain fresh in the hearts of his friends and comrades. The record of his honorable service will be preserved in the Archives of the American Expeditionary Forces. Signed: John J. Pershing, Commander in Chief."

Arthur Vermeire

Does Not Know of a Finer Place

The interviewee was born in the city of Łódź, Poland, which had a population of about two hundred thousand people, of which one-half was Jewish. Łódź was the textile center of Poland. The interviewee's early life in this country was hard at first. Two days after her arrival in New York, she came to Paterson and lived with her brother. Many factories were anxious to secure foreign labor because they were more serious, better workers and could be hired for less money than the American help. A few days after her arrival in Paterson, she secured a job in a paper-box factory through the help of some friends. Her salary was started at seven dollars a week, working eleven hours a day. At first, she did not care very much for the American types of food, but she became accustomed to them after being here a few years. Jewish and kosher food stores were along River Street and Water Street, on both sides of the river.

The sections adjoining the river, particularly River and Water streets, were the only Jewish sections of Paterson. There were several synagogues here, fish and herring stores, kosher butcher stores, and many other types of Jewish food stores. There were very few Jews in Paterson who did not live in this Jewish section, and these few came to this section for their Jewish and kosher foods. The interviewee came to Paterson in 1905 and lived in this section until 1927. She moved several times during these years, from River Street to Water Street to Godwin Street, always remaining near the river.

Many times during her early years in this section, bands of loafer kids would walk through this section, shouting "sheeny," "Jew," etc., at the Jews, especially if a man had a beard. Many times rotten fruit or other objects were thrown at Jews who had beards. These kids never gave the Jews much worry, and the Jews called them "loafers" and "bandits." During the Halloween holiday, these groups would come through River Street and do quite a bit of damage.

There were no conflicts between the various types of Jews. The Polish Jews had their own groups, named after the cities from where they came in Poland. The German Jews, who were the merchants of Main Street in Paterson, lived in the East Side residential section of Paterson. The Jewish peddlers, clothing and junk dealers, lived on the north side of the river—mostly on Water Street, where they had their own synagogue, which was called the "Junk Man's" shul.

About 80 percent of the Jews of Paterson at this time—1895–1925—earned their living in the textile mills. The heads of the family in most

cases were the weavers; the daughters were the winders and quill winders, and the sons were warpers.[56] Many of the wives also worked on
two looms as weavers. The German Jews controlled a great many or
most of the clothing stores on Main and Market streets. A few German
Jews owned a great deal of property in the city, and the head of this
group was Nathan Barnert. Many Jews who never had a trade and those
who were in poor health became peddlers. All they needed was a few
dollars and a horse and wagon. Some bought junk. Until this day, you
will find that 90 percent of the junk dealers are Jews, and they still live
around the Water Street section. Most of the stables and yards are still
near the river. Other peddlers who went from house to house and
through the country, selling housewares and clothing, received their
wares from the German Jews on Main Street on credit and settled their
accounts every few days. A great many Jews had grocery and candy
stores, and in the past fifteen years we find more Jewish store owners
than any other group.

Most of the Jews who worked in the textile cities of Poland came
directly to Paterson to obtain work in the silk mills here. There were a
few who went to Astoria, Long Island, where there were a few mills;
some to Easton, Pennsylvania; and to other cities that had a few mills.
But just as soon as work slowed up in these towns, they moved to Paterson because of the great many silk mills there and to be near their
friends and relations. In most cases, Jews who lived in Warsaw, Łódź,
Białystok—which were the textile centers of Poland—had correspondence with their relatives in Paterson and with other textile workers
who came previously.

The interviewee came to America on the SS *Poetonia* in the year
1896. Before coming to America, she never thought she would work on
Saturday; but she found things different when she got here. In order to
keep her job in the paper-box factory, she was forced to work on Saturdays. In the old country, Saturday was a day of rest and reading after the
services in the synagogue; but, in this country, she was forced to work
half a day, and then she received her pay. On Saturday afternoon, she
would go out shopping. On the other side, ladies would always wear a
shawl over their heads on leaving the house, but her friends advised her
differently; here she dropped the habit of wearing shawls. She mingled
with the other girls from the factory, learning the American ways and
customs.

She read no Jewish papers in this country, but spent a lot of time
reading books from the Paterson library and books secured from School
No. 10. Whenever she heard of someone receiving a letter from Łódź,
she called on these people and was very interested in hearing from

home. She went to night school at No. 10, where she learned to read English, but she picked up the spoken language by talking with the people in her shop.

She does not know of a finer place to live in the world than America, especially the past few years. Many times in our conversation she remarked in Jewish: "Thank God for a United States." She believes the younger generation does not worry and does things the easy way. American children have it so much easier than the early life she had in Łódź, where she had to care for and bring up five children and do all their washing and ironing by hand. Water was brought from distant pumps in large pails, and wood was brought and chopped from the forest because they burnt wood in their stoves. American children have their parents do the worrying for them, and, as a rule, they don't help much at home. Her children don't have the respect for her that she had for her parents in the old country. She now realizes how old-fashioned her parents were, but she believes this is because of the more modern ways we have in America.

In the old country she did mostly housework, bringing up five children even though she spent two years in a woolen mill, which was similar to our silk mills in Paterson. At present, she is a housewife and a mother of four children. She worked for several years after her marriage as a weaver, helping her husband. She never made any other changes in her work because the only work to be found in Paterson was in the silk mills unless one had the education to work in an office or become a saleslady in a store.

She does not belong to any Jewish organizations at this time because most of the women's organizations were charitable, and she felt that she was in no position to give to charity. She now belongs to the Lodzer Relief Society and the Zionist movement.

American life did not change her Jewish customs very much. She still keeps the Sabbath and other Jewish holidays. She still boasts that her home has always been kosher. She claims she speaks American perfectly, but she speaks with a very strong Jewish accent. She talks Jewish to her husband and children, but the children talk back in English. She believes local politicians are the biggest bunch of grafters on earth, but she likes the American democratic form of government. When she first came to this country, she went to Night School No. 10 for one year and then to Eastside High School for another year. She attended a few classes in American at the YMHA during the past year, but she discontinued them.

Murray Koch

Unless He Worked on Saturdays

The interviewee was born in the city of Białystok, Russia-Poland, one of seven children who survived. There were two deaths at childbirth in the family.

Having come from a very religious family, and his father being a rabbi, he ate nothing but kosher foods. His father usually brought home the meats from the slaughterhouse. He claims the foods in America were little different than the foods in Poland. In the old country, baked goods were never bought; all baking was done at home by his mother and sisters. Fish, chicken, and noodle soup were always on the menu for Friday nights and the evenings prior to the Jewish holidays; cold foods were served on Saturdays and holidays.

He started his schooling in Białystok at four years of age. After seven hours a day at school, he would go to a *yeshiva* and study Hebrew.[57] Many of the men and he himself would sleep on the floor of the yeshiva, and their families or friends would bring in their meals. There was no talking at all there, and the younger boys would study for ten or fifteen hours at a time. This gave him a great deal of Hebrew knowledge.

The interviewee moved to Paterson two months after his family's arrival in America, and in 1901 they lived on Godwin Street, a very short block from River and Washington streets. Three years later, they moved to River Street. In both of these places, there were dark hallways, gas lights in all rooms, and water in the kitchen only. The Jewish food stores were all around the neighborhood, and the streets in this section were very filthy with strong odors from the various fish and herring stores. There were six synagogues within the radius of two blocks.

There were no difficulties with other ethnic groups. Several times a year groups of bums would come along River Street and think it fun to steal from the grocers, who kept a great deal of their stock in front of their stores. Nor was there any trouble between the various Jewish groups, because each had its own synagogue that was controlled by the chief rabbi of Paterson. The German Jews met at the Barnert Temple at Straight Street and Broadway and lived east of the temple. The Conservative Jews met in the Temple Emanuel, which was on Van Houten Street near Church Street, in the heart of the business section of the city. At present, their new temple is on Broadway and Thirty-third Street. The wealthier Jews of the city met here. The Russian Jews had their synagogues on Godwin Street—one on each side of Washington Street. The Polish Jews had a small synagogue on Godwin Street near Bridge Street. The Polish and Russian Jews lived together on River Street and Godwin Street near their synagogues. The Russian Jews had stores in the downtown section, mainly on River Street. There were many Russian Jews who peddled clothing and junk. The Polish Jews were the silk workers of Paterson. There were quite a few candy and grocery stores owned by Jewish people that were scattered throughout the city.

The Russian, German, and Latvian Jews had no reason to come to Paterson directly, unless they had relatives here. Many Polish Jews located in Paterson because there were Jews here in the textile mills. Paterson became one of the greatest Jewish centers in the East. Those who came from the textile centers of Poland—Poland was noted for its textiles—came directly to Paterson because of correspondence with relations and friends who came from their hometowns several years previously. Wages in Paterson were higher than those in Łódź, Białystok, Ozorkow, and other towns in Europe, and living conditions were on a much higher level here. Many Russian and Polish Jewish families came here to avoid the Russo-Japanese War, because they did not want to fight for the country they hated.

Our interviewee's family arrived in this country in 1896. His family did not lose many of their old Jewish traditions, probably because of the fact that his father was a rabbi and his mother the daughter of a great rabbi in Białystok. His early life was spent in a yeshiva. Every Saturday morning, the entire family attended services. They invited some friends home to a cold dinner, mainly fish and chicken. These friends were mostly officers of the congregation and their wives or a traveling rabbi who stopped in town over the Sabbath. At these various Saturday dinners, a great many religious blessings were said over the dinner. After the meal, the men went into the parlor, got into a discussion of various Jewish stories, and ended up singing religious songs. Several hours before sunset, the men returned to the study in the synagogue, where they sat around the table with the other men and studied the Talmud, with the rabbi as an instructor. After the study, they held two services—*minche* before sunset, and *maariv* after sunset.[58] Many Saturdays, they would break a bread to pieces and enjoy a bit of herring. They read a great number of Jewish books in his house because his father had quite a library. They also received by mail several Jewish papers and magazines from organizations in various cities. He read *Uncle Tom's Cabin* in Jewish several times and found it very interesting. He has a great many books by Sholem Ash—*Three Cities, God of*

Vengeance, and many others.[59] Some of these books were given to the Labor Lyceum.

His early life in New Jersey was spent in various schools in and near the state. He arrived in this country when he was twelve years of age, and finished grade school at age thirteen. Four years later, he finished Paterson High School, where he played violin in the high school orchestra. He had no time for play because he was very anxious to learn and take advantage of our free school system. He finished the last two years of public school and four years of high school in this country, learning English very rapidly. His father and older brothers also took a great interest in learning the language, and he was their teacher after his own schoolwork. His mother took no interest at all in English. They always spoke Jewish at home, now and before. When gentile visitors called, Jewish was immediately dropped, and everyone spoke English.

After graduating high school at eighteen, he attended a farm school a few miles outside of Philadelphia for two years. He gave this up and then tried to find a job without Saturday work. This was impossible, so his father decided to send him to the New York Electrical School to learn a trade. Spending two years at this school and then being unable to get a start, he decided to go to the West Coast. He spent several years in California holding various jobs. During his stay in California, there were many times he was without funds, and at these times he went to the synagogues and received food and shelter. In 1918, his parents mailed him the fare to come home, and he settled down in Paterson as an electrical contractor, without working on Saturday.

He believes the younger Jewish generation are not getting the proper Hebrew education, and the fault lies mostly with the mother at home. He would like to see a combined American and Hebrew school. He believes the children should attend services at the synagogues. Some of the children of today are breaking away from the old Hebrew and Jewish customs and traditions, and the only way to keep the children from being led further away from the Jewish life is for all mothers to arrange to have their children attend classes at the Talmud Torah, or Hebrew Free School. He had no difficulties with his own children. They have a great deal of respect for their parents, obey the Hebrew laws, and attend services at all times. Nor has he difficulties with his parents.

He does not belong to any economic organizations or labor groups. There have been no family-life changes in America in regard to Jewish or religious customs. This was because of the fact that his family are very religious people. Home conditions were a bit different because of the more modern conveniences here than in Białystok. He explained me that on the other side, on Friday evening before sunset they would light the candles, and several hours later the candles would burn out. This was OK because, according to religious custom, one was not supposed to turn on or off lights on the Sabbath. He now has an arrangement so that he turns on his electric lights on Friday before sunset, and at eleven P.M. the lights turn off automatically by a time clock. This gives him plenty of light by which to read.

His family always had a great deal of love and respect for this country. At the Sabbath morning service, his father always led the synagogue in a prayer for our government, the president, and the cabinet of our country. Many of his father's sermons helped to encourage patriotism among the members.

He takes quite an interest in politics. At election time, he picks out all the Jewish candidates on the list and votes for them. He is satisfied with local politics. He is also very much interested in national politics and is pleased with the actions of our president, secretary of state, and other government bodies in regards to European affairs. Many times, the Jews of America appealed to our president to seek relief for the Jews in other parts of the world, and our government has been of a great help. These actions are making the Jews of America more interested in our government than ever before.

Murray Koch
October 31, 1940

The Only Thing He Knew Was Textiles

The interviewee was born in Łódź, Poland, in the year 1878. His parents and grandparents were also born in Łódź. His early life in New Jersey was spent in the River Street section of Paterson. In 1900, his family lived on River Street, near Washington. In 1902, they moved across the river to Clinton Street, where the Talmud Torah is at present. In 1907, they moved about four blocks away from River Street to 121 Governor Street; and, in 1914, to 11 Governor Street, which is just a few houses away from River Street. Most of the Jewish people of Paterson lived near River Street, between Main and Straight streets. There were quite a few Jewish merchants who lived up Main Street around the four hundred block. They were the wealthier Jews, who were scattered about the East Side section of the city. There were a great many Jews who lived in the Carroll Street and Grahm Avenue section, but this was considered a continuation of the River Street section as it was only five blocks away.

There were some changes in family life upon coming to America. In Poland, the wives worked just as well and as hard as the men. In America, the wives are ladies with their nice clothes and makeup. The American custom of ladies smoking would be a disgrace in Poland, because only the wealthy Russian ladies smoked there. Homes were more modern in this country, with gas lights instead of oil, and water in the kitchen instead of a pump a block away.

Their food habits were almost the same as in Łódź. His wife arrived in this country two years after he did. During this time, he ate many of his meals at the free lunch counter in the corner saloon. This was done when his funds were low and when he wanted to save money. There were a greater variety of fruits and vegetables in this country, and the fruits here were very cheap.

There were little difficulties with the other ethnic groups. There were many times, however, when he was called various names such as "sheeney," "kike," and "Jew" by groups of gentile boys. There were no conflicts between the various types of Jews because each group kept to itself. The Russian Jews had their congregation on Godwin Street; and the German Jews, who lived on the east side of Paterson, had their congregation on Straight Street and Broadway. The Polish Jews did not build their own synagogue until 1914 on lower Governor Street, a short block from River Street. Each Jewish group had its own rabbi, its own synagogue, society, etc.

The Polish Jews were the silk workers in Paterson, and later, in 1920, owned most of the silk mills in Paterson. The German Jews owned the stores on the main streets of the city. The Russian Jews were the custom and junk peddlers of the city and owned the Jewish stores on River Street. The Polish Jews came directly to Paterson—some with short stops in New York City, and some with short stays in Plainfield, New Jersey, and Astoria, Long Island, where there were a few silk mills. But these few Polish Jews were dissatisfied for some minor reason and came to Paterson.

After a two-day stay in New York City, this man went to Astoria, Long Island, where he secured a job as a weaver. He stayed at a boardinghouse that was run by a party who had come from Łódź five years previously. There were seven other boarders, who all had come from Łódź. Two years later, he and his family, who by this time had come to America, moved. During the two years he worked in Astoria, he made several trips to Paterson on Sundays to see some of his Łódźer friends and relatives; and he arranged to secure a job and move to Paterson.

At first, this man, like many others, was forced to work on Saturdays and holidays. The American silk mill owners did not allow the weavers to have beards because they would get caught in the looms. The Polish Jews had no synagogue of their own until 1912; but, during the Jewish holidays, the Polish Jews rented halls on River Street. So the Polish Jews departed from their religion for a time.

This man joined the IOBA (Independent Order B'rith Abraham) in the year of 1906, when there were only eighteen members; they now have sixty-eight members. He joined the Polish synagogue in 1912, when the Polish Jews were wealthy. The membership here has not increased; rather, it is on a slight decline. This man claims that when a Jew has money, he wants everyone to know about it. In the synagogue, it give a Jew great pleasure to donate large sums of money in the presence of other members.

Saturday was a half-day of work in this country. Saturdays in the old country were spent in the synagogue, and the afternoons were for rest. Jewish papers were about the only things that were read in those days, and these papers were sold by an old Jewish man, who carried his papers in a boy's express wagon.

This man went to night classes at Central High School for six months about twelve years after his arrival in this country. Most of his learning of American reading and talking came from the foreign schoolchildren, who were anxious to teach what they had learned in school that same day. He always spoke Jewish at home to his wife and children, but the children answered back in English. He speaks Russian, German, and Polish well. He had very little adult education. He believes it won't do any good, so why bother? He went to night school for six months in 1910, and speaks a broken English. He can write very slowly, but he can't spell very well.

He claims to always have had a great love for this country. He contrasts the freedom of thought and speech in this country to Poland. When a boy came of age in Poland, he was forced to serve two years in military training. He does not mind his sons' undergoing military training in this country, but he was always against serving a country he hated and in which he received ill treatment. He believes local politics are as fair as can be expected. He is interested in national politics, and is very much in favor of the actions of Roosevelt and Hull.[60] He believes they are great men and that their actions in the present European affairs are making the Jews of America more interested in and better citizens of this country today.

He believes the younger generation does not receive severe training in this country. The schooling here is too playful and should be far more serious. Boys of eighteen were married in Poland and were supporting families, whereas in this country all they think of is play and sports. He has had no difficulties with his children, but he claims his daughter gives him some trouble in buying her clothes. She spends more than she earns. His children think of music and play all the time. He had no difficulties with his parents, and he always has had a great deal of respect for them. He helped to support them in their old age.

This man worked on cotton and wool looms in Łódź, as did many other Jews. There were also many Jewish store owners in Łódź and in this country. This man experienced no occupational changes in America because the only thing he knew was textiles, and Paterson was the textile center of the country. For a short time, he had a grocery store that his wife took care of, and he helped along in the evening. He bought eight silk looms in 1922 and was considered a silk manufacturer for a few years. Because there were so many of his Polish-Jewish friends becoming rich overnight being manufacturers, he sold his store to raise cash and bought eight looms. As a silk worker, he was always a union man when he worked in a union shop. If a shop had no union, he forgot it. He was not active in the six-month silk strike in Paterson, but he was a member of the IWW.[61]

Murray Koch
October 31, 1940

As Silk Worker and Boss

During the later part of the nineteenth century, there was a mass emigration of Polish and Russian Jews. Most of these emigrants earned their livelihoods in the textile centers of Łódź, Białystok, and Warsaw. Upon arriving at Ellis Island, these groups made inquiries about where the textile centers were; seventy-five percent came to Paterson, and the rest of them went to Astoria, Long Island, and various towns in Pennsylvania. There were only five mills in Astoria at that time, and there were only a few in Pennsylvania. During the slow season, these families moved to Paterson because there were more mills there, resulting in a greater chance to find work. Many mill owners of that time were of

English and French stock. In many cases, the head of the family and his wife were employed as weavers, the daughters employed as winders and quill winders, and the sons as warpers. In the early part of the twentieth century, wages were approximately twelve dollars per week. In the year 1913, there was a general strike in the silk mills of Paterson that closed up all mills for twenty-four weeks. The Jews were quite active during this strike, and at many meetings there were Jewish speakers. The Jews were given much relief by their friends in the clothing unions in New York City. Before the strike, the workers were working ten and twelve hours per day on a four-loom system.[62] After they went back to work, the weavers earned as high as eighteen, nineteen dollars per week.

Then, the world war broke out, and various ammunition factories became very busy. Many of the weavers left their looms to work on war contracts, where wages were much higher. Thus, there became a labor shortage in the silk mills. Weavers started to work in silk mills, with as many as five people from the same family employed. Because of the shortage in labor, many of the manufacturers started to increase their salaries to attract help from other factories. When the United States entered the war, many of the weavers went into the service of the country, and there was an even greater shortage of labor, resulting in a gigantic increase of wages. Weavers before 1913, who were earning twelve dollars per week, were now earning forty to fifty dollars a week. Warpers were earning seventy-five dollars per week. These families accumulated considerable sums of money.

Various textile manufacturers opened offices in Paterson, so that those employees who were becoming interested in buying their own equipment could order locally. Many of these silk workers got together and formed a corporation and transacted their business in the following manner: They would purchase just enough machinery so that they and their families could operate. On weekends, they would hold their business meetings and decide upon operations for the future. In many cases, floor spaces were rented out to the heads of ten or twelve families and was subdivided by chicken-coop wire. Thus, each family, having its own subdivision, was classified as a manufacturer of broadsilks. During that time, Jews became the owners of the silk looms. From them, the manufactured silk passed into the hands of commission merchants, who sold it to wholesale and retail outlets, very often financed by the manufacturer. In later years, the number of small silk manufacturers increased enormously. The manufacturers of looms generally extended credit, and, consequently, little capital was required to purchase a single loom. Raw silk was almost always sold on a promise to pay in the future. Thousands of silk weavers, especially recent immigrants, took advantage of this state of affairs.

The procedure was simple. A weaver bought a loom on the installment plan and had it set up in his own home. He and his wife worked alternate shifts. Very few minutes out of twenty-four hours was the loom idle. When a piece of silk was woven, the weaver took it to New York by train or trolley and sold it directly to the retailer. He could afford to sell at a lower figure than the manufacturer, who had rent, taxes, overhead charges, and labor unions with which to deal. It did not take long before the loom was paid for. It was seldom that a weaver did not find a ready market for his product; but, when this happened, he could pawn the silk in Paterson, where brokers were always ready to make advances on such security. Should the weaver receive an order from a retailer for several hundred yards of silk to be delivered in one consignment at a certain time, he could make the silk piece by piece and pawn it piece by piece.

At this time, there were very few Jews who finished grade school, because their parents forced them to work in the mills on account of the shortage of labor and the high earnings. Those who were in high schools and colleges were taken out by their families to work in the silk mills.

In the year 1891, only four of the 130 silk mills in Paterson were owned by Jews. In the year 1920, there were 976 silk mills owned by the Jews. This represented 90 percent of the silk industry in the city of Paterson. Most of these manufacturers became quite wealthy at this time. And these Jews, who had come from the textile center of Łódź, Poland, built a one-story synagogue at Eight Governor Street. The Jews continued to grow more wealthy, and two years later they built a more elaborate synagogue on the corner of Fair and Paterson streets. The leaders of the synagogue were Louis Taback, president, and Sam Sommer, treasurer. These officers came from Łódź as poor men in the later part of the nineteenth century. Ninety-five percent of the membership and officers also came from Łódź, Poland, during the mass immigration. These men donated large sums of money to build this temple, realizing that they had come to this country as poor men not many years before. As these men became wealthy, they sent their children to schools and colleges, resulting in the great abundance of Jewish professionals. In the later part of 1929, the Jewish silk manufacturers, working on a promise-to-pay system, lost their fortunes and had to return to what we now consider an average standard of living. Many are old and living on the income of their children, who became professionals.

Murray Koch

Cursed the Day He Came to America

When I was one week old, there was great rejoicing in our family. I was the fifth child born, but the only one who lived even to be a week old. The deaths of my four brothers, who died within a few hours after birth, caused great consternation among the old and wise Jews of our community. As usual in such cases, one went to the chief rabbi of the community for advice. He told my father and mother to take a new-born black puppy of a first litter and drown it. Then, within ten months, a child would be born who would live. This was done in good faith, and so continues my story. Four more children were born to my mother. The two youngest died of a scarlet-fever epidemic in Odessa, when they were, respectively, seven and two years of age. And so, of this large family, we remained—my parents and three boys, Vladimir, Grisha, and Misha.

My mother was a very tall and stately woman, who was an accomplished singer and pianist. My father owned one of the largest men's clothing stores in Odessa. His factory was in Vienna. He was utterly fearless in all his undertakings, and I frequently heard him say, "I fear neither God nor man."

My brothers and I received a thorough education in Hebrew. We also attended the government schools, or *gymnasiums,* where we were taught Russian, German, French, and mathematics. It was unusual for three Jewish boys from one family to attend the government schools. The two requisites were gold or brains. In my case, it was gold; Grisha and Misha were very brilliant.

I remember in 1880, when the tsar and the tsarina of all Russia honored the city of Odessa with a visit. The maneuvers of the cavalry, the exhibitions of the schoolchildren, the singing of the Russian hymn by ten thousand people, these things I will never forget. It was not long after this that the Jews in the marketplaces had their stalls shoved over by little boys. When they protested, they were joined by others, older than they, who wreaked havoc and destruction for three days. In spite of gold and protests from the rich Jews of the city, these pogroms became more frequent. My father saw the handwriting on the wall, or was it my brother Grisha's influence? In the meantime, Grisha had graduated from the gymnasium, and with a school chum he visited the large cities of Europe and spent four months in the United States. My father finally sold his business in Odessa to three brothers who were in his employ, and we prepared to leave the land of our birth and go to Vienna. All passports, tickets, and papers were in order, but when we reached the Rumanian border, Grisha and I, who both were of military age, were refused permission to cross. Transactions were finally made with certain "agents of credentials," who for five thousand rubles would arrange for a peasant to have his son substituted in our place. The transaction concerning my brother was worked out in the same manner, and we proceeded to Vienna without any further difficulty.

Oh, how my father pleaded with us to remain here instead of going on to America! Could he have had a premonition that his best years were behind him? From Vienna, where we sold our factory, we went to Berlin—the most beautiful city I ever saw. There, we were invited to the homes of wealthy German-Jews and distant relatives. Our family was originally German. Here, too, my father wanted to remain, but Grisha was very persistent. Once we had started, we must complete our journey to America. From the port of Bremen, we took a French boat. The German boat we were to take was damaged, and we did not wish to delay our departure until repairs were made.

At Southampton, England, my father made his last plea. He was perfectly willing to destroy all tickets, passports, and other papers necessary for our trip to America and take another boat from Southampton back to Bremen and settle in Paris, Berlin, or Vienna. He did not wish to go on. I, too, was willing to return, but we were completely overruled by Grisha. As usual, he won. After fourteen days on the Atlantic Ocean, we arrived in New York on a cold January day in 1885.

We stayed in New York for a few weeks and visited friends, who had learned of our arrival and offered advice as to the kind of business we should undertake. We had a cousin in New York who left the faith of Israel for that of his wife. Since he was dead in the eyes of my parents, they would not see him. And so, my two brothers and I paid a visit to our "dead" cousin. As I see it now, it was very unfortunate that I followed his advice. He told us to see a Michael Heilprin, well-known as a scholar, author, and idealist, who devoted his time and energy to the Hebrew Immigrant Aid Society. After an appointment, we met with Mr. Heilprin, who suggested that we go to North Dakota or New Jersey. Again it was Grisha who decided for us. It was to be Vineland, New Jersey, since it was close to Philadelphia, where he could continue his studies at a medical school.

A farm was bought in Vineland, New Jersey, and my father, who had been a merchant like his father before him, did not know whether potatoes grew above or below the ground. This venture proved unsuccessful, and a large amount of money was lost. My brother went to school in Philadelphia. I wasn't particularly adapted to such strenuous work, and my mother certainly would not help, as did the Italian women on the surrounding farms near us. We visited the Jewish colony of Alliance, and found many men who had been tailors or clerks of my father in Odessa. We sold the farm in Vineland and bought one in Alliance. My parents were very unhappy here. My mother had no use for her gorgeous clothes and jewels. My brother Grisha was sent to Philadelphia to dispose of the jewelry. He returned a few days later, accompanied by a policeman, who was sent to verify that the jewels were not stolen. My parents then went on to Philadelphia and planned to stay a week or so, the season being too early to plant crops. My brothers and I decided, as a result of a mild spell, to rebuild one wall of the little wooden farmhouse. The new wall did not go up as readily as the old came down. As a result, we would have perished in the Blizzard of 1888 but for our nearest neighbors, who dug a tunnel between the two farmhouses. Their suspicions were aroused when no smoke arose from our chimney.

Time went on, and my father still continued to hate the farm and the New World. His youngest son died as a result of an accident on the farm. He cursed the day he came to America and took his spite out on everyone. On the Sabbath, when all the Jews of Alliance attended the new synagogue to offer thanks unto God for this free country, he chose the Sabbath to spread manure on his farmland, cursing the very poor soil, the intense heat, and the day he heeded his children's advice. Nevertheless, on the day he died, in Vineland again, many of these people, his former employees, the men who feared and hated him, walked behind his bier to the cemetery.

Time passed, Grisha, now George, became a doctor, married, and opened an office in Reading, Pennsylvania. I opened a store in Vineland. While to the outside world, I seemed successful, I wasn't the businessman my father was before me. There was still in our possession my Russian *bulletin*, or bonds, which were cashed during emergencies. I realize now I should have continued or used my knowledge of languages. I have many pleasant memories to look back upon, the beautiful cities of Europe—Patti, Bernhardt, Lehman, and even Lillian Russell, whom I had seen and heard many times.[63] I realize now, too late, that I should have utilized my abilities in languages. An inadequate sense of values impeded my real development in the United States. For generations, success in our family was determined by business interests. The offer of foreign language interpreter, I considered beneath my dignity. Perhaps it may be rationalization, but my memories of the beautiful cities of Europe—of Patti, Lehman, and the unforgettable Bernhardt—have sustained me. In America, I saw Lillian Russell and other celebrities. Perhaps my life would have been different if had I lived in some European city. That guess is venturesome, and I believe that the spirit of freedom prevalent here compensates for any questionable material success that may have been mine.

Mazie Berse

Notes

Introduction

1   Ann Banks included a few case histories from the Federal Writers' Project's Social-Ethnic Studies in her book *First-Person America*. C. Stewart Doty edited a collection of French-Canadian interviews from New England (*The First Franco-Americans*), but they came from the Federal Writers' Project's Folklore Studies Program, not the Social-Ethnic Studies Program. Other Federal Writers' Project published collections include the case histories of Southern tenant farmers and sharecroppers in Federal Writers' Project, *These Are Our Lives* (Chapel Hill: University of North Carolina Press, 1939); Tom Terrill and Jerrold Hirsch, eds. *Such as Us: Southern Voices of the Thirties* (Chapel Hill: University of North Carolina Press, 1978); the interviews with former slaves in B. A. Botkin, ed., *Lay My Burden Down: A Folk History of Slavery* (Chicago: University of Chicago Press, 1945); Charles L. Perdue, Thomas E. Barden, and Robert K. Phillips, eds., *Weevils in the Wheat: Interviews with Virginia Ex-Slaves* (Charlottesville: University Press of Virginia, 1976); Norman R. Yetman, ed., *Voices from Slavery* (New York: Holt, Rinehart and Winston, 1970); and George P. Rawick, gen. ed., *The American Slave: A Composite Autobiography* (Westport, Conn.: Greenwood, 1972–1979), 22 vols.

2   For a summary of the literature on this transformation of European society and how it affected emigration, see Bodnar, *The Transplanted*, 2–56.

3   The importance of letters home was recognized as early as 1927 in Thomas and Znaniecki's classic study of Polish immigrants, which contains extensive correspondence between family members (*Polish Peasant in Europe and America*, vol. 1).

4   Stuart Galishoff, *Newark, the Nation's Unhealthiest City: 1832–1895* (New Brunswick and London: Rutgers University Press, 1988), 188, 203.

5   Ronald A. Foresta, "The Evolution of the Modern Urban Core," in *New Jersey's Ethnic Heritage*, ed. Paul A. Stellhorn (Trenton: New Jersey Historical Commission, 1978), 77–78, 84–86.

6   Saul Bellow, *The Adventures of Augie March* (New York: Viking, 1949).

7   Ruby Jo Reeves Kennedy, "Single or Triple Melting Pot? Intermarriage Trends in New Haven, 1870–1940," *Journal of American Sociology* 49 (1944): 333.

8   Ibid., 332.

9   Stephan Thernstrom, *Poverty and Progress: Social Mobility in a Nineteenth Century City* (Cambridge, Mass.: Harvard University Press, 1964); Dean R. Esslinger, *Immigrants and the City: Ethnicity and Mobility in a Nineteenth Century Midwestern Community* (Port Washington, N.Y.: Kennikat Press, 1975); Gordon W. Kirk, *The Promise of American Social Mobility in a*

Nineteenth Century Immigrant Community: Holland, Michigan, 1847–1894 (Philadelphia: American Philosophical Society, 1978).

10   Frances W. Gregory and Irene D. Neu, "The American Industrial Elite in the 1870s: Their Social Origins," in *Men in Business: Essays on the Historical Role of the Entrepreneur,* ed. William Miller (1952; reprint, New York: Harper Torchbooks, 1962), 193–211; Herbert G. Gutman, "The Reality of the Rags-to-Riches 'Myth': The Case of the Paterson, New Jersey, Locomotive, Iron, and Machinery Manufacturers, 1830–1880," in *Work, Culture, and Society: Essays in American Working-class History,* ed. Herbert G. Gutman (New York: Vintage, 1966), 211–233.

11   There is a remarkable similarity between the purple prose of the Prince Street essay and the description of "Jewtown" on the Lower East Side of New York City written by Danish-American newspaper reporter Jacob Riis in his 1890 book *How the Other Half Lives.* Riis uses similar, vaguely anti-Semitic statements parading as mere description. Note the similarity between Kornmann's description of Prince Street and the following passage from Riis's description of "Jewtown": "Thursday night and Friday morning are bargain days in the 'Pig-market.' Then is the time to study the ways of this peculiar people to the best advantage. . . . The Pig-market is in Hester Street, extending either way from Ludlow Street, and up and down the side streets two or three blocks, as the state of trade demands. The name was given to it probably in derision, for pork is the one ware that is not on sale in the Pig-market. There is scarcely anything else that can be hawked from a wagon that is not found, and at ridiculously low prices" (Jacob A. Riis, *How the Other Half Lives: Studies Among the Tenements of New York* [1890; reprint, New York: Hill and Wang, 1957], 85).

12   For histories of the Federal Writers' Project and other WPA arts projects, see McDonald, *Federal Relief Administration and the Arts;* Mangione, *The Dream and The Deal;* Penkower, *The Federal Writers' Project.*

13   Hirsch, "Portrait of America," 655.

14   Horace M. Kallen, *Culture and Democracy in the United States: Studies in the Group Psychology of the American Peoples* (New York: Boni and Liveright, 1924).

15   John Higham, "Ethnic Pluralism in American Thought," in *Send These to Me: Immigrants in Urban America,* rev. ed. (Baltimore and London: Johns Hopkins University Press, 1984), 198–232.

16   Morton Royse, "Manual for Social-Ethnic Studies," 5. WPA Federal Writers' Project, Social-Ethnic Studies. Manuscripts Division, Library of Congress.

17   Caroline T. Ware, *The Cultural Approach to History* (Port Washington, N.Y.: Kennikat, 1940), 87.

18   Hirsch, "Portrait of America," 553–556.

19   Federal Writers' Project, *WPA Guide to 1930s New Jersey,* 124–125.

20   Churchill, "Italians of Newark."

21   Emory S. Bogardus, *Immigration and Race Attitudes* (Boston, Mass.: Heath, 1928), 10.

22.   Thomas F. Gossett, *Race: The History of an Idea in America* (1963; reprint, New York: Schocken, 1965), 418–424.

23   In 1943, Ruth Benedict, who was a student of Boas, and Gene Weltfish wrote a pamphlet entitled *The Races of Mankind*, in which they noted the differences between racial, language, religious, and nationality groups. It is reprinted in Ruth Benedict, *Race: Science and Politics* (New York: Viking, 1945), 169–193.

24   Mangione, *The Dream and the Deal*, 280.

25   Thomas and Znaniecki, *Polish Peasant in Europe and America.*

26   Bogardus, *Immigration and Race Attitudes*, 257.

27   Maurice R. Stein, *The Eclipse of Community: An Interpretation of American Studies* (1960; reprint, New York: Harper and Row, 1964), 16.

28   Robert E. Park, *Race and Culture* (Glencoe, Ill.: Free Press, 1950); Robert E. Park and Herbert A. Miller, *Old World Traits Transplanted* (New York and London: Harper and Row, 1921).

29   Bogardus, *Immigration and Race Attitudes*, 3–6.

30   Oscar Handlin, *The Uprooted: The Epic Story of the Great Migrations That Made the American People* (Boston: Little, Brown, 1951). The degree of uprootedness experienced by immigrants has been questioned in recent years by scholars who note that immigrants retained certain old institutions and built new ones very soon after their arrival in America. See, for example, Nelli, *From Immigrants to Ethnics*; idem, *Italians in Chicago*; and McLaughlin, *Family and Community.*

31   Charles W. Churchill, interview with author, April 12, 1988. Frank Hague's relationship with the New Deal public works projects is explored in Edward H. Michels, Jr., "New Jersey and the New Deal" (Ph.D. diss., New York University, 1986), 321–372.

32   House Special Committee on Un-American Activities, *Hearings*, Nov. 19–28, Dec. 1, 5–9, 14, 1938 (Washington, D.C.: GPO, 1939).

33   Jerre Mangione suggests that Fuhlbruegge resigned because she was unwilling to fire two writers to make room for some political appointees from the Democratic machine of Frank Hague, but Mangione concedes that the congressional investigation may have hastened her departure (*The Dream and the Deal*, 88).

34   Vivian Mintz Barnert, interview with author, April 12, 1988.

35   Churchill, "Italians of Newark."

36   Peter T. Bartis, David S. Cohen, and Gregory Dowd, *Folklife Resources in New Jersey* (Washington, D.C., and Trenton: American Folklife Center and New Jersey Historical Commission, 1985).

37   Charles W. Churchill and Abdulla M. Lufiyya, comp., *Readings in Arab Middle Eastern Societies and Cultures* (The Hague: Mouton, 1970).

Irish

1   Susan E. Hirsch, *Roots of the American Working Class: The Industrialization of Crafts in Newark, 1800–1860* (Philadelphia: University of Penn-

sylvania Press, 1978), 3–51; Raymond Michael Ralph, "From Village to Industrial City: The Urbanization of Newark, 1830–1860" (Ph.D. diss., New York University, 1978), 2–3, 12, 24; John T. Cunningham, *Newark* (Newark: New Jersey Historical Society, 1966), 24–25, 109.

2   Hirsch, *Roots of the American Working Class*, 47; Charles Stephenson, "Class, Culture, and Ethnicity in Nineteenth-Century Newark," in *New Jersey's Ethnic Heritage*, ed. Paul A. Stellhorn (Trenton: New Jersey Historical Commission, 1978), 96.

3   MacDonagh, "Irish Famine Emigration," 350.

4   Blessing, "Irish," 529.

5   Vecoli, *People of New Jersey*, 77.

6   Ralph, "From Village to Industrial City," 78.

7   Federal Writers' Project, *WPA Guide to 1930s New Jersey*, 315.

8   Schwartz, "Overturnings in the Earth," 19.

9   Frank J. Urquhart, *A History of Newark*, 2 vols. (New York: Lewis Publishing, 1913), 2:666.

10   Schwartz, "Overturnings in the Earth," 21, 23, 27–28.

11   Vecoli, *People of New Jersey*, 105.

12   Ibid., 114–115, 136.

13   Shaw, "Political Leadership," 94.

14   Vecoli, *People of New Jersey*, 162.

15   Paul A. Stellhorn, "Depression and Decline: Newark, New Jersey, 1929–1941" (Ph.D. diss., Rutgers University, 1982), 36, 49.

16   Vecoli, *People of New Jersey*, 83, 85–86.

17   Ibid., 107–108.

18   Edward Balbach came from Germany in 1850 and opened a precious-metals refinery, known as Balbach's Smelting and Refinery Company, on River Street in Newark.

19   Jozef Piłsudski (1867–1935) was a Polish patriot who led the movement to liberate Poland from Russia. He was the first chief of state and minister of war in Poland after it became a republic in 1918.

20   Cash-and-carry was the United States foreign policy embodied in the Neutrality Act of 1939, which repealed the arms embargo and authorized exports of arms and munitions to belligerents in Europe.

21   In 1923 Sebastian Kresge purchased Plaut's department store in Newark.

22   Adoph Hoffman, brewer, is listed in the 1897 Newark directory.

23   The Boer War (1899–1902) was a conflict between Great Britain and the two Afrikaner republics—the Orange Free State and the South African Republic (the Transvaal).

24   Hurling is an Irish game resembling field hockey.

25   A steeplejack builds, paints, or repairs smokestacks, towers, or church steeples.

26   Commodore John Barry (1745–1803) was an American naval officer, born in Ireland, who fought during the American Revolution.

27   The Lafayette Escadrille was a military organization formed in 1916

to fight against the Germans prior to the United States' formal involvement in World War I.

28   Newark Technical School was founded in 1884. Today it is known as the New Jersey Institute of Technology.

29   The Public Service Corporation was a public utilities company that supplied electricity, transportation (especially trolleys), and gas.

Italians

1   Starr, *Italians of New Jersey*, 1–2.

2   Ibid., 6–7; Archdeacon, *Becoming American*, 139.

3   Vecoli, *People of New Jersey*, 223–224, 225, 235.

4   Churchill, "Italians of Newark," 29, 30–31, 53–54; Samuel H. Popper, "Newark, New Jersey, 1870–1910: Chapters in the Evolution of the American Metropolis" (Ph.D. diss., New York University, 1952), 136–137.

5   Churchill, "Italians of Newark," 121; Vecoli, *People of New Jersey*, 228, 230.

6   Nelli, "Italian Padrone System in the United States."

7   Federal Writers' Project, *WPA Guide to 1930s New Jersey*, 314.

8   United States Immigration Commission, "Immigrant Banks," in *Reports of the Immigration Commission* (1911; reprint, New York: Arno and New York Times, 1970), 37:209, 318, 321.

9   Rosa, "Recollections of Peter B. Mattia," 38–39.

10   As one of his first official actions in 1933, President Franklin Delano Roosevelt closed all the banks in the United States to determine which ones were solvent and which were not. He thereby ended the so-called bank crisis of the Great Depression.

Poles

1   Bukowczyk, *And My Children Did Not Know Me*, 11, 21; idem, "Transformation of Working-Class Ethnicity," 57, 60.

2   Baretski, "History of the Polish Settlement in New Jersey," 355–360; Federal Writers' Project, *WPA Guide to 1930s New Jersey*, 317.

3   Bukowczyk, *And My Children Did Not Know Me*, 49.

4   Howard F. Stein and Robert F. Hill, *The Ethnic Imperative: Examining the New White Ethnic Movement* (University Park, Pa.: Pennsylvania State University Press, 1977), 36–37.

5   Bukowczyk, *And My Children Did Not Know Me*, 36.

6   Ibid., 22.

7   Nelli, *From Immigrants to Ethnics*, 115.

8   *Schnapps* is German for brandy, wine, or spirits.

9   United Electrical, Radio, and Machine Workers of America.

10   The speedup was a practice of management to gradually increase the pace of work in factories.

11   The HMS *Batory* arrived in New York City on September 6, 1939,

with refugees fleeing the war in Europe. The Polish crew mutineed because they thought the ship was to be used as a British munitions carrier. The sea men became an immigration problem because they could not be returned to Poland.

12   This is probably a reference to the panic of 1893.

13   *Ameryka-Echo* was a Polish-American newspaper established in Buffalo in 1902.

14   In continental Europe a *gymnasium* is a high school, specializing in preparing students for the university.

15   *Sokol* was a Polish-American newspaper published in Pittsburgh.

16   *Pan* is Polish for landlord or gentleman.

17   Kreuger's Auditorium on Belmont Avenue in Newark was built by German beer baron Gotfried Krueger.

18   Maria Konopnicka (1842–1910) was a Polish author and poet.

19   He was referring to the *Index Librorum Prohibitorium*, a former list of books forbidden by the Roman Catholic church.

20   Simon Freed, tailor, was listed in the 1926 Newark directory.

Lithuanians, Russians, and Ukrainians

1   Davis, *Russian Immigrant*, 8.

2   Magocsi, "Russians," 8.

3   Stein and Hill, *Ethnic Imperative*, 23.

4   Budreckis, *Lithuanians in America*, 1–2; Baretski, "History of the Polish Settlement in New Jersey," 344.

5   Magocsi, "Are the Armenians Really Russians?" 142–143, 151n.; idem, "Russians," 893–894, 885; idem, "Carpatho-Rusyns," 201; idem, "Ukrainians," 1000.

6   Magocsi, "Ukrainians," 1000–1001; idem, "Carpatho-Rusyns," 203; idem, "Russians," 889–890; Thomas Francis Sable, "Lay Initiative in Greek Catholic Parishes in Connecticut, New York, New Jersey, and Pennsylvania, 1884–1909" (Ph.D. diss., Graduate Theological Union, 1984), 11, 105; Stein and Hill, *Ethnic Imperative*, 25–26.

7   Kaunas was the capital from 1918 to 1940. The capital is now Vilnius.

8   This interviewee has confused the sequence of events. The Russian Revolution began in March 1917 with the abdication of Tsar Nicholas II. When the Bolsheviks seized power in November 1917, they promised to end the Russian involvement in World War I. They signed a separate peace with the Central Powers in March 1918 at Brest-Litovsk. The interviewee may be referring to the Russian civil war that broke out in the summer of 1918.

Dutch

1   Philip B. Scranton, ed., *Silk City: Studies on the Paterson Silk Industry, 1860–1940*, Collections of the New Jersey Historical Society, vol. 19 (Newark: New Jersey Historical Society, 1985), 1–5.

2   Herbert G. Gutman, *Work, Culture, and Society: Essays in American Working-Class History* (New York: Vintage, 1966), 216–218, 237–239.

3   Steve Golin, *The Fragile Bridge: Paterson Silk Strike, 1913* (Philadelphia: Temple University Press, 1988), 17.

4   Vecoli, *People of New Jersey*, 71–73; Richard D. Margrave, "Technology, Diffusion, and the Transfer of Skills: Nineteenth Century English Silk Migration to Paterson," in Scranton, ed., *Silk City*, 23; Nancy Fogelson, "They Paved the Streets with Silk," *New Jersey History* 97 (1979): 140.

5   Golin, *Fragile Bridge*, 25, 30.

6   Federal Writers' Project, *WPA Guide to 1930s New Jersey*, 352.

7   Swierenga, "Dutch Immigration Patterns," 16, 27, 30–31, 32.

8   De Jong, "Dutch Immigrants in New Jersey," 71, 76, 77.

9   *1900–1951, 50th Anniversary, Prospect Park*, 5, 7, 21, 23, 31, 53.

10   Ibid., 23.

11   Lini De Vries, *Up from the Cellar*, 26, 33–34.

12   In a winding mill the skeins of pure silk, which have been soaked and dried, are rewound from reels onto bobbins, i.e., spools, prior to warping.

13   A loomfixer handled the installation and repair of looms. It was a highly skilled job, even more skilled than weaving.

14   A *dominee* is the pastor of a Dutch Reformed church.

15   Plymouth Rock is an American breed of chicken.

16   Normal schools were the precursors of modern teachers' colleges.

17   Izaak Walton (1593–1683) was an English author known for his classic book on fishing, *The Compleat Angler* (1653).

Jews

1   Pentz, "German Jews in Newark," 1; idem, "Early Jewish Life in Newark," 1–2.

2   Shapiro, "Jews of New Jersey," 196 197; Jewish Community Council, *Essex Story*, 14–15; Cunningham, *Newark*, 195–196.

3   Pentz, "German Jews in Newark," 1–2; Jewish Community Council, *Essex Story*, 16, 19.

4   Berman, "Jewish Community," 21; *Our Paterson Jewish Heritage*, 18–19.

5   Shapiro, "Jews of New Jersey," 305.

6   Jewish Community Council, *Essex Story*, 19–20, 34, 40–41; Vecoli, *People of New Jersey*, 255.

7   *Our Paterson Jewish Heritage*, 41.

8   Howe, *World of Our Fathers*, 183.

9   *Our Paterson Jewish Heritage*, 26, 34; Snyder, "Paterson Jewish Folk Chorus"; Berman, "Jewish Community," 21.

10   Brandes, *Immigrants to Freedom*; Purmell and Rovner, *Farmer's Daughter*.

11   Shapiro, "Jews of New Jersey," 300.

12   The Jewish Sabbath, which begins at sundown on Friday night and

continues to sundown on Saturday, is inaugurated by a woman of the household, who lights candles and recites a blessing.

13   A printer's devil was an errand boy or young apprentice in a print shop.

14   Scott Nearing (1883–1983) was a radical social scientist and author of *The Conscience of a Radical* (1965).

15   Aleksandr Sergeevich Pushkin (1799–1837) was a Russian Romantic poet and author. Among his famous works are the poem *Eugene Onegin* and the novel *Boris Godunov*.

16   The Mayo brothers, William James Mayo (1861–1939) and Charles Horace Mayo (1865–1939), were cofounders in 1914 of the world-renowned Mayo Clinic in Rochester, Minnesota.

17   Count Lev Nikolayevich Tolstoy (1828–1910) was a Russian novelist, the author of *War and Peace* and *Anna Karenina*. Fyodor Mikhailovich Dostoevsky (1821–1881) was the Russian author who wrote *Crime and Punishment*, *The Idiot*, and *The Brothers Karamazov*. Ivan Sergeevich Turgenev (1818–1883) was a Russian playwright and author who wrote the play *A Month in the Country* and the novels *Fathers and Sons* and *On the Eve*.

18   *Mitlshul* is Yiddish for high school.

19   The revised Emergency Relief Act, passed by Congress in 1939, required that anyone who had been employed by the WPA for eighteen months must be removed from the payroll for at least thirty days.

20   On October 2, 1918, the German government requested an armistice based on President Woodrow Wilson's Fourteen Points, but England and France were reluctant to agree. Finally, on November 5, the Allies accepted these terms with some exceptions. The armistice was then signed on November 11, 1918.

21   John Bunny (1863–1915) was a comedian known for his large size— about three hundred pounds. His career in the movies lasted from 1910 to 1915.

22   George ("Slim") Summerville (1892–1946) was an American comedy actor.

23   Eagle Rock is a section of the Watchung Mountains in Essex County that overlooks Newark and the Oranges. Today, it is a county reservation. Singac was a bungalow colony on the Passaic River, five miles southwest of Paterson.

24   The National Labor Board was established in 1933, under the National Industrial Recovery Act, to enforce the right of collective bargaining. It was replaced in 1935 by the National Labor Relations Board, created under the Wagner Act.

25   The use of the word "confirmation" was probably an attempt to find an American equivalent for the Hebrew term *bar mitzvah*, which is the ceremony that celebrates a boy's reaching the status of manhood for religious purposes at age thirteen. Technically, however, Orthodox Jews believe that Judaism does not require a "confirmation" of faith, and many Reform Jewish congrega-

tions have had a separate confirmation ceremony at the time of graduation from Hebrew school as distinct from bar mitzvah.

26   *Kaddish* is a prayer that praises God. All but the last sentence of the Kaddish is in Aramaic, which is a Semitic language that dates back to the ninth century B.C. and was spoken extensively in southwest Asia as a lingua franca by many peoples, including the Jews. The Kaddish is recited by immediate family members at the funeral, during mourning periods, on anniversaries of the death, and on certain holidays as part of the *Yizkor* (Memorial for the Dead) service. *Shiva* is the seven days of mourning, commencing after the funeral. During this time, the family remains at home, sits on wooden stools, and there are services in the home every evening. This is known as "sitting Shiva."

27   The *ghetto* was the Jewish section of a town or city, usually enclosed by a wall in Eastern Europe. The term originally came from the name of the Jewish quarter of Venice, established in 1516.

28   Hasidism is a Jewish pietistic movement that originated in the eighteenth century in southern Poland and the Ukraine. Its founder was Israel ben Eliezer (1700–1760), who was known by the title the Baal Shem Tov, which means Master of the Divine Name.

29   Dame Quickly is a character in the play *Rosalind* (1812), written by the Scottish playwright James M. Barrie.

30   *Chazan* is Yiddish for "cantor."

31   The Hebrew Immigrant Aid Society, or HIAS, was founded in New York City in 1892. It stationed an agent at Ellis Island to mediate between the immigration officials and the Jewish immigrants.

32   Balbriggan is a knitted cotton fabric used especially for underwear and hosiery. It is named after the town of Balbriggan, Ireland.

33   *Mandlbroyt* is Yiddish for "almond bread." *Kuchen* is Yiddish for "baked goods."

34   A *sheytl* is a wig worn by Orthodox Jewish women, who are required to shave their heads after marriage to make them less attractive to men other than their husbands.

35   George Baker (1880–1965), known as Father Divine, was an African-American religious leader who established "peace missions" to provide low-priced or free food and other aid to impoverished African-Americans during the Great Depression.

36   *Shochet* is Yiddish for an authorized, kosher slaughterer. A *yarmulke* is a skullcap, worn indoors and outdoors by Orthodox Jewish men and during religious ceremonies by Conservative Jewish men.

37   *Tallessim* is the plural for *talis*. A *mezuzah* is a small box containing Biblical verses that is affixed to the front door jamb of an observant Jewish family's house or apartment.

38   Harry Bridges (1901–) is an Australian-born labor leader who led the 1934 strike of the International Longshoremen's Association as their Pacific Coast president. Samuel Francis Hobbs (Democrat, Alabama) was a member of the United States House of Representatives from 1935 to 1951. In 1939, he

introduced a bill in Congress that provided for the incarceration of criminal aliens who could not be deported because their governments refused to take them back.

39   The University of Newark was established in 1935 through the merger of the Mercer Beasley School of Law, the Newark Institute of Arts and Sciences, and Dana College. In 1946 it became part of Rutgers University.

40   Coal passers were the seamen who brought coal from the ship's bunkers, or coal storage bins, and removed the ashes.

41   The Fraser River is in British Columbia, Canada.

42   Garret Augustus Hobart (1844–1899), a resident of Paterson, served as vice-president of the United States under William McKinley. A statue of him was erected in front of Paterson's city hall.

43   Torah literally means "teachings," but it refers either to the Five Books of Moses or more loosely to the Old Testament.

44   The Talmud consists of the Mishnah (a code of Jewish laws) and the Gemora (discussions of scholars about the Mishnah).

45   The three High Holy Days are the two days of Rosh Hashanah (the Jewish New Year) and the one day of Yom Kippur (the Day of Atonement).

46   *Kosher* means "fit to eat," according to Jewish dietary laws, which include specific procedures for slaughtering.

47   *Gefilte* fish (literally, "stuffed fish") are fish cakes or a fish loaf made from chopped or ground fish.

48   *Challah* is braided white bread glazed with egg white.

49   *Tefillin*, or phylateries, are two black leather boxes containing scriptural passages, which are bound by black leather strips on the left hand and on the head during morning prayers, every day except on the Sabbath and holidays.

50   *Tzitzit* are the fringes on the corners of the prayer shawl (*tallis*) worn by men in fulfillment of the biblical commandments.

51   A *cheder* is an elementary-level Hebrew school.

52   Franz Josef (1830–1916) was the emperor of Austria and, after 1867, of Austria-Hungary.

53   Eugene V. Debs (1855–1926) was the Socialist candidate for president in 1904, 1908, 1912, and 1920. He rose to national prominence as the president of the American Railway Union, in which capacity he led the Pullman Strike in 1894.

54   *Payess* are hair ringlets worn by Orthodox Jewish Jewish boys in accordance with Leviticus 19:27: "Ye shall not round the corners of your heads, neither shalt thou mar the corners of thy beard."

55   *Twisting* is the process of turning several fibers together to form yarn in order to strengthen it prior to transferring it to *skeins*, i.e., lengths of yarn wound on reels prior to dyeing. In *warping*, the *warp*, i.e., the threads that run lengthwise in a fabric, is transferred from bobbins which are on a large frame known as a *creel*, to large *warping wheels*, on which each thread is aligned according to the designer's pattern. *Entering* is the process of drawing the warp ends through the eyes of the *heddles*, i.e., the steel wires attached to the loom.

56   *Quill winders* wind the *filling* (the threads that run at right angles to

the warp) onto filling bobbins, also known as *quills*. The process is sometimes called "quilling."

57   A *yeshiva* is an institute of Talmudic learning. It ranks higher than the cheder and the Talmud Torah.

58   *Minche* is the daily afternoon service. *Maariv* is the daily evening service.

59   Sholem Ash (1880–1957) was a Yiddish novelist and dramatist. He was born in Poland and lived in the United States during World War I and again after 1938. Among his books are *Three Cities* (1933) and *The God of Vengeance* (1918).

60   Cordell Hull (1871–1955) was secretary of state under President Franklin Delano Roosevelt from 1933 to 1944.

61   The Industrial Workers of the World, or "Wobblies," as they were known, was a radical labor organization established in 1905 in Chicago by William ("Big Bill") Haywood, Daniel DeLeon, and Eugene Debs. The IWW was active in the Paterson Strike of 1913.

62   For years the weavers in the silk industry worked on two looms. In 1913 the introduction of the four-loom system, which doubled their work load, was one of the factors leading to the 1913 Paterson strike.

63   Adeline Patti (1843–1919) was one of the great coloratura singers of the nineteenth century. Sarah Bernhardt (1844–1923) was a French actress, one of the most famous actresses in the history of the theater. Lilli Lehmann (1848–1929) was a German dramatic soprano who was a member of the Berlin State Opera. Lillian Russell (1861–1922) was an American singer known primarily for her beauty.

Selected Bibliography

Federal Writers' Project

Banks, Ann. *First-Person America*. New York: Alfred A. Knopf, 1980.

Doty, C. Stewart, ed. *The First Franco-Americans: New England Life Histories from the Federal Writers' Project, 1938–1939*. Orono, Maine: University of Maine Press, 1985.

Federal Writers' Project. *The WPA Guide to 1930s New Jersey*. New Brunswick, N.J.: Rutgers University Press, 1989. Reprint of *New Jersey: A Guide to its Present and Past*.

Hirsch, Jerrold. "Cultural Pluralism and Applied Folklore." In *The Conservation of Culture: Folklorists and the Public Sector*, edited by Burt Feintuch, 46–67. Lexington, Ky.: University Press of Kentucky, 1988.

———. "Portrait of America: The Federal Writers' Project in an Intellectual and Cultural Context." Ph.D. diss., University of North Carolina, 1984.

McDonald, William F. *Federal Relief Administration and the Arts*. Columbus: Ohio State University Press, 1969.

Mangione, Jerre. *The Dream and the Deal: The Federal Writers' Project, 1939–1943*. Boston: Little, Brown, 1972.

Penkower, Monty Noam. *The Federal Writers' Project: A Study in Government Patronage of the Arts*. Urbana, Ill.: University of Illinois Press, 1977.

Stott, William. *Documentary Expression and Thirties America*. New York: Oxford University Press, 1973.

General Immigration

Archdeacon, Thomas J. *Becoming American: An Ethnic History*. New York: Free Press, 1983.

Bodnar, John. *The Transplanted: A History of Immigration in Urban America*. Interdisciplinary Studies in History. Bloomington: Indiana University Press, 1985.

Green, Howard L., and Lee R. Parks. *What Is Ethnicity*. New Jersey Ethnic Life Series. Trenton: New Jersey Historical Commission, 1987.

Magocsi, Paul Robert. "Are the Armenians Really Russians?—Or How the U.S. Census Bureau Classifies America's Ethnic Groups." *Government Publications Review* 14 (1987): 133–168.

Merzbacher, John S. *Trenton's Foreign Colonies.* . . . Trenton: Beers and Frey, 1908.

Purvis, Thomas L. "The European Origins of New Jersey's Eighteenth Century Population." *New Jersey History* 100 (1982): 15–31.

Vecoli, Rudolph J. *The People of New Jersey*. The New Jersey Historical Series. Princeton: D. Van Nostrand, 1965.

Wright, Giles R. *Arrival and Settlement in a New Place.* New Jersey Ethnic Life Series. Trenton: New Jersey Historical Commission, 1986.
————. *Journey From Home.* New Jersey Ethnic Life Series. Trenton: New Jersey Historical Commission, 1986.
————, comp. *Looking Back: Eleven Life Histories.* New Jersey Ethnic Life Series. Trenton: New Jersey Historical Commission, 1986.
————. *The Reasons For Migrating.* New Jersey Ethnic Life Series. Trenton: New Jersey Historical Commission, 1986.
Wright, Giles R., and Howard L. Green. *Work.* New Jersey Ethnic Life Series. Trenton: New Jersey Historical Commission, 1986.
Wright, Giles R., Howard L. Green, and Lee R. Parks. *Schooling and Education.* New Jersey Ethnic Life Series. Trenton: New Jersey Historical Commission, 1987.

Byelorussians

Kipel, Vitaut. "Byelorussians in New Jersey." In *The New Jersey Ethnic Experience,* edited by Barbara Cunningham, 88–107. Union City, N.J.: William H. Wise, 1977.
Magocsi, Paul Robert. "Belorussians." In *Harvard Encyclopedia of American Ethnic Groups,* edited by Stephan Thernstrom, 181–184. Cambridge: Harvard University Press, Belknap Press, 1980.

Dutch

De Jong, Gerald F. "Dutch Immigrants in New Jersey Before World War I." *New Jersey History* 94 (1976): 69–88.
De Vries, Hille. "The Labor Market in Dutch Agriculture and Emigration to the United States." In *The Dutch in America: Immigration, Settlement, and Cultural Change,* edited by Robert P. Swierenga, 78–101. New Brunswick, N.J.: Rutgers University Press, 1985.
De Vries, Lini. *Up from the Cellar.* Minneapolis: Vanilla Press, 1979.
————. *1901–1951, 50th Anniversary, Prospect Park, N.J.* [Prospect Park: 50th Anniversary Committee], 1951.
Swierenga, Robert P. "Dutch Immigrant Demography, 1820–1880." *Journal of Family History* 5 (1980): 390–405.
————. "Dutch Immigration Patterns in the Nineteenth and Twentieth Centuries." In *The Dutch in America: Immigration, Settlement, and Cultural Change,* edited by Robert P. Swierenga, 15–42. New Brunswick, N.J.: Rutgers University Press, 1985.
Wall, Muriel F. "Benelux-American Citizens: The First Settlers." In *The New Jersey Ethnic Experience,* edited by Barbara Cunningham, 49–63. Union City, N.J.: William H. Wise, 1977.

Irish

Blessing, Patrick J. "Irish." In *Harvard Encyclopedia of American Ethnic Groups*, edited by Stephan Thernstrom, 524–545. Cambridge: Harvard University Press, Belknap Press, 1980.

Cunningham, Barbara. "The Irish-Americans of New Jersey." In *The New Jersey Ethnic Experience*, edited by Barbara Cunningham, 267–274. Union City, N.J.: William H. Wise, 1977.

MacDonagh, Oliver. "The Irish Famine Emigration to the United States." *Perspectives in American History* 10 (1976): 357–446.

Schwartz, Joel. "The Overturnings in the Earth: Firemen and Evangelists in Newark's Law-and-Order Crisis of the 1850s." In *Cities of the Garden State: Essays in the Urban and Suburban History of New Jersey*, edited by Joel Schwartz and Daniel Prosser, 17–34. Dubuque, Iowa: Kendall/Hunt, 1977.

Shaw, Douglas V. "Immigration, Politics, and the Tensions of Urban Growth: Jersey City, 1850–1880." In *Cities of the Garden State: Essays in the Urban and Suburban History of New Jersey*, edited by Joel Schwartz and Daniel Prosser, 35–61. Dubuque, Iowa: Kendall/Hunt, 1977.

———. "The Making of an Immigrant City: Ethnic and Cultural Conflict in Jersey City, New Jersey, 1850–1877." Ph.D. diss., University of Rochester, 1972.

———. "Political Leadership in the Industrial City: Irish Development and Nativist Response in Jersey City." In *Immigrants in Industrial America, 1850–1920*, edited by Richard C. Ehrlich, 85–95. Richmond: University of Virginia Press, 1977.

———. "The Politics of Nativism: Jersey City's 1871 Commission Charter." In *Urban New Jersey Since 1870*, edited by William C. Wright, 84–95. Trenton: New Jersey Historical Commission, 1975.

Italians

Churchill, Charles W. "The Italians of Newark: A Community Study." Ph.D. diss., New York University, 1942.

———. *The Italians of Newark: A Community Study.* 1942. Reprint. The Italian-American Experience Series. New York: Arno Press, 1975.

McLaughlin, Virginia Yans. *Family and Community: Italian Immigrants in Buffalo, 1880–1930.* Ithaca, N.Y.: Cornell University Press, 1971.

Nelli, Humbert S. *From Immigrants to Ethnics: The Italian-Americans.* New York: Oxford University Press, 1983.

———. "The Italian Padrone System in the United States." *Labor History* 5 (1964): 153–167.

———. *Italians in Chicago, 1880–1930: A Study in Ethnic Mobility.* New York: Oxford University Press, 1970.

Osborne, James D. "Italian Immigrants and the Working Class in Paterson: The

Strike of 1913 in Ethnic Perspective." In *New Jersey's Ethnic Heritage*, edited by Paul A. Stellhorn, 11–34. Trenton: New Jersey Historical Commission, 1978.

Peroni, Peter A. *The Burg: An Italian-American Community at Bay in Trenton*. Washington, D.C.: University Press of America, 1979.

Rosa, Kenneth J., ed. "The Recollections of Peter B. Mattia." New Jersey Historical Society, Newark, N.J.

Starr, Dennis J. *The Italians of New Jersey: A Historical Introduction and Bibliography*. Newark: New Jersey Historical Society, 1985.

Vecoli, Rudolph J. "The Italian People of New Jersey." In *The New Jersey Ethnic Experience*, edited by Barbara Cunningham, 275–293. Union City, N.J.: William H. Wise, 1977.

Jews

Berman, Karen. "Jewish Community Played Vital Role in City History." *Paterson Evening News*, September 15, 1975, 21.

Brandes, Joseph. *Immigrants to Freedom: Jewish Communities in Rural New Jersey Since 1882*. Philadelphia: University of Pennsylvania Press, 1971.

Friedenberg, Albert Max. "Jews in New Jersey from the Earliest Times to 1850." American Jewish Historical Society. *Publications* 19 (1909): 33–44.

Howe, Irving. *World of Our Fathers*. New York and London: Harcourt Brace Jovanovich, 1976.

Jewish Community Council of Essex County. *The Essex Story: A History of the Jewish Community in Essex County, New Jersey*. Newark: Jewish Community Council of Essex County, 1955.

"Jews in New Jersey." New Jersey Ethnic Survey. New Jersey State Archives. Trenton, N.J.

Katzler, William von. "The Germans in Newark." In *A History of the City of Newark, New Jersey*, by Frank Urquhard, 2: 1021–1125. New York and Chicago: Lewis Historical Publishing, 1913.

Kohn, S. Joshua. "David Naar of Trenton, New Jersey." *American Jewish Historical Society Quarterly* 53 (1964): 373–395.

Kussy, Nathan. "Early History of the Jews of Newark." In *The Jewish Community Blue Book of Newark*, 11–38. Newark: Jewish Community Blue Book Publishing, [1924].

Our Paterson Jewish Heritage. 2d ed. [Jewish Historical Society of North Jersey], 1987.

Patt, Ruth Marcus. *The Jewish Scene in New Jersey's Raritan Valley, 1698–1948*. New Brunswick: Jewish Historical Society of Raritan Valley, 1978.

Pentz, E. W. "Early Jewish Life in Newark." New Jersey Ethnic Survey. New Jersey State Archives. Trenton, N.J.

_____. "German Jews in Newark." New Jersey Ethnic Survey. New Jersey State Archives. Trenton, N.J.

Purmell, Bluma Bayuk Rappoport, and Felice Lewis Rovner. *A Farmer's Daughter: Bluma.* Los Angeles: Hayvenhurst, 1981.

Roth, Philip. *The Facts: A Novelist's Autobiography.* New York: Farrar, Straus, and Giroux, 1988.

_____. *Goodbye, Columbus.* New York: Bantam Books, 1959.

Shapiro, Edward S. "The Jews of New Jersey." In *The New Jersey Ethnic Experience*, edited by Barbara Cunningham, 294–311. Union City: William H. Wise, 1977.

Snyder, Robert. "The Paterson Jewish Folk Chorus: Politics, Ethnicity, and Musical Culture." *American Jewish History* 74 (1984): 27–44.

Lithuanians

Alilunas, Leo J. *Lithuanians in the United States: Selected Studies.* San Francisco: R and E Research Associates, 1978.

Bates, Eve Widzenas. *Sudiev! = Good-bye!: Joys and Hardships of a Lithuanian Immigrant Girl.* New York: Manyland Books, 1977.

Budreckis, Algirdas M., ed. *The Lithuanians in America, 1651–1975.* Dobbs Ferry, N.Y.: Oceana Publications, 1976.

Greene, Victor. *For God and Country: The Rise of Polish and Lithuanian Ethnic Consciousness in America, 1860–1910.* Madison, Wisc.: State Historical Society of Wisconsin, 1975.

Holy Trinity Lithuanian Roman Catholic Church, Newark, N.J. *Commemorative Mass and Banquet,* September 12, 1976.

Pentz, Ernest. "History of the Lithuanians in Newark." New Jersey Ethnic Survey. New Jersey State Archives, Trenton, N.J.

Senkus, William A., comp. *The History of a Lithuanian-American Community in Elizabeth, N.J.* Elizabeth, N.J.: Lithuanian-American Historical Society, [1984].

Stukas, Jack. "The Lithuanians of New Jersey." In *The New Jersey Ethnic Experience*, edited by Barbara Cunningham, 322–342. Union City, N.J.: William H. Wise, 1977.

Poles

Baretski, Charles Allan. "A History of the Polish Settlement in New Jersey and its Notables." In *The New Jersey Ethnic Experience*, edited by Barbara Cunningham, 343–365. Union City, N.J.: William H. Wise, 1977.

Bukowczyk, John J. *And My Children Did Not Know Me: A History of the Polish-Americans.* Minorities in Modern America. Bloomington: Indiana University Press, 1987.

_____. "The Transformation of Working-class Ethnicity: Corporate Control,

Americanization, and the Polish Immigrant Middle Class in Bayonne, New Jersey, 1915–1925." *Labor History* 25 (1984): 53–82.

Thomas, William I., and Florian Znaniecki. *The Polish Peasant in Europe and America.* 1918. 2 vols. Reprint. New York: Alfred A. Knopf, 1927.

Russians

Davis, Jerome. *The Russian Immigrant.* 1922. Reprint. New York: Arno Press and the New York Times, 1969.

Edwarda, Sister Mary. "The Russian Immigrant in the Lakewood Area of New Jersey: A Case Study." *The International Migration Digest* 2 (1965): 136–144.

Klimenki, Gennady. "Russians in New Jersey." In *The New Jersey Ethnic Experience,* edited by Barbara Cunningham, 375–394. Union City, N.J.: William H. Wise, 1977.

Magocsi, Paul Robert. "Russians." In *Harvard Encyclopedia of American Ethnic Groups,* edited by Stephan Thernstrom, 885–894. Cambridge: Harvard University Press, Belknap Press, 1980.

Ukrainians

Cohen, David S., and Donald P. Lokuta. *Ukrainian-Americans: An Ethnic Portrait.* Trenton: New Jersey Historical Commission, 1982.

Halich, Wasyl. *Ukrainians in the United States.* Chicago: University of Chicago Press, 1937.

Magocsi, Paul Robert. "Carpatho-Rusyns." In *Harvard Encyclopedia of American Ethnic Groups,* edited by Stephan Thernstrom, 200–210. Cambridge: Harvard University Press, Belknap Press, 1980.

———. "Ukrainians." In *Harvard Encyclopedia of American Ethnic Groups,* edited by Stephan Thernstrom, 997–1009. Cambridge: Harvard University Press, Belknap Press, 1980.

Rak, Dora. "Ukrainians in New Jersey from the First Settlement to the Centennial Anniversary." In *The New Jersey Ethnic Experience,* edited by Barbara Cunningham, 435–459. Union City, N.J.: William H. Wise, 1977.

Wheeler, A. Basil. "Ukrainians in Newark." New Jersey Ethnic Survey, New Jersey State Archives, Trenton, N.J.

Index